Sharing the Quest

There is a light that shines beyond all things on earth,
beyond us all, beyond the heavens,
beyond the highest, the very highest heavens.
This is the light that shines in our heart.

Chāndogya Upanishad (III, 13:7)

To Paul,
With whom sharing the Quest
has been a Joy!
Much love,
Bobby and Julia
xxx   xxx

Sharing the Quest

Muz Murray

Element Books

To
PUSSY-WILLOW
who watered this garden
and watched it grow
with joy

© Muz Murray 1989

First published in 1986

This edition first published in the UK in 1989 by
Element Books Limited
Longmead, Shaftesbury, Dorset

Printed and bound in Great Britain
by Billings, Hylton Road, Worcester

Text design by Humphrey Stone
Cover design by Max Fairbrother

British Library Cataloguing in Publication Data

Murray, Muz
Sharing the Quest – 2nd ed.
1. Religious life. Mysticism
I. Title
291.4'2

ISBN 1-85230-087-6

Contents

Acknowledgements

Firstly, to Guru Omni for his untiring efforts in trying to beat this recalcitrant lump of clay into something resembling a human in evolutionary process. I am grateful for this Grace.

To all those students whose questions stimulated me to go deeply into myself in order to answer them, I thank you.

And a thank you to Stephen Sturgess for his portrait of the author, and other drawings done in the spirit of karma yoga.

Also to Richard Austin for his wonderful "Ho-ho! Now! Go out and save it!"

To those magazines which first published some of the original versions of these articles, especially Britain's *Yoga Today*, from my regular column in which, comes the title of this book; and to *The Mountain Path* (India); *Seed* magazine, (England), *Science of Thought Review* (England), *Cosmic Paper* (Holland) and *Middle Earth* (Germany).

To Neville Spearman Ltd, for quotations from *Edgar Cayce's Story of Jesus* and *The Children of Mu* by James Churchward. Sources of other quotations are given in the Chapter References at the end of the book.

And especial thanks to the yoga students of Britain and Europe whose love and assistance from afar helped me through a long hard winter of writing (especially Uma Wurster and Dottie Hook). My heart's warmth returns to you.

Foreword

To allay any fears that my good reader may have, that because I am known mostly to dress in muted shades of orange, I must be touting for some dodgy pseudo-Hindu cult or other, let me say at the outset that I do not belong to any cult (and never have) nor do I proselytise for this or that particular Path. My way has always been to remain free to explore everything this mysterious universe has to offer us. Therefore I have always sought to assist others to open themselves by whatever means or spiritual practice most suited to their own natures.

My tendency is to see everything from all sides and to attempt a global understanding of spiritual life. How can I know the whole if I only view existence through the narrow slit of a single tradition? If we are strongly attached to any one philosophy or religion, especially to the extent where we are prepared to fight for it – either physically or verbally – then we can know without doubt that we are in bondage to illusion. We are fighting over castles in the air. Religious belief born of social conditioning is not a sound basis for spiritual *knowledge* or understanding. Those chained hand and foot to cultural concepts can make but little progress along the Path. At best they may shuffle along only to the destination – or style of 'heaven' – as designated by the keepers of that Path.

It is better to adhere lightly to any one system of belief, like a butterfly to a flower – as a mystic or a yogi adheres to the world, knowing that he may be gone from it at any moment.

Since my own awakening to the spiritual path, I have spent all the years of my life absorbing the understanding of Christian mystics, Jewish rabbis, Sufi dervishes, Sikh saints, Hindu gurus, Zen masters, Buddhist sages, Chinese contemplatives and many others, including simple *Izangoma* (African 'wise-doctors'), shamans and native American medicine-men whom I count among my friends. In this way one gains a sense of universal spirituality.

I embrace the essential aspects of all traditions and also the non-traditional paths, but without being attached to any of them. Whatever gives me Light I carry with me while it serves me well. But whichever way one follows, if it is one with 'heart' and open to all other paths, then one develops a spiritual discrimination (awareness) which prevents one from being deludedly 'taken in' by any cultishly restrictive organisation.

Although my heart may be moved by Jesus the Christ, it remains unmoved by 'Churchianity'. I may try to follow the Noble Precepts of the Buddha without feeling any need to *be* a Buddhist. Having lived among the Sufi dervishes, I may follow their Path of the Heart without adopting the Muslim faith. Although I may have been given initiation as a Hindu monk in India, and endowed with a title and the saffron robe, to consider myself as a 'swami' (being equivalent to an ordained 'priest' of an established order) would be too confining for my freedom of growth. For when one accepts a traditional role one is pressurised by too many seekers who feel that a teacher must conform precisely to what their needful image of a guru says he should be. Besides, when I came to realise that the word *swami* indicates 'He who is One with the Lord', I was too abashed to take such a title on myself, having only paddled in the shallows of such a relationship.

I see myself neither as a 'swami' nor as a 'New Age' teacher. I incline more towards the notion of the 'No Age', seeking the practices and teachings which are suitable for any age of the world, being immersed in the contemplation of the eternal verities. Perhaps what I call the 'Zen-templative' way of life comes closest to my heart – that contemplative and aesthetic mode of being cultivated by the Zen monks of Japan – but with more warmth and laughter and less severity. He who takes his path too seriously is unlikely to arrive anywhere.

The ochre or saffron robe as worn in India indicates that the wearer is (or ought to be) 'one who has given up worldly pursuits and is concentrating on the Godly life alone'. In olden days when criminals were due to be executed, they were dressed in these mud-coloured garments (this being the most cheaply available dye-stuff) to distinguish them from the other prisoners. So it was that the yogis adopted the use of the same coloured rags to denote that they too were 'cut off' from the life of the world. And this became a symbolic gesture universally adopted among the Eastern ascetics.

It is interesting to note, that of recent years, through scientific research, it has been determined that the visual effect of this colour induces a contemplative consciousness – a 'cosmic chance' if ever there was one! I have found this to be so myself and for this reason I continue to wear the colour. But that does not make me any more than a *sadhu* (a wandering truth-seeker) in this world, slowly stripping myself of psychological baggage along life's long and winding road. Thus my 'Way of Unlearning' is a simple 'Sharing of the Inner Quest' with fellow-travellers on the Way Within.

Having externally combed the earth for many years, sifting the sands of many spiritual cultures for guidance on the inner way, I have inevitably come to the same conclusion as the renowned Zen professor, D.T. Suzuki, when he says that: "Indian metaphysics are the deepest in the world, and their dialectics are incomparable. All nations of the world have to bow down to the Indians in this respect." And this from one of the world's greatest proponents of the enlightening Zen philosophy! Many other scriptural scholars throughout the world, after making exhaustive comparative studies, have also come to echo his sentiments.

In my own researches, I found that the scriptures of most 'popular' religions of the world, whilst being worthy in their own way, were unsatisfying, as they all danced around the spiritual life on a relatively superficial level, suitable mainly for the masses of mankind. Doubtless they all pointed in the same direction and gave a few hints along the path, but having preserved only a few fragments of the Master's mystical teaching, for a more introspective and serious seeker of truth, none of them got down to the 'nitty-gritty', brass tacks level as far as methods for self-harmony and Self-realisation were concerned. Eventually I found it was only the Hindu and Buddhist texts which really explored in depth every aspect of the spiritual path and showed the way – *all the way* – to the Source: or at least, as close to arrival as any text can show.

From time immemorial, the sages of India have been known to have delved deepest of all into the psycho-spiritual nature of human existence, and have left a practical legacy unequalled in any other culture for achieving Oneness with the Absolute. Such scriptures prescribe the perfect path for every type of temperament and at every level of development. It is not to be wondered at, therefore, if my writings naturally have an Eastern flavour here and there – like a whiff of curry in an English street.

But because the Sanskrit language of the seers and yogis of India contains the most extensive and subtle spiritual vocabulary this planet can boast, one is able to enter into levels of spiritual profundity for which we in the West do not even have concepts – let alone words! And one Sanskrit term often needs a whole paragraph, or even a complete book to explain its subtle ramifications. However, not being a grammarian or any kind of a Sanskrit scholar, where necessary I have done my inadequate best to restate whatever intuitive understanding I have gained of the ancient wisdom in a way which I hope is absorbable by the seeker of today.

As many of these chapters were originally written as single articles for spiritual and yoga journals, there are a few places where inevitable explanatory repetitions occur, when a key concept or word had to be qualified to make the article complete and understandable in itself. Whilst rewriting and enlarging the manuscripts for this book I have tried to eradicate such duplications where I could, except where it would obviously destroy the flow of the narrative, on the understanding that it can sometimes be helpful for things to be repeated in different ways in order that a tricky concept may be more easily grasped, or intuitively 'seen'. I hope readers will bear with me in this matter, as this means they may also dip into the book where they will.

In my *Sharing the Quest* I have tried to instill a little of the mystic's eye-view of the universe as a cosmic continuum from the *Heart of All* through all our hearts. For it is essentially the intuitive knowledge of the reality of this situation which has been the living experience of mystics in every age of the world. And on 'bringing through' their wholistic vision of existence, the mystic masters of every culture have spoken in a way which opened up the lives of millions.

On whatever Path we awaken to the spiritual life – in this war-weary and confusing world – we would be extremely foolish to deny the wisdom of all Paths other than our own. On the contrary, we should hail with joy and gratitude the fact that there are fellow-travellers on the Inner Journey, whose teachings may clarify what we misunderstand along our chosen way. For no matter by what road another travels, he is still steadily entering into the Divine, through his own level of understanding of the workings of the heart. So let us walk awhile beside him on his way, and each support the other in his chosen faith.

There are those – and many – who need to walk the 'safe road' through the spiritual life, supported by the standards of their inherited tradition. No blame. But if they can also be open to the wisdom of other ways, so much the better for us all. The less divisive cultural 'religiosity' there is in the world, the greater the chance there is for seekers everywhere to awaken to a universal spirituality. And by this I do *not* mean a universal *religion* (heaven forbid!) but a universal sense of comradeship in the recognition of each other's efforts on the *Way Within*.

For the hardy few – the spiritual heroes of the world – who have no faith bonded to any fold, then the clear-eyed way of the Universal Mystic is open – the way of the Open Hand, the Open Heart and the Searching Single Eye.

If you can walk a little along this way with me – then welcome to this book.

MUZ MURRAY

A MYSTIC'S EYE-VIEW
AND THE WORLD OF
GURUS

Awakening on the Mystic Path

One of the most frequent questions I am asked on my travels, is how I came to be on 'The Path'. The *Path* of course is not a path at all, but simply that condition of the spirit in which a man has become aware of an inner need to know the nature of his being. *Who am I? What am I doing here? Is there any purpose to my existence?* are the constant questions living within him. The Path can thus be understood as the yearning quest in the soul of someone seeking an answer to the aweful *Why* of existence.

Most of us can perhaps go on for years not giving the idea a thought, or dismissing it as unpractical, or pretending to ourselves that we don't give a damn. Comes a time when we are overtaken by inexplicable fears or feelings of inadequacy; we tend to cover them up by throwing ourselves into feverish and generally pointless activity – a full involvement in the daily round of life – in petty pleasures or political strife, or in sport, sex, art, music, religiosity, war or whatever. But eventually the futility of it all catches up with us if it has no underlying meaning within. There seems to come a time in the life of every human being when the shallowness of their everyday existence is revealed to them.

If a man perceives only the hollowness of his being and the meaninglessness of his life, then he may become stricken with despair, take to drink or drugs to cover his pain, commit suicide, or find himself driven on the 'Path' out of necessity to find some reason for existing. But suppose he has been made aware of the shallowness of his everyday vision of life by comparison with a greater vision – through experiencing a state of consciousness which gives him a new and enthralling insight into the wondrous nature of existence – then the chances are he has undergone a mystical experience.

The mystic is one whose 'eyes have seen the glory' of the true nature of things. To him, as to the atomic scientist, the world and the so-called 'physical' universe are no longer as material as we generally suppose them to be. He sees this apparent world as a living symbol of more glorious states of existence. He has had a glimpse of other dimensions, of other states of 'reality', of a paradise in which all things exist here and now but which he rarely perceives. Once he has seen with his 'inner eye' his conception of reality is automatically changed.

In general, even with all its unreal and surrealistic happenings, we consider our everyday world as reality – and on the relative level so it is. Relative only to our average level of conscious perception that is. If we have never experienced any other 'reality' or extra-ordinary state of consciousness (other than dream states), then we are only able to relate to this world as it appears to our feeble sensory capacities. Consequently, the visionaries, whose conscious receptivity is operating at a higher frequency, and who attempt to relate their experiences of other states of reality, are dismissed as deluded fools, cranks or madmen by those who have unfortunately never known any condition of 'seeing' or 'knowing' other than that afforded by the use of the five limited senses; but the mystical experience transcends the senses and the intellect and is *perceived directly*.

By what? one might be tempted to ask. It is by something for which we have no word in our language, but is known to Sanskrit-speaking Hindu holymen as *buddhi,* usually translated as higher mind or illumined intellect. But this falls short of its real meaning as it operates on a level beyond what we consider to be the operations of mind and intellect. Considering it to be the highest opposite pole to the 'unconscious' of psychology, I venture to call it the *sun-conscious* – or the faculty of spiritually-illumined intuitive receptivity. *Sunconscious* awareness is an awakened understanding which permeates every level of our beings without the participation, or intervention, of the mind or discursive intellect. These two latter faculties are obliged to catch up after the event has occurred instantaneously in the deepest levels of the whole organism. This effect leads to the conjecture that the 'sunconscious' faculty, being beyond the comprehension of the body-mind complex, is somewhat in the nature of the 'mind of the soul', as its awakening feeds the spiritual being with the inner light and joy it craves.

However, around the average human being there seems to be some sort of 'psychic insulating shell' safeguarding him from premature perception of the 'glory' of the light and splendour within all manifest things. As it would be disastrous for a chick in the egg to break out of its shell before the inner conditions for its maturity had developed, so it is with man. It would appear that until a certain quality of spiritual and mental togetherness has developed within him, or a ripeness through internal and external suffering, he is not equipped to cope with insight into the inner realities of existence. To actually *experience* the terrifying intangibility of this universe before the heart and mind are ready for it could drive a person insane (that is, incapable of further coherent thought and action on *this* relative plane). Its effect would be equivalent to that of a monkey suddenly overtaken by human consciousness and becoming aware of the wonders and horrors of human life.

It is for this reason that mental disorientation often occurs with the use of psychedelic drugs such as LSD or mescaline. Not that drugs disclose any of the *Whys* and *Wherefores* of existence, but they do powerfully destroy the earthbound concepts of body, space and time, as perceived by the senses. This can hurl the unprepared mind into a terrifying intra-dimensional wilderness. When the 'psychic filters' between the surface mind of man and his subconscious realms are suddenly removed by drug activity, the protective 'shell' is cracked and, if he is spiritually or psychically unready for even such low-level relations, then the results can be mind deranging. Stripped of his habitual sensory faculties and sense-of-ego (his 'psychic shell') he is exposed either to the delirious joy of mental freedom and ecstasy, or, if he retains the sense-of-ego, then he can find himself in the grip of inexpressible terror in a hellishly chaotic and demented formless universe.

The terror seems to come from being unable to adjust quickly enough to other conditions of existence and having the ground of his previous 'knowledge-of-the-world' pulled from under his feet. Similar conditions prevail, on a lesser scale, for the developing spiritual seeker as his 'psychic shell' begins to dissolve. If he tries to rush things he may soon find himself out of his depth. This is why no true Master ever tries to force the pace of a student's growth, nor promises enlightenment-in-five-minutes, but allows the student to determine his own rate of development and advocates a slow step-by-step opening up of his mind and spirit, together with the steady dissolution of his sense-of-ego.

Developing oneself in such a manner is most beneficial for creating the needful conditions in body and mind towards an ultimate harmonious union with the 'Absolute' (or the 'God-experience'), or at least, towards preparing the ground for a 'sunconscious' or insightful mystical experience. Although the mystical experience, and even full Cosmic Consciousness (which is a complete identification with, and absorption in, the total cosmic creation), are admittedly still of a relativistic nature, on variously ascending levels, they are, however, of a higher aspect of consciousness, capable of causing a catalytic elevation of the spirit and – in varying degrees – a refining of the moral and ethical sensibilities in man. Such experiences thus serve as valuable and encouraging stepping-stones along the 'Inward Path' from relative to Absolute Knowledge or Truth.

Unfortunately today's *mis*education system is not geared towards self-understanding or intuitive development, but seems bent on producing only keen intellects. (Instead of which, its main success is in producing masses of bored empty-heads). However, even a keen intellect is not necessarily advantageous for encouraging mystical experience, and can be a major disadvantage. The mystical experience occurs to simple peasants and tradesmen, whose hearts are open, as well as to profound thinkers. Although the peasant may have an inborn wisdom, it is not intellectualised knowledge, but a natural inner-knowing, and thus he may be in a far better intuitive condition to receive mystical insight. The thinker whose heart is involved in keeping his thoughts elevated towards the intuitive sunconscious, is also in a receptive condition.

For those who have experienced the phenomenon, a moment of mystical consciousness is regarded as the most real and elevating experience of a lifetime. It is a state of being which – by comparison with anything previously experienced since birth – makes our everyday world either pale into a mirage-like unreality and relative insignificance, or opens it up into a multi-dimensional super reality full of depth and richness of meaning.

At the age of twenty-four I was completely ignorant about mystical consciousness and viewed such presumed delusions with a derisive scepticism. In fact, since the age of seven or eight, I had been adamantly anti-religious, as at that time my parents, who had no religious inclinations themselves, had packed me off to Sunday-school every Sunday morning, just to keep me out of the way. It was during one of these Sunday-school sermon sessions that I suddenly perceived with an awful awareness, that those who were 'talking down' to us with their saccharine-sweet versions of Bible study, neither understood, nor, in their heart of hearts, believed what they were telling us.

It sickened me to realise that they wanted us kids to believe what they were saying in order to feel useful and comfortable in themselves. The security-seeking motivation of evangelism was revealed to me in that moment and I never forgot it. And I never went back. Through all the years of my teens I avoided anything which vaguely smelled of religion, despising churchly hypocrisy and considering myself to be a confirmed atheist, a God-less 'free-thinker' and proud of it. Therefore my about-face was all the more wondrous to me because of it.

It was in Cyprus, January 1964, during seven years of vagabondage around the world, when it happened. I had been through a great deal of emotional turmoil and privation during my travels and arrived at the port of Limassol with great relief at having left the scenes of my suffering behind me. One evening I was sitting gazing vacantly at the sea in the afterglow of sunset, having just finished a meal in a little Greek eatery, feeling very tranquil and relaxed, when I began to feel a strange pressure in my brain. It was as if some deliciously loving hand had slipped numbingly under my skull and was pressing another brain on top of mine.

I felt a thrilling liquidity of being and an indescribable sensation, as if the whole universe was being poured into me, or perhaps rather as if the whole universe was welling up out of me from some deep centre. My 'soul' thrilled and swelled and my consciousness passed out across the ocean and the land in all directions, through the sky and out into space. Within moments I was among the stars and planets and strange entities of space. Somehow I was aware of great beings, millions of miles high, moving in space, through which the stars could be seen. Wave after wave of revelation swept through my whole being, too fast for my normal conscious mind to record other than the joy and wonder of it.

In those moments I lived and understood the meaning of the esoteric dictum, 'As above, so below'. Every single cell of my body seemed to record and intuit the experience, retaining it like the negative film emulsion in a camera. I was aware that every cell had its own limited form of consciousness, although collectively they were all still subject to a single controlling consciousness which was mine. And it seemed to me that the whole of humanity was in the same condition: each 'individual' believing in his own separate mind, but in reality being *in*-dividual (that is, *indivisible*) from a single controlling consciousness – that of 'Absolute Consciousness' itself. (Nearly ten years later I was to read in a scientific journal that scientists were beginning to discover that single cells can 'see' and 'hear' and have limited autonomous consciousness. And this is only one of the instances in which aspects of the mystical knowledge given in that experience have been empirically verified in later years).

But at the time the awe and wonder of the things experienced
were beyond speech and I was unable and unwilling to express
them even to my closest friends, for fear of profaning the
experience, even though paradoxically I longed to do so. Who
would understand in any case? It took me ten years to digest
the experience myself, before I was able to talk about it at all.
But it was such that my whole secure, brash and cock-sure
intellectual world was turned topsy-turvy and inside out, and
for once I was overjoyed with existence.

All the following week I walked about in great happiness,
with a crystal vision which gave a greater luminosity to the air
and all but made the people and buildings around me transparent. It was at this time I realised that the capacity for 'seeing'
into others, which I had intermittently experienced since
childhood, without consciously being aware of what I was
seeing, was not something of which everyone was capable, as I
had imagined. Only then did I come to understand what it
was. As a diamond-merchant knows the quality of true dia-
mond from cut-glass beads, so I found I was intuitively 'seeing'
the level of 'soul-quality' in the development of those around
me.

For the next few years, as I was trekking alone down the
length of Africa, I had to rethink everything I thought I knew.
Slowly I absorbed the knowledge filtering from the sunconsciousness in my cells. But the intellect still demanded satisfaction, having been by-passed by the experience. So I began
to devour every book on mysticism I could find, until I came
across a large volume called *Cosmic Consciousness* by Dr Maurice
Bucke, MD, which chronicled what appeared to be an increas-
ing incidence of such an extraordinary phenomenon throughout history. I also found the writings of Martinus, a contemporary Danish mystic, some of whose experiences were
very similar in content to mine. Thus my intellect was satisfied.
I had done no practices to prepare me for the event. I had never
taken a drug. I was not having delusions (not that the 'inner
me' thought so for a moment, as for the first time in my life I
had a solid core to my being) and I was not going mad. Others
had seen what I had seen, had been where I had been.

As the experience soaked into me, slowly – very slowly, mellowing a savage youth, my character and lifestyle began to change. Little by little, without conscious effort or intention, I began to withdraw from stimulants in my diet. I found myself growing away from blood-foods such as meat, fish and eggs, and alcohol and tobacco no longer had a hold over me. The empty hedonism and life of the bar gave way to more contemplative pursuits. I became consumed with the meaning of life. What is existence? What is reality? What kind of creature am I? What am I supposed to do in life? I could no longer take anything for granted. I was on the 'Path'.

By the time I arrived in South Africa, I had come to the conclusion that meditation was the next necessary step for self-unfoldment, although I was still somewhat hazy as to what meditation was. (Now, after twenty years' practice I begin to ease into it and gain the first glimmerings of its true nature and value). I believed I was on the wrong continent and needed to be in India to find a meditation master. But I was unaware of the spiritual saying: 'When the pupil is ready, the Master appears', which proved to be true for me. In my time of need I came into contact with a Master on a visit from India, who gave me initiation into *Shabd Yoga,* a form of meditation involving *mantra* (mystic sound) and inner hearing, also known as *Nada Yoga.*★

Since my first spontaneous 'Initiation' by the cosmos, I have taken initiation and guidance from many teachers, but that does not necessarily bind me to follow any single one. I may hold the image of an inner guru in my heart, one in whom my spirit most rejoices, and one whose teachings lead me to the Light – yet that does not mean I must close my eyes, ears and heart to the rest of the universe.

Should I restrict myself to the fragrance of only one flower, to the exclusion of all the others? It seems a little churlish to declare the rose the only scent worth smelling, when the jasmine, honeysuckle and the flowers of autumn freely give their fragrance through the seasons and make no claim on me. Yet I attend them all in my garden and enjoy the different pleasure of them all in turn.

★See page 90 and 127

Similarly the guru – or spiritual preceptor – has many forms. Since we seemingly exist in this wondrous hologrammistic appearance of a cosmos all around us, I can do no other than see every aspect of existence as my teacher, as the universe is a learning-system which always brings us the lessons we need. I must be alert in every instant to the shaping of my soul in everything which occurs to me. What I see in the way you are or the way you act, may in the moment be as much my teacher as the sage on a mountain. Or I may gain as much from observing a frog in meditation, a child at play, or the bumbling of a bee in the light of a buttercup.

To come to the understanding that life is not a question, but an answer – it simply *IS* – and to align oneself with its workings, without getting in the way – this, we may say, is the way of a mystic.

Guru Omni and the Guruverse

Q. *A thing that confuses me is the question of devotion – to which guru? Although I know that, as Ramana Maharshi said, "God, Guru and Self are One," still, having had contact with several teachers, I go through phases of needing their darshan (visual contact) and feeling devotion towards them. And if one already has an inner guru, what then? The main teachers I have been connected with in my sadhana (spiritual practice) feature strongly in my consciousness from time to time. What to do? To whom should I direct my devotion?*

A. It is inevitable that we need the physical presence of our spiritual teachers now and again, to help boost our flagging spirits when world weariness has brought us down. And such association is one of the most vital and important aspects of our spiritual development. Without spending time in the company of a truly spiritual person we are unlikely to understand by ourselves what real spirituality means, having no model to inspire us in our everyday life. But by the subtle and influential radiation from the calm mind and heart of a spiritual presence, a profound sense of the 'spiritual' is effortlessly instilled in us.

Bhagavan Sri Ramana Maharshi (1879-1950) the Self-realised sage of Arunachala mountain in southern India, was of course speaking from the highest spiritual elevation and Absolute authority. Having been a pure channel of universal consciousness since his enlightenment at the age of sixteen, he was able to state, as Jesus, that 'I and the Father are One'. However, whereas Jesus used the term 'Father' in keeping with the patriarchal religious conception of his contemporaries, Guru Ramana spoke of the 'Self', a more precise technical term as used by the ancient seers and yogis.

Of course, this capitalised 'Self' should not be confused (as it often is) with the ordinary everyday ego-bound personality of one's individual self. What we consider as our normal ordinary self (which is mainly a self-centred little package of ego, mind, intellect, memory, will and personality, suffused with soul for animation) is no more than a temporary 'contraction' of the Universal Self, much as a small cloud is only a temporary 'contraction' of elements in the clear blue sky it is 'made' of.

This Universal or *Omni*-Self is variously known as the Absolute, the Omnipresence, the Indwelling Presence, the Ground of Being, Universal Spirit, *Brahman,* God, Allah, Christ or Krishna Consciousness, etc. It is most easily known to us as the sense of 'being', of existing, that state of consciousness which recognises that 'I am'. In its transcendental sense of 'I AM-ness' it has been the universally perceived form of exalted consciousness experienced by sages in all times and all climes. And it is this ever-available and Omnipresent sense of 'I AM' which is eternally reflected through billions of human minds, causing each tiny consciousness to think of itself as 'I'. It is this same primordial 'I' or Universal Consciousness of the Self which is looking out of the eyes of every being in existence, be it man, woman, child, animal, bird, insect, fish or microbe. Thus we might say God is 'keeping an eye on things' at every level of manifestation.

But just how the world is seen depends on the clarity or cloudiness of the vehicles (imperfect ego-bound *mentalities) through which the Omnipresence views its own 'creation'. If the distorting lens of the mind is not clear, the view may be seen as if 'through a glass darkly'. But he who has succeeded in

---

* One should say *sense*-of-ego as ego is only an apparent malady: for more detail see chapter – Evolving out of Ego.

dissolving the incessant egoid operations of his individual mind becomes awakened in the heart-centre: that is, the centre of that 'space' where he feels himself to be. Then there can be nothing other than pure consciousness of the Self (known as Self- or God-Realisation) passing through the filament of one's being. Such a person has a crystal-clear world view through eyes radiant with the True Self.

When I want to give this Omniscient Self some conceptual 'form' I fondly like to call it *'Guru Omni'* (short for *Guru Omnipresence Divine* or G.O.D.) for I find the teaching of this Great Guru all around. And the total cosmos in which Guru Omni operates (and is endlessly dreaming into manifestation) I term the *'Guruverse'* – this universal dramatic dreamshow of an existence which shapes our souls and turns everything back on ourselves in the end. Thus everything in the Guruverse is the expression of Guru Omni's teaching to us, which appears in many guises.

If we are spiritually alert, we are unceasingly aware of guidance in everything, in everyone, and in every event around us. In this way we may understand the whole world as our 'Guru'. For the world *is* 'God, Guru and Self' in visible operation. Sometimes this may manifest in the spiritual teachers with whom we come in contact, and at other times, perhaps in an accident, or an angry associate hurling home truths at us in an argument. All are learning situations given us by the Guruverse.

We may accept this 'guru-ness' going on through the actions of other people and events, but that does not necessarily make every spiritual teacher a guru. We tend to use the word in a sloppy way, attaching it to any Tom, Dick or 'swami' who gives us spiritual instruction, if he happens to be wearing the right robes for the role. If we can also take this as a *form* of 'guru-ness' according to the level of development achieved by our teacher, then calling him *'Guruji'** should not be considered objectionable.

The word *guru* is very broadly used in India to denote almost any spiritual teacher, or person from whom you learn something, or any human or non-human entity, or inner or outer

*Ji is an honorific suffix denoting respect.

experience or event of any kind which awakens one's inner wisdom and lifts the veil of ignorance from one's eyes. Such is the operation of Guru Omni. In secular Sanskrit, *guru* is considered to derive from the root *gr* – to praise, invoke or utter, thus being one who invokes the truth in the disciple by his utterance. However, the yogis understand *guru* to mean 'dispeller of darkness' from the words *gu* (darkness) and *ru* (remover). Thus a true guru is one who is able to dispel the darkness of ignorance and doubt from the hearts and minds of his followers.

Strictly speaking, the term guru should only properly be applied to one who has totally transcended *all* of his personality problems and ego, and is thus a clear channel purely radiating the Divinity.

In such a case – as in the attainment of Ramana Maharshi – it can be said that, in a being of that quality, God, Guru and Self are truly One.

This, in effect, is the case with every one of us, only we are too attached to our self-created image of ourselves, to be aware of it. The Self is our very essence. Its nature is a bliss which can do no other than fill us whenever we can dissolve the 'Gordian knot' of our personal selfhood. We are like the filament in an electric light bulb, but with a temporary blockage between us and an omnipresent current ever ready to illumine us. This blockage is the sense-of-ego. Therefore we should encourage anything which helps to loosen such self-imposed bonds. The fostering of a sense of devotion or reverence is of great assistance in this endeavour.

Reverence is the natural attribute of the soul and its cultivation activates the soul's function as a two-way medium of interaction between oneself and the Omni-Self. In this way the deep Self is always suffusing the surface self and gently easing us towards itself from within and without.

For seekers of the Light there is a natural attraction and affinity with light wherever it is found. When a true guru emits love-light from his eyes our souls are ignited. When the clouds part in a darkened sky and the sun shines, our hearts are lifted. When walking in the dark of night we are happy when we see the stars, or the rising of the moon. The dancing flight of glow-worms give us pause for wonder. And a gladness warms us when we see the lights of home. Even city lights are cheering after a long drive in the dark. And Christmas lights brighten the spirit on drab winter days. At home the snugness of the flickering firelight can bring us mellow dreams. Even the gentle light of a candle flame has its own magic. Thus light in all its forms can move us many ways and link us with the Light within.

So it is in the life of the Spirit. All around us there are things which move us and are worthy of reverence. We are warmed in heart when we see someone show humanity to another. This reverence towards mankind is none other than Guru Omni flowing through the filaments of flesh and bone, giving and receiving in unbroken circuitry. We are thus the channels of that endless flow of grace we needs must bestow on every other form of life around us if we seek to grow. Even a drowning wasp is one with you and will cling gratefully to your offered finger, doing you no harm in its rescue. In this way we may lose our sense of separateness and fear of things 'out there', for the same Omniscient current of loving life animates and unifies all.

As all the world is thus Guru Omni the Divine, there need be no doubt as to where to bestow one's devotion. The sun shines on all alike and gives its light to the whole solar system. It does not guard its rays for one alone and refuse its warmth to another. If your heart is warming in devotion, then make it sun-like, radiating your sunconsciousness in all directions, and shine on all of creature-kind. Every living being needs to receive as well as to give. And it is a spiritual necessity to give out what we receive – in one way or another – not as an evangelist, but simply as a 'sharer' of warmth according to another's needs. We can lighten the day of the milkman, the woman in the corner shop or the snotty-nosed child in the street.

When you are in need yourself, you seek the sun in others. And naturally, as like attracts like, your reverence will be most attuned to those teachers whose presence 'speaks to you' and touches something in your heart. If a guru's gaze moves you deep inside then know that he is one who has validity for you.

Even though you may hold dear the image of another guru in your heart, but one who is no longer in this world, you must realise you also need the presence of a living master too. If you can feel and recognise the same 'vibration' or quality of being in some other teacher, then there *is* your inner guru manifesting in another form for your assistance.

When one has doubt about which guru is the best for you, it is generally because you are still in the process of 'ripening' ready for the future meeting with the one you need. It is wise therefore to associate with as many different teachers as is possible for you and 'feel your way' into what they *are*. What they are teaching is much less important that what you feel when in their presence. Just being around a spiritual teacher works its subtle alchemy in the soul. As you experience the effect of different teachers, in the course of time you will develop spiritual discrimination and will come to know who is best for you.

In the midst of the trials and tribulations of the world, in times of crisis and misery, or in moments of quiet and inner tranquillity – see who it is who comes into the mind's eye of your heart. Or whenever you try to enter into yourself seeking solace in the quiet of your soul, whoever's face arises effortlessly in your thoughts, then he is the guru for you – or at least, for your present needs. In whom do you feel an echo of the grace and serenity your soul is seeking? Whose memory lightens your heart? Mentally review all the living masters you have known and see whose incomparable smile remains most in your thoughts. You will come to realise whose endearing qualities are living in your heart and representing something high for you. And in that direction your love will flow.

Since it is that same Omnipresent current of love which is channelling through every teacher, or guru-sage, to a greater or lesser degree, depending on their level of development, it is the recognition of that current which generates the love in you. Therefore it is efficacious to direct your devotion to that flow itself – as felt from others and as arising in yourself. In this way you thereby become one with the Omnipresence. When the loving rays from a teacher's eyes kindle the blaze of devotion in your heart, this is also the working of the Self (the ultimate Inner Guru) welling up within you, and being projected outwards to form a circuit between you and your teacher (Guru Omni in disguise), which again is augmented by reciprocal action.

This process of alignment with the loving current from the heart awakens and kindles the power of your Inner Sun – the Self. Therefore we can reflect that reverential divine devotion in all our daily doings everywhere.

Shine on! Shine OM!

Problems on the Path

Q. *Now and again I get totally fed up with trying to make any spiritual progress. As I don't seem to be getting anywhere in any case, I lose all my energy for practice for quite a while. Then I see how miserable I am becoming and have to start doing something again to get me out of the dumps. But when I read in one yoga text that you must 'strive for perfection with diligent practice' and then elsewhere some top-notch guru says 'the only true way is natural and spontaneous, without any effort', I get flummoxed and exasperated. My mind is continually swayed between doing and not doing. How to resolve the paradox?*

A. At times of great frustration in our endeavours towards the Light, I think we all ask ourselves, "What am I doing this for? What's the use? Why should I bother to make any effort on the path of Self-realisation?" We find all the handed-down teachings enjoin us to practice austerities and spiritual exercises (known as *sadhana* in Sanskrit yoga terminology) of one kind or another and yet we are also told by Enlightened Ones that the true and perfect way to understand reality is effortless. How do we reconcile these seemingly disparate instructions?

In the words of one of the greatest sages of our time, Bhagavan Sri Ramana Maharshi:

Effortless and choiceless awareness is our real nature. If we *can* attain that state and abide in it, that is all right. But one cannot reach it without effort... If you do not realise your essential nature, your sight remains obstructed. What is the obstruction? Find it out and remove it... one's efforts are meant *only for the removal of obstructions* which hide the true vision. The real nature remains the same. [When] once it is realised *it is permanent*... A practiser gains peace of mind and is happy. That peace is the *result* of his efforts. But the real state must be effortless. The effortless *samadhi* (superconscious state) is the true one and the perfect state. It is permanent.

When the efforts are spasmodic... so also are their results.[1]

No doubt effortlessness is something we all crave for in our *sadhana;* perhaps from the intuitive knowledge that in reality we do not have to *do* anything: we only have to consciously *be.* But we have forgotten how. So we try out various methods to remind ourselves. If the path we find ourselves on becomes too hard to sustain in the face of flagging spirits, we begin to lose faith in it and get discouraged or distracted. It takes intensive effort merely to stay at home and (without the 'holier-than-thou' spiritual pride of self-satisfaction) conscientiously sticking to your meditation or yoga practice at specific times, day after day, when your friends are all out enjoying themselves, or inviting you to join them – especially if you feel you are getting nowhere with it all.

In my early days of practice, after a year or two of such self-imposed austerities, I can recall my own sense of glee when I came into contact with the school of thought whose motto was: *Don't push the river – it flows by itself.* What an excitement surged in me at the words! It was almost a mini-revelation in itself. 'Now why didn't I think of that before?' I wondered. 'It is so obvious! Am I not forcing the issue with all these austerities and practices? Why shouldn't I just flow with it – like everything else in nature? The river has no need to push itself, it simply flows with its own momentum, seeking its level. If inner harmony and bliss is my true nature, then why am I making all this effort to become what I already am?'

Maybe I am ignoring the flow of nature, I reasoned, if someone wants me to see a film with them and I refuse to go? Is that not in effect the natural process of the Guruverse at work in bringing me the invitation? So it was with such self-justifications that I decided with great relief to give in and abandon my *sadhana.*

However, I found that 'just flowing' was sooner idealised than done. If only one *could* just let go and relax enough to simply flow with the world, then that would indeed be the perfect way to realise the 'essential nature' of oneself. But for most of us, unhappily it does not seem to work that way. Have you ever tried to *just flow?* In the first flush of freedom it may be wonderful – but how long can you hold it?

One very quickly floats out of the conceptualised dream of

'flowingness' and gets sucked into the endless stream of conflicting thoughts instead. Such things as apprehension, worry, fear, love, lust, uptightness and so on, soon begin clamouring like flotsam on the surface of the mind. We find ourselves getting whirled around in the eddies of the social current and caught up in all kinds of unnecessary diversions destructive to one's peace of mind, without even realising where the change began. Very soon the mind is back to its habitually disorganised and chaotic condition.

It was at such a point I realised that I could carry on with this kind of 'free-flowing' until Doomsday and still not be any the better for it. This, I thought, was the state of mind of the average cabbage. But having become disillusioned with both my *sadhana* and with free-flowing I was totally without direction and succumbed to that dire affliction of spiritual aspirants – the 'dark night of the soul'. This is a condition in which life becomes utterly meaningless and loses all its savour. Whenever such a sickness came upon me I always turned to nature for solace.

Sitting in a field, or a wood, or on a mountain and soaking up the healing harmony of my surroundings, I could always experience that clouds and sunsets and birds and trees and flowers and bees were all still flowing on as happily as ever, eternally changeless in essence. What was the difference between me and nature – I wondered. Why does it flow and I don't? Where did I go wrong? The trees and flowers are not neurotic or mentally confused, yet they are as conscious and sensitive as I am. Scientific experiments have shown that even plants have some form of seemingly primitive 'emotional' or 'symbiotic' attachment to those who care for them. Plants are attuned to the thoughts of man and are in vibratory rapport with all other forms of life. Yet their reactions are *momentary* and not reflective.

A tree does not fret and worry about how it is going to manage to put out buds and blossoms and bear fruit. It has no anxiety for the future, for fear of insufficient rain or sunshine for the coming year. It does not know how, or what, it does, and yet through an effortless un-selfconscious unfoldment, it grows and opens out in glorious diversity. Like the rest of organic nature, it is conscious, but without ruminative thought. The natural world is a fantastically complex process of Consciousness in operation without the intervention of separative, locally individualised and self-conscious mentalities. That flawless flow of Consciousness which is the substratum of all existence is simply flowing through the natural world and unfolding it without resistance.

There was my answer! I had forgotten that I too, was a product of that process. The natural world has not set itself *apart* from any thing. On the relative plane, it just *is*. As a function of the inseparable Omnipresence, it is sustained by it. But man has come to think of himself as a separate entity from nature, even on the gross relative plane. In today's world he often feels estranged even from his own parents, and thus, by extension, from all of humankind. He has the illusion of being encapsulated in his own separate existence, with his own autonomous mind and an individual consciousness. He feels dreadfully alone and has the erroneous belief in the necessity of forging his own salvation, or 'unfolding' for himself. If he could overcome his sense of isolation – created by his sense of selfhood (ego and mind) – he could be as spontaneously unfolded as the rest of creation. But it is his idea of *mind* itself which obstructs the flow of that underlying Consciousness of the universe, and prevents him from experiencing his true nature as the Self, which is described in Sanskrit as *Sat-chit-ananda,* the primal formula meaning Existence=Consciousness=Bliss.

This is the nature of Cosmic Consciousness, which is always there awaiting us, whenever the tightly coiled spring of the little self is unwound. And we are immersed in it like fish in the sea. But even when we understand the problem intellectually, and accept the fact that we are constantly existing in a state of unrecognised bliss (needing only the removal of mental blockages to experience it, as shown in the mystical experience, or in the temporary effects of some psychedelic drugs), it does not help us very much. Although we may know, in essence, that we are already the Self and that there is therefore nothing more to be attained, we do not experience it as living reality, but only as a mental idea.

All mental ideas must dissolve in the light of direct 'sun-conscious' experience. Therefore since mere intellectual knowledge does not make us any the happier, it becomes futile to give up our *sadhana* or spiritual practice, which is the only conscious and well-proven means to realise such experience. If the methods of the sages did not work, they would not have been persisted in for thousands upon thousands of years. So we can opt to use the methods and work on ourselves, or remain lost, uptight, anxious, aggressive and unhappy.

But in any case, our inherent nature refuses to allow us to backslide for too long. Once we have become conscious of 'being on the Path', we may try to give it up, become tired of practice and forget it for a time, but our driving need will win out in the end. Once one knows something of the spiritual life, one cannot easily return to cabbagehood. Besides, the Omni-presence is always working on us from within. When a spring-time bud is near its flowering time an inexorable force of nature impels it to burst into blossom. And so it is with us. Some unbidden pressure builds up inside and pushes us to carry on our inner work – to make us flower. And we ignore its promptings at our peril. Even anguish stirring in the soul is a birth-pang of the spirit – a prelude to one's inner blossoming.

It is wiser to attune ourselves to these inner promptings which tell us we are drifting away from the Self, rather than relying on the wretched ramblings of the mind which lead us further astray. We cannot expect the mind to quieten by itself. We have to do something about it. The slippery sense-of-ego and its self-justifications for 'sloping off' can never be over-come without constant vigilance and awareness of its wily ways. There is no easy way out. Ultimately we have no hope of attaining inner peace without working on ourselves. As Bhagavan says: "Even if we find somebody who has achieved this supreme state of stillness [without any obvious effort – such as Bhagavan himself] you can take it that *the necessary effort has already been made in a previous life*."[2] (Italics mine).

So effort has to be made, not to gain anything new, but to wipe the slate clean and experience ourselves as we really are. To do that means we have to toss out all the concepts and conditionings of our upbringing, and also the conditionings we have unquestioningly lapsed into in our *present* lifestyle. Whilst the intellect is still swayed by its inner tendencies and predispositions, then effort is necessary, if only to get rid of them. The first step then, is to take stock of what those hidden and unformulated inner hang-ups are. Constant effort is needed at every moment to step back and be aware of them in order to know what needs eradicating. Otherwise we will always be at the mercy of the mind, being caught up and involved in its endless chatterboxing to no purpose.

But man's ticker-tape mind is so full of his daily doings, the price of potatoes, rice and beans, the newspaper headlines, the political situation, war and injustice, radio reports, television and films, bosses and boardrooms, sex and the social whirl, the family, the rent, the job, the future, the past, the harrassment of the next-door neighbour – or his kids, or dog – or *anything* other than the thing that is closest to him: the blissful nature of his Real Self. He never has a thought-free moment to realise his true condition of existence.

Even when falling exhausted into bed there is no escape from the motions of the mind. Not only does it chatter away all night long, it even creates a phantasmagorical living film show of a dream world for us to participate in at another level of reality. Whether we remember our dreams or not, they still go on and we are obliged to join in. But if *I* am fast asleep – then who is the dreamer? If I identify myself with my body, and the body is sleeping, then who is this entity who is participating in the dream? At the shallow end of sleep, when my consciousness is functioning on two different levels and I am aware that I'm dreaming, I say I and the dreamer are one. But when I am totally involved in the dream experience (in a dream body) I have no knowledge of my physical body and no identification with it, believing my dream body to be the 'real thing'. Thus I cannot *be* my physical body, otherwise I – or *it* – would be aware of it all the time.

It is the mind which is completely involved in the dream-world. Am I then the mind? If that is the case, then who is getting any sleep and rest? If I am the mind – then what is the use of going to bed if I am only going to spend the whole night gallivanting round in my own fantasies? But if the mind itself

is only one of my fantasies – as the sages assert – then what am
I? At some point in the night comes that period of deep sleep
without even dreams, when that peculiar entity we imagine
ourselves to be, and think of as 'I', disappears without trace.
My sense of 'I-ness' strangely dissolves into a blissful oblivion
of no thought, no world and no dream world. The waking and
dreaming 'I' has ceased to exist. Without that *I*-idea there is no
mind.

If that *I*-idea and what I take to be my own mind can
disappear, then my whole existence is founded on an unstable
illusion. Now you have it, now you don't. How could such a
mind, or that 'I', be myself? For that 'I' which I usually believe
to be myself to have remained in existence in deep sleep, there
had to be that very 'I' remaining consciously alert to know it.
Otherwise I am forced to conclude that I pop in and out of
existence like a cuckoo in a clock.

So who *was* the eternal witness to my existence in deep
sleep? No doubt *something* exists in that condition. Is there a
'stable' me at a deeper level, which does not fluctuate, some
sense of 'I-ness' beyond what I normally take to be myself.
Who am I? *What* is the real me? Am I some other I? With the
extinction of the limited sense-of-I with which I am familiar, it
appears that a thought-free 'something' beyond mind still
exists, in a seemingly paradoxical state of 'non-existence' – a
situation which is comparable to the mysterious condition
known as 'death' to the layman. And yet every morning one
always appears to wake up from it. By extension, can there be
then such a thing as death? For everything in the realm of Spirit
has its analogy in the world of 'matter', and everything in the
world of matter reflects an aspect of the subtle workings of the
Spirit.

Nightly sleep is nightly death of the individual 'I'. Yet we
are not afraid to enter into *that* 'non-existent' condition, which
so terrifies us in death. On the contrary, it is the greatest bliss
for us. We are only too eager to escape into it after spending
only sixteen hours or so of wakefulness in this workaday
world. Why is it so? The sages say that with the dissolution of
thought, we enter into the 'Consciousness of the Self' (God-
Consciousness). And that is where 'we' emerged from. We are

only conscious in the present because of 'awakening' out of That. But this condition into which we awaken is equivalent to a dream about being alive, compared to the vital reality of that original state.

In deep sleep we return to that condition – but without conscious awareness. There comes a period when all the unreal and superimposed gabblings of the waking and dreaming worlds become finally stilled. In this 'night of the mind' we blissfully abide for a brief time in our true condition as the substratum of existence. And this short contact with our real nature is the only experience of the day which refurnishes us with enough mental strength to go on through another sixteen to twenty odd hours of what can sometimes be absolutely hellish non-stop thinking. Even a few minutes of that blissful mindlessness each night, is enough to recharge us. If we were denied access to that condition by being kept at the surface level of sleep for a few days, then we would soon become physically uncoordinated and mentally disorientated to the point of madness. Therefore the deep sleep state, or nightly entry into the Self is a vital necessity – at least for those who are not experiencing 'effortless awareness' in meditation.

It is frustrating to realise that every night we effortlessly enter into a similitude of the *sat-chit-ananda samadhi* state, but with veiled awareness. Like the flowers and trees unfolding themselves in the flow of universal consciousness, we are not cognisant of it. We can only infer the 'existence' part of that condition because the mind-body-ego-complex we take our-selves to be, still appears to exist on waking – but the 'consciousness and bliss' experience is lacking altogether. Yet even in the oblivious ignorance of that nightly event we are re-vitalised and refreshed.

If we could experience that condition while remaining conscious and alert, how much more powerful might it be? Is it possible? Not only is it possible, but it is the ultimate joy of joys expressed by the mystics down the ages who have entered into that divine state by the practice of meditation. What they have done, everyone can do. Such is the assertion of all those who have ever attained to the realisation of the Self. And their methods have been refined and perfected over countless centuries, for the dissolution of the sense-of-ego and the vagaries of the mind. If we have misused our minds for most of our lives, we cannot expect to have instant results from our practice. But gentle and persistent efforts will eventually bear fruit, providing of course, that one is *constant* in keeping the flighty mind from butterflying out into the delusions of the world.

As Bhagavan says: "Though all the scriptures have said it and though we hear it daily from the great ones and even from our guru, we are never quiet but stray into the world of *Maya*★ and sense objects. That is why conscious, deliberate effort is needed to attain that effortless state of stillness. Now [in the early stages of development] it is impossible for you to be without effort. When you go deeper, it is impossible for you to make effort."[1]

★*Maya* is the veiling power over the mind which makes the illusion of the world appear as 'reality', giving the impression of being something distinct from the Omnipresence.

Following the Fat Cats of Gurudom

Q. *I get concerned about the difference between self-hypnosis and enlightenment. One of my closest friends is very critical of the sheep-like nature of most people; they tend to want to follow, be told what to do, etc. He especially condemns Rajneesh (who does have quite a hypnotic voice!) and I myself would seriously question many sannya-sins'* motives for following him. They find his way attractive because it offers:*
1. An identity ('I am a sannyasin')*
2. An instant circle of friends
3. Excitement (free-love, etc.)
Also a lot of money is made by many gurus, especially Rajneesh. It annoys me that enlightenment is still for the rich and those with no money are tied to the struggle for survival. Do you think I have a too high ideal or just misunderstanding? I'd much appreciate your thoughts on the subject.

A. This problem of self-hypnosis is a tricky one. There is no problem with enlightenment. When genuine enlightenment occurs it is known to be unmistakable. If one reads the lives of the sages, whose awakenings were often sudden and ecstatic,

*A *sannyasin* is an initiate.

but which left them in a state of permanent Realisation, it is obvious that there was never any doubt as to the authenticity of the phenomenon. It is therefore only with self-deception that we need concern ourselves.

After a breakthrough in his meditation, a yoga teacher of my acquaintance began telephoning everyone he knew in great excitement to let them know he had become enlightened! The very fact that he needed to tell everybody about it was proof enough of his delusion. He had, in fact, undergone what the Japanese monks call *satori* – an illuminating experience, which he had taken for the final thing. He would have been wiser to wait awhile, but he was bubbling over with self-gratification at his achievement. Had he not been so caught up in spiritual pride he might have recalled that Self-realisation also brings about a chastening awe and a humbling of the soul in which the sense-of-ego and the sense-of-separateness disappear. For a Realised Soul – when he and the Omnipresence are One – who is there left to tell about it? Much to his chagrin, the yoga teacher's 'enlightenment high' fizzled out very soon after.

Another time, a yoga teacher came to me bursting with similar enthusiasm, to tell me of a wonderfully transforming experience which had 'changed her life', at a local Christian Charismatic meeting. I could tell from the somewhat scattered and glazed look in her eyes and the agitated atmosphere, that she was suffering more from religious hysteria than anything profound. And this was further confirmed by her very uncharacteristic and pious exclamations of *'Praise the Lord!'* with which she punctuated her speech every few minutes, with an evangelical fervour. Coming from a *yogini** whose heart was more naturally inclined to Eastern teachings, this was all the more disturbing.

Had it been a natural and genuinely heart-opening conversion, there would have been no problem. But at this period my friend had been going through a very trying and nerve-racking crisis in her personal life. She was also emotionally involved in the falling apart of her marriage to the very Christian leader of the Circle and had been struggling to mend their relations by

*Female yogi

bridging the gap between their physical and philosophical lifestyles. The highly charged atmosphere created in the Charismatic Circle had tipped the balance of her sensibilities, evoking a rush of false euphoria to take her out of her troubled mind. But the result was in the nature of psychic disorientation rather than of spiritual revelation.

Having seen such signs before, I knew the 'come-down' and return to her former nervous depression would be heavy. Not having the heart to destroy her pseudo-euphoric illusion all at once, I was obliged to insert a carefully worded psychological pin, suggesting she closely evaluate the experience relative to her emotional attachment to the group-leader, so as to bring about a steady deflation without sudden trauma. And so it turned out. She came out of it gently in a day or two, observing the event as I had suggested and coming to realise the desire-prompted psychological factors, borne of desperation, which had brought about her mental disequilibrium.

There are of course, many examples of spiritual euphoria in the lives of Christian, Muslim and Hindu sages. But the 'God-mad' ecstasy of the saints is worlds apart from a sudden outburst of psychically induced mental imbalance. The energy generated by long-standing spiritual practice is characterised by a radiation of great love emanating from the mystic, whose eyes are often shining with a piercing light (not at all glazed or glassy!) And his atmosphere or 'vibration' is of a gently joyous energy rather than that of agitation and distractedness. But even this is a phase on the path and subsides into a quiet glow after a time, in which the experiencer gently abides ever afterwards.

A completed guru has usually passed through the phases of his own madness and his discerning eye knows immediately if a student is crazy, illumined or merely deluded. He perceives at once where a student stands on the level of spiritual ascendency. If you imagine you are realised and you are not, then a guru can show you exactly where you are at. Such is one of the worthy functions of a guru: to administer a swift kick to your presumptuous rear if you are fantasising with yourself. And if you feel yourself to be 'too advanced' to be checked out by a guru, or on the other hand, perhaps afraid of a guru 'seeing into you', then you can know right away you are not where you think you are. Even if such a guide is not available for this necessary function, you might try instead going to stay with your mother for a while! If you can pass this simple test with equanimity and unruffled feelings, then you are well on the way.

When working in group situations, the energy generated can bring on varying degrees of 'collective euphoria' which can be an aid in spiritual 'quickening' if wisely guided. But in badly controlled groups, where anything goes, the more wild and unchannelled energies can also run to the lowest common denominator, such as sensuality, aggression or a fervid 'contact high' of religious delirium. It all depends on the forces at work. In many 'guru-groupie' circles, whatever happens is usually attributed to the guru, who may not even be the slightest bit involved. But the disciples often desperately *want* it to be the 'power of the guru', whether he has the ability to generate it or not.

The atmosphere of a so-called 'spiritual intensive' is thus often charged with the collective fantasy of the participants. The excitement which is generated appeals mostly to the mind and emotions, rather than the spirit, which can sweep the spiritually unwary off their feet – or out of their heads. Some feel that bizarre effects are 'expected' of them, or their spiritual pride demands that they are seen to be 'spontaneously' experiencing *kriyas* (automatic movements), while others work themselves up into a crazily explosive state. And the resulting aberrations such as 'holy-rolling' speaking in tongues, '*shakti-jumping*' or whatever, are therefore generally of a psychic rather than of a spiritual nature.

This is not to say that these things do not also occur naturally in advanced adepts, but they often tend to be forced among dilettantish beginners. But whatever occurs in a group situation, it creates a group togetherness, bonded by the shared experience. Although some of these outrageously expensive weekend 'Enlightenment Intensives' of differing groups (as promoted by Madison Avenue sales techniques) may bring about a mental-emotional breakthrough here and there, such happenings cannot be equated either with Self-realisation or the value of steady inner development under the guidance of a spiritual master. So there is no need to feel that one is missing out on anything.

According to my (participatory) observation, such events serve mainly to swell the ranks of the organisation, and create an evangelical fervour in the participants, which is always dangerous to spiritual stability and clear-sightedness. A fanatical in-crowd loyalty tends to develop among those who are smugly 'in the know', or at the mildest it breeds a cliquish élitism, which seems to make the participants unfit for the company of any but their 'in-group' peers, or their *Guru-bhais* ('Brothers of the same Guru').

On the other hand, the genuine 'family feeling' which gathers around a real spiritual master and his teaching, is alluring and heartwarming for those involved in it. And why not? Never mind the specious speculations as to why they are there. The experience of *Satsang* – or association with the wise and True – is one of the most vital aspects of the spiritual life. Providing that such involvement does not ostracise outsiders (nor evangelise them) and one remains open to the rest of the world, it is a worthy way to live.

But alas! such groupy-ness most often tends to alienate outsiders and diminishes the insider's capacity for dealing with the rest of the world. And in the Hindu-oriented sects, to become a special 'something', like a *sannyasin,* an initiate, or a *swami* may add colour to an otherwise humdrum life, but it also brings about a bolstering of the spiritual ego which is hard to overcome. In the case of Rajneesh, however, he maintains that he feeds his followers with ego-inflating titles and *swami*-hood to make them realise how ridiculous they are. Many take the titles, but not the point. And often non-red/orange-wearing 'lesser mortals' are looked upon askance. Belong to a *Guru-bhai* family-brotherhood by all means, but it is as well to remember – while in the body – that the world you live in is still your house and home, and the rest of the human race your family.

As to why others choose to join a particular group or sect – are the motives of others really our concern? Let us each look to our own. We all have our reasons for doing what we do: or think we have. Yet we also may be moved by forced beyond our ken. But in any case, each of us gets what he karmically deserves – whether he has money or not. Even supposing you were well off and you find a guru who is mainly into making a mint of money for himself – do you imagine you will gain enlightenment from such a one?

Can you show me *anyone* who has ever gained enlighten-ment from paying heavy fees?

Of what do you imagine you are being deprived? One has to cultivate spiritual discrimination in such matters. You can better assess the effect of a guru on yourself from a quiet interview, than from a 'wham-bang sock-it-to-me' weekend devised by his disciples. Beware of the words of devotees for they speak with coloured tongues. Nor can you evaluate a teacher's quality by the trumpet fanfare from the advertising angels heralding his coming. Some 'masters' appoint a publi-city agent and others operate quietly and unobtrusively, working personally with their students. The attainment and loving rapport of a lesser-known teacher may well be worth much more to you than the famous guru you must pay vast sums to see from afar. But in any case, we have to realise that both need some kind of financial support. One is free to choose what seems most reasonable. No one is obliged to follow the fat cats of gurudom.

Many gurus in India are able to teach freely, because they are supported by the donations of wealthy householders, as are the *sadhus* still struggling towards enlightenment, because the Eastern peoples realise that the cultivation of sages in their midst is of inestimable value to themselves, and thus the world. In the West there are also many teachers who would like to work for nothing, but are obliged to ask a fee, since travel funds, food and housing, etc., must be found. Unfor-tunately there is no tradition of gifting or supporting a spiritual master in Western society, if his vision happens to be outside or beyond the borders of the Christian tradition. He is gener-ally unable to devote himself wholeheartedly to the total awakening of his spiritual potential, being obliged to either set up some semi-commercial spiritual enterprise around himself, or take on some form of worldly work to live by.

Even so, many naive Western seekers tend to feel affronted when their spiritual teacher appears to be even nominally involved in any sort of commerce to survive (thereby labelling him 'worldly'), and seem to imagine that he should magically exist like a being in a fairy-tale without the need for money. Yet they are the last to offer anything to ease his burden, under the impression that a teacher's time is theirs and needs no recompense. I feel that this lack of economic support, and the general absence of cultural encouragement, are perhaps a part of the reason why we have so few mystic masters of distinction in the West.

We judge our teachers according to our lights, dim as they are. But can we really judge from the appearances of what we see and hear? Some Hindu *swamis* disdain to touch money at all, snootily considering it 'vile and dirty stuff'. They may impress the gullible, but are we to take them seriously as holy men, or as neurotics suffering from a form of spiritual one-upmanship? We can also find ascetics vainglorious in their self-mortifications (such as holding one arm in the air for twenty years until it withers), as a means of creating public wonder and support. There are others who take no other food but milk, and are proud of it, adept at the holy game of being 'more renunciate than thou'. Are these then, any more venerable than the money-makers?

In any case who knows what works a guru may intend to do with his hoarded wealth? We may see him spending it on luxurious hotels and mixing with high society. Does this mean he is a profligate or is he a 'Guerilla of the Inner Planes' doing 'undercover' work where it is most needed, in influencing the leaders of the land? Or perhaps he intends to establish spiritual centres everywhere, or collective farms, orphanages, hospitals and schools. Some 'gurus' may actually *be* frustrated playboys let loose in the permissive Western world. But is it really our concern?

Is it not the impact of the Master on our lives which matters most? Whatever he does should be related to how *we* see life within our own psychological make-up and not to what we think *he* should do. It is our choice to take or leave what any guru gives. To try to bind a guru to your idea of what you have preconceived, is to deny freedom for him and to ignore the opportunity for growth his actions have prompted in you. There is no 'ideal' guru. Even the most illumined sage may act outrageously according to our cultural conditioning. Mahatma Gandhi was known often to sleep between two women as part of his *sadhana* and self-observation. So what seems obvious to outsiders may be something else again. A sage may be doing it to awaken you, or he may have other reasons of his own. In any case you cannot fathom his motives.

A real guru is a walking *koan*.★

And the only answer to it is your own awakening.

★A *koan* is a seemingly nonsensical and enigmatic phrase used by Zen Masters to awaken their students to an intuitive awareness beyond the limits of mind and intellect.

ON CHANGING THE
WORLD

Those who want to take over the world and improve it will never succeed.
Lao Tzu

Q. *How does one help to change the world, to make it a better place to live in?*

There are so many problems and so much suffering in the world, people starving, wars, famine, floods, political upheaval, suppression of the people, etc., etc. Yet for outsiders the yogic way appears to be a retreat from the world in order to work on oneself. Therefore some people say the yogi is being selfish and that it would be better if he became a social worker or something, to really help the afflicted. I would appreciate it if you would clarify your view of this issue.

The Way of the Worldly Man –
Revolution

A. This problem is extremely complex and has to be looked at from many different angles. Let us first look at the ways of the world, and then at the workings of the subtle world and its mystics, who – like the Omnipresence – 'move in mysterious ways, their wonders to perform'.

I'll begin with a little parable:

Once upon a time God said to all Creation: "Now everything is running smoothly, I think I'll take a little holiday. Who will look after things while I'm away?" The gods blanched at the responsibility. They looked uncertainly at each other, twiddling their fingers and coughing a little self-consciously. The devas and angelic beings all shuffled their feet and looked elsewhere, trying to hum. Suddenly up piped Man, who said, "Go on Gaffer! We can manage things all right, don't you worry!" So off went God and Man began to shape his own destiny. And since then God has never been allowed another chance.

Man still imagines he is in charge of the world. But for some reason it's not working out so well. He surveys his handiwork and sees the endless wars and riots, the graft and inequality, the corruption of those in power, the mindless racism, the exploitation and rape of the earth, the famine and suffering and suppression of peoples and the ever-present threat of total annihilation. He is not altogether impressed.

In fact, in spite of his wealth and technological power, when he allows himself to feel, he finds he is downright miserable. Therefore it must be somebody's fault. Forgetting he has taken over the role of God, he shakes his fist at the heavens and snarls, "What sort of a God allows a world like this?" It is always helpful to find a scapegoat. On getting no satisfactory response from God, one can always accuse his supporters. "Look at all these spiritual escapists! These yogis, gurus, and mystic hermits living in selfish seclusion, or walking about with their heads in the clouds! What use are they to the world? If they have any answers, why don't they get back in the world and sort things out?" The idea is that even if there are those who are not contributing to the troubles of the world, they must have their noses rubbed in it and be made to feel guilty about it.

Man's memory is short. He forgets that almost every time a holy man has attempted to put the world to rights, he has either been crucified, burned at the stake, shot dead, or otherwise hounded and harrassed. Hardly a conducive method for encouraging involvement in the world! Yet even so, many a sage has laid bare his breast for the world's welfare and paid the penalty. It would seem that only history reveres a holy man. Rarely, if ever, is he acclaimed by the 'madding-crowds' of his contemporary world. For the problem is that the Seer inconveniently speaks the Truth, and people do not care very much for the Truth. The *status quo* is much more comfortable. And truth has always been bad for priestly, commercial and governmental business.

People much prefer to live in their illusions and yet fondly imagine they really want the world to change. "It's not me, it's the others" is the prevalent attitude and belief. And preferably the 'others' should do something about the state of affairs. Hence the insistence of some that the yogi or the contemplative should become social workers instead of 'selfishly' seeking their own salvation. Yet the world is already filled with uncountable numbers of 'unselfish' social workers, welfare institutions and well-meaning do-gooders of all kinds, attempting to ameliorate the problems of the planet; but do we find anything changing as a result? Although their work is worthy, does it really affect the way of the world at all? Are they not simply involved in the patching-up of the miseries of man's endless inhumanity to man? And do our political and governmental paper legislations, treaties and suchlike really hold water or effect social change? Or are they usually ignored (like the Race Relations Act for example) because the majority of mankind is unready for the change?

At least those working towards these ends are doing what they can according to their limited world view. But those who complain the loudest about what others are not doing, what are they doing to help the world? Often they are living un-happily in it, begrudgingly 'doing their bit' and caustic in their attitudes towards those who are doing what they feel drawn to do. The craftsman who is happy in his work does not feel the need to tell others what they should do with their lives. Those who are miserable in their own occupations or mode of living, but are afraid to change them, simply grumble their way through life, generally casting gloom and despondency all around them.

It is of little use to profess concern for the world at large if we are not daily working to promote happiness in our immediate surroundings. If I am not consciously engaged in lightening someone else's day, then chances are I am darkening it. We seem unable to see the futility of wanting to help the oppressed in Latin America or wherever, if we are constantly uptight at home or work, suppressing our children, or having rows with our life partners, parents or flatmates. We are often unaware in the way we allow ourselves to get drawn in by the tensions of others. We see the chain reaction when the boss-man puts the pressure on at work: the next man down tends to release his humiliation by testily asserting his meagre authority where he can, causing *his* subordinates to vent their spleen on someone else in turn and so on, way down the line. Those at the end of the chain may take it home with them, abusing fellow motorists in the traffic on the way, and throwing a domestic tyrant 'moodie' on their families for the evening. Such pressures, among many others, (duplicated in a billion homes and factories and offices) all add to the stressful mental climate almost everywhere today.

If we are already pressurised within, almost anything outside can light the fuse. Thus we all carry the seeds of mental, verbal or physical warfare in our emotional instability and uncontrollable minds. If my nervous system is so easily inflamed, am I any better than the warmongering 'others' I condemn? Surely all the miseries of the world begin with attitudes like mine? If I cannot control my own escalating reactions, how can I hope to effect any worthwhile change in the world?

But the mass of mankind is not so introspective. It prefers immediate external solutions to what it believes are external causes. And on the surface at least, it would appear that the causes are from the outside. For example, a large percentage of children who grow up under the constant pressures of parental, scholastic and social control, eventually lash out blindly (or calculatingly and revengefully) at the 'world' ('society', 'women', 'wogs') or any other conveniently unrealistic label. Hence the resulting riots and revolutions, racialism, political wars, dictatorships and all kinds of criminality. But the retributive smashing of rioters (or governments) changes nothing intrinsically. The fires of the losers merely go underground and smoulder with a deeper fury. "When hatred follows hatred, where will it end?" said the Buddha. We have to break the chain somewhere.

But why are the pressures there in the first place?

No child brought up lovingly becomes a dictator. Simple as that. But our parents were perhaps unable to give their all, being pressurised by *their* parents and social norms and financial difficulties and war, as were their grandparents by their war-struck world and so on, back as far as you like. Thus we can always blame the system, society, police, parents, the government and the like. And certainly all these have something to answer for.

Does the petty power-seeking bureaucrat ever wonder if his thin-lipped loveless attitude bears any relation to the explosive nature of today's world? Were all such persons to have a change of heart and suddenly realise that they are in fact 'public servants' and sincerely try to help (rather than hinder, as is usual) the people who came to them, they could, by that alone, astoundingly change the spirit – not only of a nation – but of a New World struggling to be born. Must it always be miserly spirits who seek to place themselves in such occupations?

But we cannot change the attitudes of others either by force or legislation. Others change themselves when their time has come. We can only live our own vision. If it is pure and selfless, others will change by our example. Therefore we must first look to ourselves. It is our own mental attitudes which have moulded our lives so far and will continue to determine them for the future.

Although our minds may be coloured and conditioned by past events, it is unworthy of us to use this as an excuse for our present actions. For it is the way each of us reacts NOW – from moment to moment – that is the 'cause' of future events. Where one person explodes in a given situation, another takes things calmly. Therefore it is not the events in themselves that are the problem, but our fearful or aggressive reactions to-wards them. If we react with an inflamed ego we escalate the warring attitude of the world. But if – like the contemplative – we have worked on ourselves to dissolve the sense-of-ego, then the nature of the world itself becomes changed in our eyes. If the ego no longer leaps at every real or imagined provocation, we find it is not the world that is at fault, but our view of it which needed adjusting. Once we begin to 'see' without the 'scales' of conditioning over our eyes, we realise something of the 'Oneness' of the world. We come to understand that all in all it is the way it was meant to be.

"That's all very well," I hear the worldly reply, "but can you call all this violence and senseless savagery the way things were meant to be? Are we supposed to sit back and watch it all without doing anything about it? Suppose some great lout is about to attack you, you can't just turn the other cheek, muttering 'Oneness brother' and loving your neighbour as yourself, now can you?" True enough. Or is it? It depends on how we understand the mysterious workings of the world.

It is recorded that the Methodist preacher John Wesley once went to a village to give a sermon, but was confronted by the village bully laden with an armful of stones. The bully warned Wesley that he would be stoned if he opened his mouth to preach. Wesley neither ran away nor attacked the bully. He looked thoughtfully at him and said, "You cannot throw a single stone unless my heavenly father permits you." The authority with which he spoke stopped the bully in his tracks. This 'authority' was the fact that Wesley was living what he spoke. They were not merely empty words. Wesley was convinced that all was God and, that being so, the bully was also a process of God going on for his benefit. Therefore he was prepared to be stoned if necessary, as God would be teaching him something thereby. This attitude opened the mind of the bully, who dropped his aggression and later became Wesley's staunchest supporter.

Wesley had internally 'seen' the true nature of the world. By living in his vision he created a bastion of spiritual strength around himself. Supposing a whole nation could steep themselves in such a vision? What need then would there be for the dubious 'protection' of H-bombs and the like? I do not doubt that the prayers and righteousness of a nation steeped in Godward consciousness in times of war contributes mightily to their freedom from an unjust regime.

But the worldly man's answer has always been to fight fire with equally vindictive fire. "When words and legislations no longer suffice," he says, "we must take to arms!" Such a rabble-rousing cry creates what I call the usual 'Orthodox Revolution'. There is nothing new in it. The seething suppressed (or simply uptight), suddenly have a vehicle for the release of their pent up emotions and another free-for-all bloody revolution occurs. But do such antics ever get us anywhere? The great Mao Tse Tung revolution has vanished almost without trace in today's China.

During the 1968 'May Revolution' of France, the student 'revolutionaries' won the day, the Government crumbled and handed over the power. But then it was embarrassingly discovered that the 'people' had no idea what to do once they had had their fling and taken control. The students no longer had faith in 'personality cult' leaders, but had no better ideas with which to replace the old system. They also failed to enlist the aid of the 'workers', the backbone of the country, who 'stubbornly' stuck to their old way of life. Thus for lack of a visionary blueprint living in the hearts and minds of the masses, they lost impetus and the old establishment school obligingly returned to power.

But even if the 'revolutionaries' had been successful in the old way and installed a strong new leader, with such 'orthodox' attitudes whenever has this type of 'changing the world' done any lasting good? Here and there, no doubt, in the beginning, a revolution may make a few changes for the better, at the cost of destroying other worthwhile 'institutions' loved by others. But because revolutions have always been based on an 'Us and Them' mentality, charged with anger and violence, the means by which they have been accomplished have always sowed the seeds of their own degenerative destruction in the end.

Each time, the protagonists of revolution fall for the idea that 'the ends will justify the means', believing in the 'war to end all wars' – but do we ever see any evidence of an end in sight? Once the first 'end' is accomplished (by expedient means) there are always other ends to go for. And how many hearts have changed for the better in the process? The dispossessed go underground and find other ways to fight back. Thus new expedient means are brought to bear and have to be enforced. Since there appear to be no ends, we must conclude we live by endless means. How then can we hope to justify the means which are self-perpetuating and never end? Our way of acting *is* our way of life. And if we feel the need to justify our actions at all (if only in our own hearts) then they are incorrect.

Not that we should avoid a 'just war' against a despot (or despotic government) if we have allowed things to reach such a state. But it were better we avoid the 'orthodox revolutionary' attitudes of the past. So many unhappy and disturbed people want to change the surface appearance of things 'out there' rather than realising they need to get rid of their own psychological problems first. And the world is the way it is precisely because it is full of emotionally unstable people interfering in the lives of others. Thus although they may be sincere in their intentions, revolutions by such deluded people are always doomed to failure.

Take any revolution in history, study the aims and ideals (if any) behind it and look at today's conditions in the place it occurred. What happened in every case? Need we ask? How long did it take before the revolutionaries became the power-seekers and the glory-boys of the Establishment? How many years was it before their irritating rash of idealism was absorbed by smothering grey-minded bureaucracy? How easily did they learn the ways of governing, still steeped in the conditioning of those who went before? And how long before the 'freed' people felt the yoke descending on them once again and sought to escape from the authoritarianism of their so-called 'liberated' country?

The 'Glorious Revolution' is a fickle mistress. In a few weeks, months or years, we are always back where we started. The names of the leaders are changed, a new set of self-bolstering egocentrics are installed and 'Bureaucracy rules, O.K.?' Meanwhile the needful pressures of government are put on, the life of the people changes not at all and the whole tedious cycle comes around again. Any orthodox revolution based upon the average materialistic and intellectually myopic conception of the universe cannot hope to lead anywhere.

Given the apparent nature of gross life on this planet, if any kind of change is possible at all, it is only a 'grass-roots' revolution that could hope to bring about anything worth-

while. Unless the majority of people of a nation have cultivated a vision – an awakened wholistic consciousness – one
concerned for the welfare of all, then the superimposition of
any new regime can come to nothing. The real essence of
change and transformation of 'society' (which is no more than
you and me, multiplied *ad infinitum*) is therefore brought about
only by the evolution of each individual consciousness into a
higher state of receptivity. Then only can we naturally treat
each other as we wish to be treated ourselves. Thus in little
ways, step by step, we can all play our part in changing the
consciousness of the earthbound mass mentality.

Happily this is at last beginning to happen all over the
world, as the Old Age patriotic separatist mentality is being
suffused with an influx of 'Planetary Citizen Consciousness'
from those of us who believe in the Oneness of All Mankind.
There are also many others sensitively extending this
ecological consciousness to all other forms of life on this earth,
for we are all members of a chain-reactive unity, bound to live
or die together.

A former United Nations Secretary General, U Thant,
declared many times during his office, that it was only the web
of meditators spread out all over the globe which was preventing the planet from descending into complete chaos. By meditatively sinking deep inside ourselves, unity with the world is
no longer a mental idea but a living experience. Then the
barriers between ourselves and all life dissolve. In such experience lies true transformation. Those who meditate daily, the
sages and yogis, religious contemplatives and the growing
millions of awakening spiritual seekers could be called the
'Guerillas of the Inner Planes' for it is in them that the real
revolution is occurring, before being brought into manifestation. In this way the steady flowering of each individual heart
is bringing about a truer blossoming of the world.

Where there is no vision, the people perish.

Proverbs 29, 18

The Way of the Wise Man —
Revelation

In Part One we reviewed the 'Way of the Worldly Man' in attempting to change the world by legislation and/or revolution and found an endless succession of recurring cycles. Finding his own way unsatisfactory, the worldly man rebukes the 'escapist' seeker and the sage for 'selfishly' following their hearts rather than 'helping to change the world'. But does the world need changing or is it our conception of it that needs readjusting?

To begin with: what is our conception of the universe? Do we have any notion of its true nature? Do we believe it is obviously that which we see in front of our noses? Do we follow the scientific explanations which purport to tell us how things actually are? Or do we have a more visionary view, in which we are able to see what is beyond the physical manifestation? The spiritual Masters of all traditions, throughout the ages, have always stressed that the world is not what we take it to be. Being so emotionally involved in it, we are generally unable to see the wood for the trees. Unless we step back and take a good look beyond our conditioning, we can have no real understanding of the workings of the world and our position in it.

It has long been known that our senses give us a totally erroneous picture of the universe in the way we perceive it. For example, science has shown us we see the light of stars which no longer exist. We see the sky as blue, which it is not. Even the red rose is any colour *but* red, since it absorbs all other colours but reflects back the red. Many people are colour-blind; yet if they were in the majority, the 'visionary' who saw colour would be laughed at, as are those today who can see beyond the 'physical' appearance of the world. Most humans also see, hear and smell in an extremely limited spectrum compared with many other creatures on this earth.

The authority of the senses has been experientially exploded for the 'man in the street' in the last few decades by the advent of the mind-releasing drug LSD. It changed the lifestyle of a generation bringing visionary experience to the 'ordinary man' and removing his conceptual barriers between mind and so-called 'matter'. Even modern scientists have found themselves becoming mystics on discovering that nothing exists which can be called 'solid matter'. Everything we see is purely a creative vibrational energy oscillating in the Cosmic Flux. The eminent physicist Sir James Jeans stated that 'the Universe begins to look more like a great *thought* than a great machine'. Science thereby corroborates what the Seers have known intuitively from the first – that the world in which we imagine we live, has no tangible existence!

Then what in the name of wonder is it we may well ask.

What appears to exist (both under the electron microscope and the inward gaze of the Sage) is nothing but a pattern of energies thrown upon the 'screen' of consciousness. This mess of vibration we decide to perceive as 'the world', for the time we are involved in it. But without our participation in this wondrous three-dimensional hologrammistic cosmic film show, is there anything there at all? What happens when the light from the projector (mind) goes out? 'Withdraw the mind,' say the sages, 'and the Universe is not.'

So at best we can say that the world is *relatively* real. Just as a film is relatively real, being unreal as a tangible event or substance on the screen, but 'real' as a film show. We could say that the world is 'real' relative to the quality of perception of the individual consciousness at any given moment. From an esoteric viewpoint, the world may be compared to something like a rainbow. A rainbow has no 'tangible' existence, yet it temporarily appears to exist because of a combination of the moisture in the air and the angle of the sun in relation to the position of the beholder. It has no substantial actuality, yet it is relatively real as a phenomenon we perceive, because of our angle of vision.

We see the world in a similar way. It appears thus because of

our 'angle' of vision. Or, perhaps it does not appear and
something else does. We may see other dimensions of experience, according to the interior condition or 'angle' from which
our level of awareness views things. From the 'angle' of what
we call 'death' we may see a relatively different universe
altogether. Similarly for the period before conception and
birth. Again, from the 'angle' of profound deep sleep it appears
that no universe of any kind exists. "But we know it is still
there, because it appears to others!" is the usual objection. But
does it? Are there in actuality, any others? Here the rationalist
and the mystic irrevocably part company, for we are getting
into really deep waters.

Only a vaguely graspable essence of this experience can be
conveyed. For example: on coming out of the non-conscious-
ness of deep sleep into shallower sleep, we somehow find
ourselves within a dream universe. It is usually a seemingly
real enough world we awaken into. We find it well populated
with millions of people, cities and continents and oceans and
all the complexities of life. It is an existence we absolutely
believe in whilst living it. How could we doubt it? We are
experiencing it. Everything appears to be solid to the senses. If
someone in the dream told you 'this is only a dream' you
would laugh it off as absurd, pointing out how graspably real
everything is. You realistically taste all the pleasures and
believe utterly in the terrors. Then suddenly, or gradually,
you 'wake up' to find it was 'only' a dream. This whole
phantasmagorical 'external' world you pleasured or suffered
in, simply blossomed out of your 'sleeping' consciousness.

But into what do you 'awaken'? You emerge from one level
of sleeping consciousness into yet another relatively real
dream world – the one in which you are dreaming you are
reading this – and imagine that *this* is the only real world,
simply because it endures a little longer than the previous one.
But even four score years and ten (in short sixteen-hour bursts)
appear only a moment in eternity. 'That which does not
endure, is not the *Real*' say the profound scriptures of the
Seers. They also tell us that only when we awaken from this
daily dream of life will the 'Great Illusion' be ended.

What the dreamer dreams is nothing else but the dreamer.

All the people and events of your dreams are only a projection of yourself. The remarkable variety of personalities and incredibly detailed minutiae of your dream world were no more than the fantastic Cosmic Drama of your mind. We scoff at the idea that we are 'inventing' this whole universe in which we find ourselves. Yet we daily 'awaken' into this one out of another no less amazingly complex. Where are the dividing lines?

In your dream world you may suddenly have been killed and the shock of it threw you 'awake' into this world. (And what then, if you are killed in this world?) Meanwhile the terrifying calamities of your dream world evaporated when you woke up. But what of the 'other people' in your dream catastrophe? Are they all still suffering there? Do you campaign for their assistance from your friends? Do you still try to help them once you have woken up into *this* world? Obviously in the 'waking' consciousness you realise they were simply projections of your own mind. If your psyche had been in a good space – in a peaceful state – then your dream world and the 'others' in it would have been equally tranquil.

The same 'law' operates in the so-called waking world. This world is also a reflection of yourself. If there was nothing wrong with you, there would be nothing 'wrong' with the world you are in either. Each night the world we know disappears altogether. Each morning we find it coming into focus again. We open our eyes into all our habitual memories, frustrations, fears, anxieties and imaginings, making a little self-created world of our own. Everyone sees only an approximation of the commonly accepted 'actual' world, according to the colour of his conditioning. It is our view through the distorting lens of the mind that projects the world as it seems to be. But were we to become illumined in the night, our experience of the world would be transformed on awakening.

Perhaps this gives us some idea of the condition of the Sage, or Self-realised (God-Conscious) being. Once he has 'Awakened' from all the relative realities and relative dream universes, there is no longer any world for him to change. For him, as for the awakened dreamer, there are no 'other' people either. He is appreciating the enormity of the 'Cosmic Joke' that those he sees are all himself, reflected in the universal 'Dream of God'. Is it possible therefore, for the truly realised Sage to do anything about 'changing the world'? Having found himself to be the Totality, the Source of All Existence, there is nothing separate from him. Thus he can only be what he is.

On occasion, Sri Ramana Maharshi, whose spiritual attainment was renowned throughout India, was rebuked by the worldly-minded for sitting silently in his life-long *samadhi* state (and thereby attracting suffering seekers from all over the world), instead of going out and preaching to the masses for the emancipation of the world. He told them:

"How do you know that I am not doing it? Does preaching consist in mounting a platform and haranguing the people around? Preaching is simple communication of knowledge. It may be done in silence too.

"What do you think of a man listening to a harangue for an hour and going away without being impressed by it so as to change his life? Compare him with another who sits in a holy presence and leaves after some time with his outlook on life totally changed. Which is better: to preach loudly without effect or to sit silently sending forth intuitive forces to play on others?"[1]

To ask such a Master to help change the world is like asking him to throw a bucket of water at a raging inferno on the cinema screen when even a child knows it is only a film. Yet in Guru Ramana's presence, seekers found their sorrows dissolving and their minds becoming tranquil. When they returned to their respective places in the world with wonder in their hearts, their relationships with others reflected what they had received. Thus the benign effect of a Realised Master spreads out into the world from soul to soul, like ripples on a pond.

A Master is not indifferent to the sufferings of those to whom they are real enough. He is deeply moved, although he appears to simply sit doing nothing. However, it is the very quality of the Sage's non-doing which is his greatest gift to the world. His apparent stillness is like the illusion of immobility in a rapidly spinning top. He is, in effect, more like a generating dynamo, a vortex of dynamically radiating energy releasing endless waves of concentrated 'God-ness' out into the universe.

Having become one with the clear light behind the 'projector', the distorting lens is no longer there and we see Reality directly through his eyes. Thus simply receiving a loving look from the eyes of a Self-realised being can change the heart of anyone who is ripe for transformation.

'Only those who have seen beyond the world can improve the world,' says Sri Nisargadatta, another Self-realised sage, and simple shopkeeper, who vacated his body in 1981.

The existence of a true Sage, suffusing the world with spiritual sustenance, is a beacon of light for the soul-sick and suffering seekers lost in the labyrinth of worldly inanities. The recorded words of past Masters are the most venerated, profound, and inspiring writings existing on the planet. The lives of Self-realised Sages, by their example, have changed the lives of the masses throughout history. Even just to know that a Jesus or a Buddha lived, has been enough to kindle the hearts of millions since their time. Without such models to inspire us, can we imagine the visionary poverty of the human kind?

Once a Master has achieved Self-realisation – Oneness with the Omnipresence – he need do no more. He is then free to play in this dream world of ours according to his lights. But it then becomes a matter of what I call 'Cosmic Collusion' when he chooses to participate in the Divine Tragi-comedy of this world, as if it was real – or as if it mattered. In the books of Carlos Castaneda, it is the same thing that his Yaqui Indian teachers, Don Juan and Don Genaro, call 'controlled folly'. They know the foolishness of the situation, yet they still participate in it, humorously and without attachment.

Jesus said 'Render unto Caesar that which is Caesar's' – in other words, give the world what it requires of you, but keep yourself focussed in God. We are clearly told to act dispassionately in worldly affairs, for it is not the tangibles which ultimately matter. We should therefore be grateful that a Master remains to grace our paradoxical dream world at all, rather than demanding that he do other than he does.

Meanwhile, back in the body, we lesser beings believe ourselves to be stuck in this weird and wonderful world. Yet which world are we really inhabiting? Don Juan's world shows us superimposed 'separate realities'. There seem to be so many 'worlds', dimensions or levels of existence perceptible to clairvoyants, spiritualists, deep meditators, mediums, *siddhas,* shamans and magicians. We also hear of many authenticated accounts of 'ordinary people' who have been pronounced clinically dead (for minutes, hours and even days) and then who miraculously revive again, to tell the tale of entering realms beyond death. Their experiences were variously of a hellish or heavenly nature. What are we to make of that? Obviously suicide is no way out for the tortured mind.

It would seem that asleep or awake, alive or dead, in whichever relative universe we find ourselves, we still have the impression of some kind of 'worldishness' going on. Until we are illumined, we are stuck with operating in a 'world' of sorts for most of the time, a world which seems to be the place (or series of 'places') where we are obliged to act out the problems of our mental creations. Our position in it (or them) is not only self-made, but even 'tailor-made' to suit our own needs for growth. If this is so, as the Sages say, could this 'creation' ever be any other than the arena of gladiatorial combat it appears to be? Perhaps this wildly paradoxical positive-negative (yin-yang) play of opposites *is the very nature* of 'temporal' existence. And if so, can we ever hope to change it? Does it not seem more feasible that we are here to change ourselves? Are we to cover the whole earth with leather, or simply to put a pair of shoes on our own feet?

If we understand our 'earthly' lifetimes to be the 'School of the Soul', are we not here to learn precisely those lessons we need in each life? According to the Law of *Karma* – as we sow, so shall we reap – by repercussion of the words, thoughts and deeds we have previously released into the 'psychesphere' (the mind-soul etheric 'atmosphere' of the planet) in this lifetime or another, we attract to ourselves the experiences we need to go through to correct (or enhance) our inner attitudes. If we realise that we have brought about the situations that confront us, that alone should be enough to humble our aggressiveness towards those events of an unpleasant nature.

It is of little use bemoaning our fate if we find ourselves in miserable circumstances. Every problem which confronts us is a 'God-given' opportunity to transcend an inner problem which is preventing growth. The outer trouble is only the reflection of the inner one. Try to see to what it relates. We are always in exactly the stressful situation we need to be until an inner change occurs. Thus every seeming obstacle is a door to another dimension of living. The key is confrontation with our entrenched and incorrect attitudes. Our 'worldly existence' is the battleground of the mind made visible.

Such is the message of the Hindu epic, the *Bhagavad Gita,* in which Lord Krishna (God incarnate) instructs a despondent Prince Arjuna regarding his unwilling duty on the battlefield. Arjuna is reluctant to fight because many of his old beloved teachers and relatives are in the opposite ranks. But Lord Krishna points out that as his self-created karmic destiny has unavoidably brought him to this position of power and its consequences, the only fit and proper thing for him to do in the circumstances is to fight. He says in effect: "If you are a Prince, then fulfil the duties of a Prince – if you are a road-sweeper then sweep the roads. Do not try to avoid what comes to you. But do what needs to be done by you, *impeccably* – in a spirit of sacrifice and devotion to the Absolute, without self-interest. Keep your petty personality out of it and no karmic debt can accrue. If you fight whilst your sense-of-ego is aflame, then you fight alone. But remove your sense of self and God will be operating through you. As all is God there is no one who slays nor anyone who is slain. The whole drama is taking place on the battlefield of the mind." Arjuna's doubts were eventually cleared and his army went on to carry the day.

If we have allowed the idea of war to percolate the 'psyche-sphere' of our own relatively real world, then we are obliged perforce to participate in it when it arises. But it were better in the meantime to keep brighter ideas in the mind and actively work for the 'Forces of Light' by removing the processes of war inside ourselves. Until we are 'centred' within, we can do nothing of real value for ourselves or anyone else. Centring by creating a constantly contemplative attitude throughout the day, allows us to experience the actuality of everything being 'just God going on' as a living reality. 'His Will' in all things will be done in any case, whether we ask for it or try to prevent

it. So we might as well save ourselves the heartburn of worrying over things we can do nothing about and surrender to the
process of life unfolding.

This is not to say we should sit back and do nothing. The
nature of life will not allow us to in any case. If our hearts are
moved to do great deeds, to protest against injustices, to
march against atomic power plants, to succour such movements as Greenpeace[2] or Green Deserts[3] or other environmental groups, to aid Amnesty International,[4] or support the
worldwide spiritual communities which are the new heartbeat
of the Earth, or join Planetary Citizens[5] or any other worthy
organization working towards a Wholistic World – then may
the 'Force' (of our love) be with us!

Yet we do not have to be made of such heroic stuff to make
our changes in the world. As shown by the sages who 'simply
sit' the most sensitive stay-at-home has a part to play. By
virtue of the fact that *we are the centre of the situation we are in,* we
are presented with what we have to do at every moment. If
everyone were to remain aware of their creative capacity for
enlightening their own environment, it would be enough to
make a world where wars did not exist. We can change the
'climate' of our own little world, by a loving word or gesture,
which opens up the worlds of others. Let each act according to
his capacity, doing those things which come within reach of
his hands and heart.

Since we are obliged, in any case, to act whilst in the body
(dream or physical) we might as well cultivate the attitude of
impartial impeccability as the most appropriate in all our daily
doings. Only those actions are free from karmic 'comeback'
which come from the heart rather than the head, without
thought, and in which the life-shrinking sense-of-ego plays no
part. For example, should an old lady stumble on the road
before you, you instinctively reach out to help her up. You do
not think about it. This is the spontaneous doing of 'Nature'
without mind or ego involved. The deed is simply done. Life
is there at every moment awaiting our response. If we can
remain aware that whatever confronts us in our daily round, is
simply 'God going on', we became capable of allowing the
Omnipresence to act through our bodies, without the do-

gooder's self-gratifying sense of involvement. Otherwise, do what we will, without becoming 'flowing channels of the Divine' is it not mere vanity to imagine we can change anything but ourselves?

As Sri Nisargadatta replied when asked if there was any hope of salvation for the world: "Which world do you want to save? The world of your own projection? Save it yourself. My world? Show me my world and I will deal with it . . . What business have you with saving the world when all the world needs is to be saved from you? Get out of the picture and see whether there is anything left to save."[6]

In case this remains too frustrating for those with unashamedly active temperaments, I quote the saying of a Zen Master:

Shame! (on me) *Once I wanted to save the world.*

Ho! Now I see there is no world to save – to which a friend of mine, an activist Buddhistic shop-steward, has added, with a brilliant twinkle in his eye:

Ho-ho! Now! Go out and save it!

In other words, do that which needs to be done which is within your grasp. But with all your good intentions, try to keep in mind that one day you may wake up to find the world is just a hologram.

UNBINDING THE MIND

Contemplation or Meditation?

Q. *I don't seem to be getting anywhere in my meditation. Maybe I'm just not able to concentrate properly. I received instruction for seeing the inner light and hearing different sounds . . . but nothing like that has ever happened to me in meditation itself. Is there something else I should do for a more positive effect?*

Also I am confused as to the difference between contemplation and meditation – if there is any. The dictionary seems to think it's the same thing. I'd be glad if you could enlighten me?

A. There seems to be a great emphasis on the 'doing' of meditation these days. Whereas the reality of the process is more in the nature of 'non-doing' and in allowing the meditative consciousness to come of its own accord. We cannot 'do' meditation. If anything, we might say that meditation 'does' us – or rather, allows us to *be* – as we are. And meditation either happens to occur during our *practices towards experiencing it,* or it doesn't.

Since what we are seeking is a stilling of all movements of the mind, one can hardly meditate 'on' something. If we are concentrating upon a mental concept or idea, then we are *contemplating* it, and not meditating. The contemplative philosophers of old were considered to be primarily great *thinkers* who 'contemplated' or cogitated upon the profound subtleties of existence.

The Shorter Oxford Dictionary gives us six basic definitions of contemplation, namely: (1) *The action of beholding* (indicating the holding of an image by either the inner vision or the outer physical eye); (2) *The action of mentally viewing, attentive consideration, study, meditation.* (The word 'meditation' is here very loosely and inaccurately included in this category.) (3) *Religious musing;* (4) *Matter for contemplation;* (5) *The action of taking into account; consideration, regard, view;* (6) *Prospect, expectation, intention.*

All these definitions embody the idea of deep and profound thought and mental activity of some kind. Meditation, on the other hand, for simple differentiation could be defined as *an absence of thinking*. However, in its definition of 'meditation', the same dictionary gives three interpretations which would be more appropriately applied to the practice of contemplation; as follows: (1) *Serious and sustained reflection or mental contemplation*. (2) *In religious use: the continuous application of the mind to the contemplation of some religious truth, mystery, or object of reverence, as a devotional exercise*. (3) *A discourse, written or spoken, of a meditative character*.

All three 'definitions' inaccurately describe meditation as a *thinking* process. They refer to a manner of beholding something with the inner eye, or mentally ruminating on something, or putting oneself into a receptive state for the understanding of some specific theological or spiritual idea. No doubt this has been the sloppy usage to which the word 'meditation' has been put in the past by a non-meditating and lay public, unaware of what meditating monks were 'doing', or rather, 'not doing'.

The problem is compounded by the fact that Christian monks were evidently *not* meditating, but their conception of the word meditation – as being synonymous with 'cogitation' – has made this error widespread in the Western world. But in light of the fact that there are now countless numbers of Western meditators following Hindu, Buddhist, Chinese and Zen methods of meditation, a little more precision is required to clarify the difference between the two practices.

We can hardly blame the editors of dictionaries for a lack of exactitude, when the two terms have been so confusingly and interchangeably used in our own Christian monastic orders. Canon Peter Spink in his book *Spiritual Man in the New Age*, points out that his *Oxford Dictionary* gives two brief definitions of the word meditation (different again from mine) which are: (1) *To plan mentally and exercise the mind*, and (2) *Contemplation upon a subject*. Both are equally misleading, the first being precisely what meditation is not, and the second is of course simply contemplation. Rather than tossing these inaccuracies out of the window, Canon Sprink bravely tries to wrest some significance from these slender 'interpretations'. He says:

It is important to grasp the distinction between the two definitions; that is, the difference between a mental exercise involving the brain and an exercise in contemplation involving, as we shall later indicate, another faculty. In the first of these two activities the word meditation may be qualified by 'reflective' and the second with that of 'contemplative'. In the Western Christian tradition, *apart from the experience of the mystics,* the word meditation has been equated almost exclusively with the activity of the intellect. So in traditional Christian vocabulary meditation means simply that. However, in today's popular use of the word its meaning has been largely identified with that of the second aspect, that which the Christian mystics have described as contemplative meditation or simply contemplative prayer.

It is a curious anomaly that amongst the religious orders of the West, both Roman Catholic and Anglican, those who have been called Contemplative Communities have frequently emphasised the first aspect of meditation and often practised reflective meditation under the name of contemplation. 'Contemplative' has become the description given to those religious communities which are not 'active' in the sense of involvement in teaching, nursing, or works of mercy.

Be that as it may, with respect to the worthy Canon, I find that his admirable effort to define these terms as used within the Christian tradition may clarify matters for those within its bounds but, for those outside them, it might only serve to further confuse the issue, since the Christian definitions are at variance with the more universal usage. In virtually all other traditions of the world meditation is equated with the cessation of all activity or movement of the mind. However, Canon Spink qualifies the Christian distinction by stating:

Reflective meditation is parallel to the Western scientific method which is one of analysis and dissection. Contemplative meditation relates to the methodology of Eastern science which is not to analyse and dissect in order to touch reality, but rather to develop an awareness of the whole and the interrelationship of all things. (*Ibid*).

What he here calls 'Contemplative *meditation*' is perhaps a near-perfect definition of *contemplation* pure and simple. Contemplation in its deepest sense, that is, rather than that of worldly contemplation which is, according to the common and poetic usage, the ruminant enjoyment of a pastoral scene or inward vision. But the linking of the word contemplative with 'meditation' were better avoided in such a context as the two words together are contradictory. It is clear that contemplation implies reflection on a *content* of consciousness of some kind, no matter how rarified. Therefore even spiritual contemplation is still contemplation on something specific, be it a holy phrase, an inner vision, or spiritual ideal. It is something 'set up' in the mind at the onset as a basis for inspiration.

From the writings of the old Desert Fathers and Christian hermits, it would appear that this was the form of 'contemplation' they used. But contemplation of this nature was something far more subtle than the merely reflective 'thinking about' a subject. In its most profound aspect it was a matter of 'setting the scene', as it were, of an idea or subject in heart or mind, and then respectively and supplicatively awaiting what would come of it.

They may, for example, have taken the theme 'Make me closer my God with Thee', allowing their whole being to become saturated with the concept, and then leaving their hearts and minds open and empty for the 'Grace of God' to enter them. This attitude may account for the difference in definition of meditation as 'intellection' by the uncomprehending scholarly theologians whose understanding was distinctly *'apart from the experience of the mystic'* as mentioned, but sadly not expounded upon, by Canon Spink. But this practice of the elder Christians could, if anything (and really stretching a point) be called a 'Contemplative-meditation', inasmuch as it begins with a contemplative ideal, but could eventually lead into a meditative and conceptless, but ecstatic absorption in the Omnipresence ('God') or 'That-Which-Is'.

Thus the basic difference between contemplation and meditation is that contemplation requires something on which to contemplate and meditation does not.

Although there are innumerable mental or physical practices to bring one towards the experience of meditation, meditation itself is not in any way a mind-based activity. It has no relationship with the use of the mind during the experience, although mental functioning may be clearer *afterwards*. While the contemplative practices involve mentation, that is, the *thinking process,* in one form or another, the meditator seeks to withdraw from the movement of his mind altogether.

So the currently used phrase 'I'll meditate on it' is evidently inaccurate when speaking of a problem to be thought about. As most of us are guilty of this abusage, I would like to suggest the word *mentemplate* as a possible working alternative to replace it. *Mentemplation* can be considered as 'thoughtful mental activity within the temple of the mind', or as 'seriously considered thought with an air of expectancy in awaiting an inner answer, or the solving of a problem'. We could either 'mentemplate *upon*' a matter, or simply 'mentemplate' it. In its strongest focus the 'mentemplative' process might be considered analogous to the Eastern practice of *samyama:* fixation of mental focus, identificatory reflection, and absorption in the chosen idea. Using it in this way we might have some hope of correcting the misuse of the word meditation and retaining it with its universally known content as a *thought-free* condition.

Most of us, once we have been given a technique for *approaching* meditation, and begin to sit for twenty minutes a day at first, fondly imagine that we are 'meditating'. We are not. We may be repeating a *mantra,* or watching the breath, listening to or for internal sounds, getting caught up in our mental chatterboxing, or trying to blot it out by following whatever specific technique we have been given with which to do it. These are all mind-based activities. It would be more accurate to say we are practising *'Stilling'* rather than meditating, as our major effort consists of attempting to still the endless waves of the mind. The greater part of our 'meditation' period is spent in coming to grips with the technique of concentration (focussing and channelling the mind's energy) by which we will eventually be able to enter into the condition of meditation itself. In the early years of practice, if we manage to slip into it for one or two minutes in half an hour of stilling, we can consider ourselves fortunate.

Too many 'meditators' miss the point entirely, by expectantly waiting for something to 'happen', having been given the incentive to look out for strange phenomena. This attitude is a tremendous obstacle to entering the meditative condition.

Internal firework displays may be a spectacular and joyous bonus along the way (after years of practice) but it is not the manifestation of such transient phenomena which is the purpose or main concern of meditation practice.

This is something which appears to be overlooked by instructors of 'instant' forms of meditation in trying to make their 'package' more interesting than other brands. Teaching people to expect fascinating phenomena (which may or may not occur, depending on your particular developmental needs) takes the meditator out of the experience of the moment by loading him or her with expectations. If you are 'looking towards' something else, you cannot 'be with what you are' within the moment, and may miss the subtleties of what is actually going on in the present. And being in the 'here and now' is basically what meditation is about. So waiting (or straining) for something to 'happen', cannot be called meditation by any yardstick.

Many would-be meditators become disconsolate and give up their practice simply because the pre-programmed pyrotechnics or celestially musical diversions they have been led to expect have not occurred. They imagine that nothing is working for them. Never give up heart. No moment of sincere practice is ever lost or wasted. A student is rarely aware of the progress he or she is making and the endless changes that are occurring within. The practice of 'stilling' itself is having its curative effect.

It cannot be said often enough: the purpose of meditation is not to have the experience of an internal sound-and-light show, nor to gain this or that power (which may come as by-products) – but *to give time to the flowering of the spirit.*

It is to become harmonious and at-one-with-ourselves and the Essence which underlies the universe. More often than not our spiritual being is sensed as a stifled, suffering and shrivelled entity, repressed by the tensions of life and locked in a vice-like grip by the rigidity of the body-and-mind vehicle it inhabits. A period of stilling into meditation allows a softening of the mental and bodily armouring against life. It gives us a time of grace in which the spirit is allowed to 'expand' and penetrate the whole physical being and overflow into the radiational 'field' around us. Meditation is a process of purifying the physical and subtle bodies of the inhibitive tendencies of the mind.

As the movement of mind gradually ceases, the experience of meditation becomes apparent. On going deeper, the realisation may dawn that there are no barriers between ourselves and the Omnipresence of the universe. For in meditation one's whole concept of oneself as a distinct, separate ego-bound entity is dissolved. When this condition of entering freely into the 'Cosmic Flux' occurs in total thought-free clarity, it is known as *samadhi*.

This unconditioned 'condition' has many levels, from shallow to everlasting, and is named according to its fluctuation or permanency in the meditator. There are technical terms in Sanskrit for every stage of *samadhi*, according to the levels of profundity and whether the experiencer is still able to recognise the world or not. In its highest stage there is no experiencer; no thought of oneself, no thinker and nothing to be thought about. It is the state of pristine, pure clarity – a flawless flow of conscious awareness – but without thought. Those in the past, as in the present, whose minds have subsided permanently into this form of consciousness, have become the greatest sages the world has known.

Yet all of them insist that this is not a condition to be 'gained'. It always exists. It is our natural condition. We experienced it (in an uncomprehending form) in infancy, before the development of mind intervened. We may experience it fleetingly at any moment during the day when thoughts are momentarily suspended between successive flows of internal dialogue. Mind itself is not a 'thing' but simply the process of thoughts moving in transit. Without those thoughts, mind is not. We have only to remove our belief in the dictatorial necessity of the mind and its movement, and we find that we *are* that clear consciousness.

Samadhi is not something far from our grasp, and only for the great sages. Our periods of stilling into the state of meditation are simply for allowing us the time to recognise what is there already – our original condition before mind arose. Seeing that is analogous to viewing a landscape before, during, and after fog. The landscape always remains as it is in pristine clarity. So it is with consciousness and the fog of mind. When the fog lifts we see clearly. Even if we feel nothing is happening for us in our practice, we can rest assured that little by little the veil is lifting. And in any case, we are giving time to the harmonisation of the spirit.

As says Sri Nisargadatta, the Self-realised shopkeeper of Bombay:

'For a seeker of reality, there is only one [form of] meditation – the rigorous refusal to harbour thoughts. To be free from thoughts is itself meditation.'

Author's note: This article has been sent to the reference department of *Oxford Dictionaries*.

Never Mind the Mind

Q. *My mind is driving me crazy with its endless worrying about everything and nothing. It makes me ill and depressed, but I can't seem to stop it. The trouble is, when I start going into meditation I have the fear I'm losing my mind. What I read about* samadhi *states and loss of identity is a bit frightening. You see? I even worry about not having a mind. I mean, how would I be able to function without it? Don't we need the use of our minds in normal life?*

A. As you do not appear to be functioning so well *with* 'a mind' perhaps it is worth investigating the alternative. If we observe closely what is going on, we might seriously question as to whether there is *a* mind at all. Granted, there is a garrulous thought-flow always going on like a babbling brook, but is this 'thoughtless' chatter really *the* mind? The reality of its activity seems something more in the nature of 'mental inter-ference' in what would otherwise be the smooth functioning of the body.

What we take to be mind appears rather like the erratic static we get on a radio set when we are trying to tune in to the correct station. Is it static we are after, or a clear programme? We might consider that maybe in our 'normal' functioning we are somewhere 'between stations' and are just not operating on the right frequency. And most of us do not appear to be searching – or not searching seriously – for the right pro-gramme: let alone considering switching 'mind' off altogether!

Mind is a useful blanket-term for the operation of all our thought-processes in general, but should not therefore be taken to exist as a thing-in-itself*. This endless 'stream of thoughts' we fondly like to call our 'mind' is a form of mental disease which, when left to its own devices, generally tends to run amok, resulting in the enervation and degeneration of the

* *This should be remembered whenever I speak of 'the mind' elsewhere, for the sake of convenience.*

body. If we are really convinced of the need for this mind-flow, then we are free to accept its destructive mental processes and carry on suffering. Accepting 'mind' as a personal 'possession' places us in bondage to its machinations. Our very idea of *having* 'a mind' possesses us, and we feel obliged to go along with it. If, however, we decide we have had enough of it, we must first see what is going on, to be convinced we no longer require it. Otherwise we can be caught up in its flow of flotsam and spend most of our lives prematurely worrying over problems which never actually occur in reality.

Such negative, worrisome or fearful attitudes of 'mind' prepare the way for the development of bodily malfunction. Thus most, if not all, illnesses of the body occur as a result of our mental condition. For example: the relationship between mental stress and cancer is now well documented and firmly established. So worriers can create a thought-induced vicious circle, by making themselves prone to internal diseases purely from the fact of worrying that they *might* be prone to them. Also many people are afraid of 'catching' some germ or other, whereas the reality – as shown by the miracle of electron-microscopy – is that our bodies are filled with uncountable bugs and microbes (a whole universe of living beings within ourselves) from birth to death. There are three to four pounds of micro-organisms in the average healthy human being!

Any new 'bugs' we may ingest are absorbed by our interior 'eco-system' or flushed right through. Rarely do they manifest as ailments unless we have created a suitable breeding ground by both our physical and mental 'diets'. It is the basic 'climate' of our thoughts which determines whether we shall be ill – or remain ill – no matter what our healer or doctor tries to do. Thus every illness may be seen as a form of subtle wish fulfilment, or poetic justice, according to the cosmic law of: 'As we sow in the soul – so shall we reap in the body'.

It is not difficult to determine how this state of affairs comes about. We all have experience of how 'the mind' works on the body: embarrassment gives us flushed faces and throbbing temples, and fear makes us tremble and turn white, with palpitating heart, shaky knees and goose-fleshed skin. And stomach-knots from jealousy, anger or apprehension are known to everyone. Since every thought has such an immediate effect on the body, it is suprising therefore, that so few people seem to recognise the fact that the *habitual* mental climate – or content of consciousness – also has a lasting influence on the vitality of the whole system.

'Mind' saturates the body as water does a sponge. Thus what we allow our minds (thought-flow) to dwell upon, not only creates the quality of our lives but also the energy of our bodies. As we think, so we are.

Fortunately, when we are growing towards illness or depression, there is always a period of grace in which to realise what we are doing to ourselves. But how many of us take the trouble to avail ourselves of it? It takes time for our negative thoughts to densen through the layers of the subtle bodies and manifest as illness in the physical organism. Therefore at the first signs of tension or unease (another word for dis-ease) in the body or mind, we would do well to stop and take stock of how we are stifling the spirit by our mental habits.

Physical illness is often a question of repression, of self-strangulation, of fearful conformism contrary to our own natures. It is the revolt of the organism against not living the way we were meant to be. Illness is basically a case of *not being who you are*. It is a lack of sensitive 'listening' to your inner needs, or of repressing what you know you need because of your outward circumstances and the demands of the situation you are in. But to ignore the inner 'voice', which tells us what is fit and right for us in life, is to create intolerable stresses in the soul. For many of us, however, it would seem that our early conditioning has too great a power over us. Even when we *know* what we want (or what we don't want) we unwittingly sabotage our own efforts to free ourselves of life-negating attitudes by our pre-programmed thought patterns from the past.

Perhaps because of lack of love, or neglect, in childhood, or by the active suppression or ridicule of abusive parents (or elder brothers and sisters) we have developed an internal self-image of inferiority, feeble unworthiness, stupidity and an inability to cope. Although this does not represent our true reality, this kind of unreal self-evaluation reinforced over the years by habitual inward acceptance and confirmation, is so firmly embedded in the consciousness (and subconscious) that it negates any action we may desire to undertake to improve our situation.

Without being aware of it, many of us are often indulging in a life-long form of negativity I call 'anti-mantra'. Just as a *mantra* (a sacred sound-syllable, holy word or phrase) is repeated to cleanse the consciousness of impurities, so by the repetition of 'anti-mantras' – or life-deadening thought habits – we obtain precisely the opposite effect, which burdens the conscious and subconscious 'mindstuff' with toxically negative suggestions. How often do we suppress our desires and aspirations with such 'anti-mantras' as: 'I don't think I'm capable – I could *never* do it – I don't think I should – I don't really deserve it – I'm not worthy of it – I'm a born loser – I will never make it – It always happens to me – I haven't got the time (the energy, the money, etc.) – What would my mother say? – I'm always alone – Nobody loves me – I am hopeless – I can't do anything right – Well, next time, perhaps – If only – Yes, I would, *but . . .*' and so forth.

'*Yes, but . . .*' especially is a well-known life killer. Are we aware how often we use it? How many of these negative mantras do you recognise in yourself? Become aware of your own favourite 'anti-mantras'. See what you use them for and why, and try to find their origins. We can notice that as soon as this 'mind' of ours decides on doing something, then the habitual 'anti-mantras' of self-deprecation begin to arise. This same 'mind' then struggles indecisively, swinging back and forth between conflicting considerations and sub-conscious counter-proposals. This inevitably causes stress in the system and the resulting tensions have a tendency to slowly solidify into the various forms of bodily and mental illness. But even then, this is only the natural purging process of the body-mind complex attempting to cleanse itself of the toxicity of our thoughts.

It is evident that we also often have a semi-conscious predisposition towards *not* getting what we want, or thinking we want. For example, if we are already pre-programmed to feel **unworthy of it, even if we manage to realise our 'day-dream** desire', this mental interference of a 'mind' will not allow us to enjoy it. If we desire to be wealthy but suffer from an ingrained 'anti-mantra' such as: 'Poor me, I am miserable and money-less', (and it shows in your face and spirit), then neither friendly assistance nor money is likely to flow your way, as your inner attitude has destroyed virtually all possibility from the start.

Even if you become rich, like so many rich people, you are likely still to feel poor and insecure. Whereas, if in your heart of hearts you feel supported and rich, then your needs are few, and money and needful situations will easily flow towards you. Such is the assertion of Jesus when he says that those who have, will have everything added unto them and those who have not will have even what little they have taken away. Thus we enhance or destroy our own future. We may wish for a long and healthy life, but if we have a lurking fear of being maimed, this tendency can draw us into a situation where we are injured in a car crash or an accident at work.

Even what we call 'accidents' are happenings we draw to our selves, attracted by our inner attitudes of mind. I always find it helpful to ask what are the advantages of the 'illness' or the 'accident' one has 'decided' to have. The answers can be revealing. For many it seems to be a form of self-punishment for real or imagined misdeeds. More often than not it is a form of escape from something we did not want to face. Perhaps it came as an answer to an unconscious prayer to free us from a stressful situation or decision, in an attempt to flee from the contradictions of the mind.

But can we hope to escape the machinations of our 'mind games'? All the great sages from antiquity to the present day have diagnosed the 'uncurbed mind' as the major source of all ills. But how to be free of it? Is it possible to live without mind?

Consider the facts. We began life without a personalised consciousness. How did the original 'mindless' spermatazoon know how to seek out the egg, fertilise it, then divide into self-reproducing cells, all differently developing themselves into divers organs, bones, skin, hair and nails – all without the aid of an individually conscious mind? Eventually, passing through all evolutionary forms of life in the womb, all these multiplying little particles happily know when to stop, and miraculously end up as a human being. The much vaunted brain (which many mistakenly assume to be the source of thought), is developed last of all. Even then, it only becomes fully operational after the first *three years* of bodily existence.

Where is 'mind' all this time?

During these wonderful early years of infancy, we exist as innocents in the world. We are awed by all of creation and have no self-conscious sense of identity. It is this very lack of an ego-conscious mind in tiny children (and saints) which delights the hearts of we impoverished mind-bound adults. Only slowly comes the sorry awakening of self-centredness and 'mind', by contact with the mind-bound world around them. The myth of Adam and Eve spells out this story of Everyman.

The innocents in Creation are said to have 'fallen' into self-consciousness from the state of '*Self*-consciousness'. In other words, they became aware of an individualised movement of consciousness (namely the ego-prompted thought-flow we know as 'mind'), as distinct from the free-flowing '*God*-consciousness' which was previously operating through them. It is that free-flowingness of the Omnipresent conscious energy which is effortlessly animating and unfolding all other beings, birds, animals, insects and plantlife of the world in perfect harmony. And that includes *us*.

But as we awaken to existence, each one of us slowly tumbles into the trap of 'mind'. Man is the only self-conscious creature on the planet, thus making himself the Eternal Outsider in this 'Garden of Eden'. He has built a life-shrinking barrier between himself and the Omnipresence and all creation and calls it – 'My Mind'.

Man thinks, therefore he suffers.

But everyone has known a magic time without self-conscious thought, as every child is born with 'Eden Consciousness'. When Jesus suggested that we 'become as little children', he was doubtless referring to those very young children who are aware and clear eyed, before the movement of self-conscious mind has come to cloud them over. It is only when we can return to a similar condition, to the state of being without a sense-of-individualised-mind (but this time *with* awareness), that spontaneous and free-flowing thought arises from the

Original Source as and when necessary.

"That's all very well if you are a Sage," you might say. "But how can I stop my mind from rabbitting on? I'm only little old me." Yet every Self-realised Sage was once 'little old me' to himself; just an ordinary man in the street to begin with. And each one found his way (starting from the same place as everyone else) by investigating this thing called 'mind'.

How to begin? Firstly we need to realise that 'mind' and 'me' are not one and the same thing. When we say, "My mind is playing tricks on me", or "My mind is driving me crazy", we intuitively understand it as something *apart* from ourselves. It is *my* mind, we say, considering it like a possession. Even if it were true, a possession is always *other* than its owner. *My* house, *my* car, *my* family, *my* body, *my* hand, are all separate objects from my-self. And so it is with *my* 'mind'. Except that 'mind' is not an object or *thing* which exists in itself that one is able to 'possess'.

If mind *was* an entity in itself, it would always be self-luminous and therefore impossible to extinguish. If self-consciousness was the actual inherent nature of 'the mind', then it would always have to be self-aware and conscious of itself. But 'mind' is not a permanent entity, This wishy-washy, changeable, unreasonable and fluctuating thought-flow disappears entirely in deep sleep, swoon or *samadhi* states. If I *was* my mind, then neither 'I' nor 'mind' could ever be non-conscious in these conditions. So the best we can say of our 'sense-of-mind' is that it is no more than an occasionally observable fluid process which only exists for the time we choose to participate in it. We are not obliged to do so.

We have no need to consider mind (mental static) as 'mine', any more than accepting a headache as a 'possession'. Nor do we have to take its ramblings seriously. Yet we have become so accustomed to its endless chatterboxing that we take it as the natural state of affairs. It is like having a radio left on forever, being unaware that it is switch-offable. Having let it play for so long, it is extremely difficult to switch off. Difficult, but not impossible. We just have to remember how to adjust the controls.

As a first step, with practice, we can stand back from the

'mind' and simply watch what is going on. The very fact that I can watch my mental activity shows that it is something other than myself. If I begin to investigate it seriously, watching it as in meditation, it disappears altogether. But even without meditation, if we simply focus our attention on 'mind' itself, seeking its source of arising, we can find nothing there. It is too much of a phantom. Then we say the 'mind' is clear. But clarity is our true nature. Mind is a curtain across that clarity. Thus as soon as we lose our attentiveness, this wretched thought flow starts up again like an unstoppable spring.

However, if we get into the habit of watching our thoughts we shall soon see that the 'mind' is mainly involved in a very sterile process of turgid recapitulation or preparation. This I call the 'Repetition and Rehearsal' syndrome. We find ourselves constantly mulling over (and over and over, *ad nauseam*), past events and conversations to no purpose. And these are often of a negative nature, mental grumblings, or turning over affronts to our sense-of-ego: 'She/he was unkind to me... What I should have said to her,' etc. Or we are endlessly preparing ourselves for possible (or unlikely) future events and conversations: 'What I shall say next time.. What I shall do if...?'

This is the life and energy-draining 'repetition and rehearsal' misery-go-round. Nothing is spontaneous. We choke the vitality of life before it arises. In this way we are compounding the habitual enfeeblement of our constitutional mental atmosphere. But where is the necessity to be involved in this tedious mental shuttling from past to future and back again? Who obliges us to listen in to the interminable discussions the 'mind' is always having with itself? When we begin to become aware of what is going on, we can realise how ridiculous it is. This is the first step.

Becoming conscious of the pathetic nature of our normal 'mind' is the first step towards freedom from it. If we come to disbelieve its validity we are not so easily caught up in it. In this way we begin to deny the mind its supremacy over us. Everything we see as 'repetition or rehearsal' we can releasingly disown and discount. Never mind the mind: let it chatter on if it so desires, but have no part of it. Many times you will find

yourself caught up and involved in the thought stream again.
But smile indulgently at yourself, murmur 'codswallop' at the
mental wafflings and concentrate on the work you are doing,
or on the thought-free observation of your surroundings.

At first, you will *see* without thought for only a few
moments at a time. Try to extend the period between one
thought-flow and the next. This demands constant attention
and application. As you continue to give the 'mind' no credence or attentive interest, little by little, its habitual flow
weakens. With perseverance, eventually the movement of
mind will evaporate altogether. Where its turbulence once was
we find a wondrous healing peace and stillness which was
always there underneath.

This is by no means a vacant or alarming condition. A great
many inventions and scientific discoveries have been made
during this 'pregnant calm' when the movement of mind was
absent. When gazing thoughtlessly into the fire, or idly at the
sky, the solution to a mind-baffling problem has come in a
flash of inspiration. The answer has been 'given' rather than
elucidated by an arduous process of thought. We have the
possibility of always being in this state, by the constant refusal
to give credibility to the wasteful effluents of our habitual
stream of thoughts.

This I call my 'carpet pulling' method. Whenever any unbidden thought arises – *whoosh!* I whip out the 'carpet' from
under it and let it fall. Untiring effort in this practice is the
shortest road to *samadhi*.

Samadhi is the state of pure, primal awareness, untainted by
thought, in which the 'mind' is absorbed in one's own true
nature, the spiritual 'ground-of-being' or the *Self*. It may be
experienced on many deepening levels, according to the practitioner's development, and at its profoundest results in the
uttermost existential experience and the total fulfilment of
human existence. In its early stages, too, the *samadhi* experience
is not something to be fearful of, or too far away from our
possibilities.

But it is unlikely to occur simply by 'doing' a daily meditation session. We have to be constantly vigilant in debunking
the authority of the mind flow by our carpet-pulling practice at

all times. And in this way a taste of the *samadhi* state can come in a relatively short time. Or so it was for me.

One New Year I made an inner resolution to rigorously refuse every unnecessary thought which came into my head. For the next three months I toiled away at my carpet-pulling tactics, refusing to participate in any of my 'mind games'. Every time an irrelevant thought cropped up, I decided – 'It's only the mind (doing its damn-fool thing to make me miserable)', and let it go. Fortunately at the time I was mainly occupied with putting the last finishing touches to my cottage, which I was renovating before selling. So the work needed little thought and simple concentrated effort. When things I had to remember spontaneously popped into my mind, I immediately wrote them down on a list, so there was no necessity to have to think of them again. This practice paid dividends in the end.

One morning in April I suddenly woke up to find my mind flow had ceased altogether. The endless interior dialogue was no longer operating. What a wonder! This time however, there was no great ecstasy, nor any revelations as in the Cosmic Consciousness experience: but pure clarity and a gentle joy. As I could no longer feel my usual mental pressure, I saw clearly as if without a head. I was *totally there* in everything. There was no longer any veil or distance between me and my environment, as is usually the case when mind is there to create distinctions. The very fact of thinking – 'being in our heads' – cuts us off from the world and others. But without a mind to encase me in my body, I found that the Self was everywhere!

I had the 'sensory' impression that I was no longer limited to the body. My sense of *being* extended through the walls of the body, the walls of the house and out to infinity. What I realised myself to be, interpenetrated everything I saw. There was no need to think about it, as I *was* it. Yet it felt 'right' and far more 'normal' than my usual mind-bound condition. I found it wondrously amusing to feel my body 'located' in the centre of an endless continuum of 'me-ness'. I was like a diver moving about in a calm and lucid ocean of myself. And I walked about in chuckling awe all day, like a marionette on strings, being operated by the Omnipresence.

There was no difficulty in relating to people. When visitors came I could carry on conversations in a regular manner, but without formulating responses in my 'mind'. My answers came spontaneously and I listened as interestedly to my replies as theirs, being fascinated by watching the process of words coming out of the place where the 'centre' of this vague impression of a body appeared to be. If no unbidden response arose, I would remain silent, simply resting in the pristine awareness.

For more than three weeks I remained in this state, which I later learned is known among yogis as *samprajnata samadhi*. It is the first stage of *samadhi* in which the flow of mind reposes in the Self, but the distinction between the knower, knowledge and the things known is not yet lost. This condition might well have lasted much longer, but during the third week I became involved in the details of selling my cottage, and as I was doing my own conveyancing, I was obliged to study books of law to make up the deeds. This is a head-breaking task at the best of times, and for several days I began to feel the return of 'mind' – like a distant balloon on a string – being slowly wound back on a spindle into my head. Soon I returned to a semblance of 'normality'.

Since then, things have never seemed the same. My mental flow now comes and goes like the tide, so that I am sometimes with and sometimes without 'mind'. I hope this assuages any fears and shows that entering into *samadhi* can be a gentle process with nothing to be afraid of. We can proceed as slowly as we choose; in the same way as a child overcomes its fear of the wavelets of the sea, slowly penetrating deeper, wading the bigger waves and braving the breakers before finally plunging joyously into the ocean itself. The mind-free ocean of the Self awaits us all.

But not all of us can so easily carpet-whip our thoughts away at first if they are constantly coming thick and fast. So an alternative practice is to keep the mind-flow focussed on one thing to slow it down, whenever we do not need our full attention on the task in hand. We might perhaps hold an image of our chosen master in our heart of hearts, remaining in his vibration there, instead of in our heads. Otherwise there are only two time-honoured methods of cleansing the toxicity of the 'mind' and that is by meditation or by mantra. Only these practices are capable of consuming our accumulated negativity from the past and previous lifetimes.

Japa-mantra, or the repetition of sacred syllables, is known in many cultures as one of the most effortless and efficacious ways of clearing the mind and transforming the spirit. The repetition of mantras enhances the quality of one's consciousness and redirects the mind flow into purifying channels in the process of refining it away altogether. Its practice can bring galloping intellects to heel and awaken joy in the most incorrigible worrier.

Once one has begun to experience the joy of 'mindlessness' all early fears are forgotten in the urge to attain permanency in the natural delight of this utterly satisfying condition. The more we 'lose our minds' the more we find our true selves and the more we function to perfection. Whoever heard of a Jesus, or a Buddha, or Krishna, Moses, Dattatreya, Patanjali, Gorakhnath, Milarepa, Ramana Maharshi, Hui Hai, Hui Neng, or any other of the spiritual giants who inspired the world, being unable to function after experiencing *samadhi?* The subsequent quality of their lives is testament enough.

Therefore we may safely follow in their footsteps.

Sonharmonic Stilling

Q. *I find it an awful job trying to meditate in a flat with noises all around. In fact, rather than concentrating on the meditation, I find myself edgily waiting for the next noise, and I come out of it more tense than when I began. Is there any hope for a nervous wreck like me?*

A. You don't say what form of meditation practice you are following (or trying to follow!) But perhaps your preparatory practice of stilling is inadequate. Many techniques are similar in essence, but some are more suited to one type of personality than another. Naturally, as mantra yoga is my major pre-meditative practice, I usually favour a mantric method of stilling the mind into the meditative condition. This is especially efficacious when there are noises all around.

Chanting loudly to begin with, creates a vibratory effect and a resonance in your head, which positively charges the whole system and drowns out the external noises at the onset. Continuous repetition of certain sequences of syllables channels the habitual mental chatter and dissolves it effortlessly, as the energies of a spiritually higher frequency are manifested in the consciousness. However, if you are too inhibited by thin walls and the ears of neighbours, you might try an alternative method of entering into a *non-resistant* awareness of the sounds around you, as a focus for your practice.

Once when stilling into meditation in an *ashram* in India, someone working nearby in a cowshed outside the meditation hall dropped the handle of a bucket. The vibration of this sudden clatter thrilled through all the cells of my body. An enormous joy and laughter welled up inside me. I suddenly had an overwhelming insight into the ludicrousness of existence, and the deadly seriousness of the average aspirant's view of his spiritual practice (including my own) made me fall about laughing for a good twenty minutes. If I had been tensed up and fighting against all the noises round about, it could never have happened.

Another time in Agra I was on a bus, when a wild crowd of rioters, several thousand strong, swept down the street, roaring with rage and hammering on the sides of the bus with staves. They began rocking the bus from side to side and I thought I was about to die. Yet strangely enough, I didn't mind a bit. The tumultuous noise of the crowd was so exhilarating that it had sent me into a condition where I was beyond care of life or death. And the crowd swept by.

Another example of beneficial noise in meditation was related to me by one of my mantra masters, Sri Ramamurti, regarding the time when he was still in practice as a doctor and psychologist. One day he was meditating in his office when suddenly the telephone rang, and the sound of it was miraculously transformed into light! The whole room erupted into shining particles with every ringing tone. The effect filled him with bliss. This shows that if we go deep enough, noise need not always be a disturbance to our practice, but can even be an asset.

When I spoke to the *Siddha Yogi* Swami Muktananda of Ganeshpuri about my cow-pail experience, he confirmed its value and suggested that I find some way to teach this experience to others. This led me to develop a form of practice which involved the absorption of environmental sounds. I call it 'Sonharmonic Stilling' – *son,* meaning sound, plus *harmony;* being a method of calming the mind by harmonising the body with outside noises of the world around.

Of course, it is far preferable to practice this in the country, but it can work equally well in town. One begins by sitting in a comfortable posture, preferably cross-legged, tailorwise (in the yogic *siddhasana,* or half-lotus); otherwise one can sit normally in a chair if need be. Be sure to keep the spine erect, but have the body relaxed around it, like a coat on a post. It can be helpful to try to visualise the body as a large transparent polythene bag, covered with tiny 'breathing and hearing' holes, and filled up with ping-pong balls. Then be aware that every sound you make, or external noise, shakes the light-weight balls and makes them vibrate against each other.

Next, exhale in a slightly more intensive fashion than normal, in a smooth flow from both nostrils, until the lungs are as empty as possible. Then breathe in deeply and slowly, listening to the passage of air in the nostrils and expanding the rib-cage outwards in all directions. When the chest is full, lock the chin down onto the chest with a firm pressure *(jalandhara bandha)* and retract the muscles of the anus *(mula bandha)* and hold the breath for the count of six seconds.

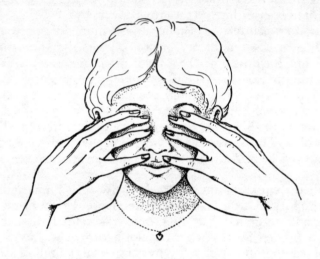

At the moment of release of the anal and chin 'locks', plug the ears with the thumb-tips (keep the nails out of the way); lightly bring down the upper skin of the eyelids with the middle fingers, and cover the upper part just above them with the forefingers. The ring fingers should lightly press into the indentations half-way down each side of the nose to restrict the air, resting your little fingers above the upper lip. Keeping your lips closed, part your teeth slightly and hum resonantly, getting the 'ping-pong balls' to vibrate in your head. Fill yourself with the sound. Lose your mind in it and keep on humming until the end of your breath. This is known as *Bhrāmari pranayama,* from the *bhrāmara* – a large black humming bee of India. Do at least six rounds of this practice.

As you hum, also try to resonate downwards into the body.

Imagine all your light-filled ping-pong balls are bisecting with the vibration, like amoebas, each one separating into two smaller balls. And in the next round of humming, each two vibrate into four smaller ones, then into eight even smaller, and so on. Eventually you realise your whole body is composed of millions of tiny vibrating particles, which are all sensitive to the slightest sound. Thus you arrive at the reality of your own form, which is precisely that. 'Physically' you are a dynamic force-field holding together a mass of vibrating molecular particles, dancing to both internal and external sounds!

When lying in the grass on a summer's day and staring at the sky, you may have noticed millions of tiny points of light 'swimming' in the air like electric tadpoles. These light-charged particles, which I call 'lightrons', I believe to be the basic 'building-blocks' of light, suffusing all matter. And after the bee-humming breathing exercise, we visualise breathing in millions of these pranically-charged *golden light particles. With long and steady inhalations, we internally visualise these 'lightrons' massing together into a sparkling vibrating ball in the region of the solar plexus, like a swarm of golden bees or a shimmering sun.

After a long inhalation, when the chest is full and puffed out, apply the *jalandhara* and *mula bandhas* (for about six seconds) and interiorise your consciousness into the glowing ball in the solar plexus. When you exhale, release the locks and visualise sending streams of lightrons flowing down the inside of the front of your body, rolling around your legs, knees and feet (as if pushed by the pressure of the exhalation) and then rolling up again through the back over the shoulders and neck and over the crown of your head. Finally you are breathing them out radiantly through your closed eyes and open nostrils with the last of the outbreath. After several rounds of this, with the solar ball growing larger and larger with each inbreath until it fills the whole body, begin to breathe the lightrons outwards from the inner sun in *all* directions through the skin.

At this stage you may experience being composed of noth-

---

* *Prana* is the Cosmic Intelligence inherent in vital air energy which regulates the breathing mechanism.

ing but vibrating golden particles. Lightrons are flowing along illumined veins and cleansing every dark corner of the body. Your transparent sheath of skin has dissolved away. You have no solidity and you are boundless. You are breathing your own self in and out in an endless exchange with your 'environment'. The plants, the birds, animals and human beings around, are all breathing your golden lightrons in and out of themselves. Where then, do they begin and you end? All is an inter-changing.

Entering into such an experience, 'external' sounds and noise cannot disturb one. Unresisted sounds become a part of your own vibration and flow through and away, scattering the lightrons like sparks from a blacksmith's heated iron. Try to feel the sounds coming from outside with every part of your body. Feel them as waves passing through. If one is 'loosely' in the body in this way, one could accommodate even a nearby explosion, without too great a sense of shock.

At first it is useful to try and listen to all the sounds assailing the left ear only. Then after a while switch to all the sounds entering the right ear. Try to determine any differences. Then become aware of the sounds coming from all directions, with both ears and with the sensitivity of your 'body-of-light'. Since your 'extended-body' has become a part of the ebb and flow of all nature, then all its sounds are also you.

Feel each sound as it occurs and get right into it. But have no thoughts *about* it. Simply *become* it. Actually feel yourself as the chirrup on the bird's tongue. Feel the kind of vibration it is. Get into the feeling within the bird as it sings. Or feel yourself inside the motor of a tractor as it ploughs the field and enjoy its chugger-mugger sound. Or, if you are in the city, relax into the traffic hum, horn blare and street cries, the clatter of milk bottles, the shudder of the building as people tramp up the stairs, the voices and the banging doors. Feel the reverberation of all the sounds rippling through your lightrons as a pleasurable sensation, instead of a distraction.

If someone is shouting or arguing nearby, do not try to hear *what* is said (and thus lose concentration by mental involvement), but let your being flow with the vibration of the sound itself, as a moored buoy bounces lightly in a passing current.

Simply feel your molecules dancing as the sound goes through. It then becomes *your* voice, *your* shout, bump, chirrup or other noise. If it is your own sound, you cannot be annoyed with it. You delight in it. It is your own vibration. You can thrill vibrationally to the starting of a motorbike, or soar and roar 'inside' the thundrous feeling of a jet, or hum with the traffic, or a bee, with equal pleasure. *If* you go with it. The motor of the universe is your own motor.

Even in a crowded street, or on a tube train or bus, you can still evaporate yourself into the sound.* Once you have grown accustomed to taking in all sound, the overall hum of sound begins to become soothing, and sudden noises are only a ripple of disturbance. And as you begin to interiorise, you can hear underneath all sounds a subtle singing in your ears. Relax into all the daily sounds around you, until they are no more than a background hum and then begin to listen to the sounds within. When the inner ringing sound occurs (like the after sound of a once-struck bell), hold on to that alone. You can then forget about all the outer ones.

This inner sound is the true 'motor of the universe'. It is known as the 'Song of God'. It is the key to deeper dimensions. The deeper your alignment with this Source of Vibration itself (when no longer aware of any external sounds), the closer you come to your own true Self. And the greater the harmonious integration of yourself in the All.

---

*This method was also known to the ancient sages as *samyama* (*mentemplation* or mental focus on, and experiential analysis of, sounds or other phenomena), as spoken of by Patanjali in his *Yoga Sutras* (approx. 300 B C).

SOUND SENSE

The Science of Sound

Q. *I came across this quote from* The Gāyatri Mantra *by Satyavan:* "*The chanting of a mantra has been defined as 'a way of ascent to Supreme Realisation'. The rationale of the Japa, or chanting, can be appreciated only when one understands the metaphysics and science of sound.*" *Do you agree with this, and if so, what is the 'metaphysics and science of sound?'*

A. I have no quarrel with the good Satyavan's assertion, as this is really a matter of individual inclination. There are those whose innate curiosity impels them to take a clock to bits to find out how it works, and those who can happily accept that it does work and simply use it to tell the time by. It depends on your inherent nature. There is certainly no absolute necessity to know the whys and wherefores of something to experience its benefits.

For example, when we switch on the television, are we interested in the rationale, or fundamental principles of how television works, or do we simply want to enjoy the programme? If we only want to be entertained, no one censures us for not knowing how the set functions. Then again, if while watching it, we are caught up with wondering how the aerial picks up signals and transforms them into pictures via the cathode-ray tube, or wondering whether the wires are too hot inside the set, we are likely to be distracted from our enjoyment of the programme.

For some people it is impossible to function without first being intellectually satisfied as to the technicalities of whatever they are involved in. Yet for others, too many technical or intellectual details are experienced as a hindrance to their practice. They would sooner intuitively feel their way into something. This type of person, for example, is more easily able to understand that perhaps the heartwarming quality of being, radiated by their guru or teacher, is evidence enough that his methods must be sound, for him (or her) to have arrived at that level of tangible 'presence'. Thus their intellects need no convincing and they are inspired to follow in good faith the practice prescribed, without prior knowledge of how it works. And in so doing, the knowledge of its functioning may become apparent through practical experience. This is the beneficial attitude to cultivate on the mantric path, since theoretical explanations must inevitably fall short of the actuality: like trying to describe the taste of a strawberry, or even the taste of different kinds of strawberries.

The Science of Sound is known as *Nāda Yoga* – a study involving contemplative immersion in Universal Sound of audible and inaudible frequencies. This practice is considered the highest culmination of all yoga paths, containing them all and to which all forms of yoga eventually lead. One of the most celebrated yoga texts, the *Hatha Yoga Pradipika*, after describing all the beneficial disciplines for yogic development, enumerating various *asanas* and breathing exercises, *shatkarmas* and *bandhas*, devotes its final section to this science, under the name of *Laya Yoga* – the unification of the individual with the Supreme, by the practice of immersion in *Nāda*, the mystic sound.

This sound is ringing throughout the universe and can be heard internally by everyone, once the mind is attuned to it. "All the seven heavens are echoing with the Sound. The ignorant do not hear it, or catch the strains," says Hafiz, a Muslim mystic poet. But saints and sages throughout history, including Moses and Mohammed, have had their lives opened up by hearing it.

"Search for the Sound in the body, and thou shalt be saved!" said Guru Nanak (founder of the Sikh religion). "By devotion to the master's word, I enjoy perpetual peace, for in me is Sound, the crest-jewel of all virtues."

In the *Gheranda Samhita*, the sage Gheranda declares that of all the inner concentrations for purification of mindstuff, that of "*Anahata Nāda* (the unstruck sound) is best of all." As in the *Hathapradipika* and also the *Kurma Purana*, the yogic texts describe all the major physical practices and invariably culminate in prescribing concentration on the inner sound for final perfection. When the mind becomes so absorbed in that sound that one is no longer 'listening' to it, but is vibrating in unison with it, then the final state of *Laya Yoga (Nāda Brahman* – or Oneness with God/Sound) is achieved.

Such an attainment gives one divine hearing and attunement to the dynamic source of mantric sound. The Seers (or rather, 'hearers') claim that it removes all mental and physical defects, destroys ignorance '(sin) and burns up residual karmas. A contemporary master of mantra, Sri Ramamurti (previously a psychologist and medical doctor specialising in brain surgery), says:

> . . . *nādam* controls all afflictions and obstacles of the mind. If one who is addicted to any intoxication will concentrate his mind on *nādam,* he will not have to try to control his mind by alcohol, narcotics, or hypnotic and sedative drugs. There is no better known method to control restlessness, uneasiness and anxiety than the practice of *nādam.* When any problem arises, sound current, *nādam,* increases.[1]

The deeper one delves into *Nādam,* or *Nāda,* the closer one comes to understanding what Satyavan calls the 'metaphysics of sound'. The metaphysics of the expression of *Nādam* is the fundamental process of cosmic manifestation, according to the laws of which, unmanifested sound (*Para-nāda* – the underlying principle of universal energy in potential form), burgeons forth from the 'creative void' through progressive levels of densification until it becomes audible, and ultimately visible, through diversification into form, light and colour: much as white light is diversified into many colours when seen through a prism. But in this instance, the prism through which universal manifestation is viewed, is the narrowed–down 'lens' of normal individual human consciousness.

It is therefore true that one can only *truly* appreciate the awesome wonder of the workings of a universe brought into existence by mantric sound, when one begins to intuit the mystico–scientific sonic principles of such manifestation. But this is an incredibly complex and profound study of the greatest magnitude and is generally only accessible to mystics, highly developed yogis and those with spiritually illumined intellectual capacities. Not for nothing does the Sufi master Hazrat Inayat Khan make the statement: "The knower of the mystery of Sound knows the mystery of the whole universe."[2]

But to try and understand this process with the untrained mind (the worldly consensus-consciousness) is hardly feasible, since the metaphysics of ultrasonic sound (being beyond mind and ear) only becomes experientially comprehensible once one has passed beyond the confining bounds of intellectuality and soars into realms beyond imagining. This fact, however, need not be a deterrent to investigation, but rather a spur to appreciating the remarkable effects that mantra practice, and especially a mantra like the *Gayatri*, has on one's conscious experience, even without understanding the processes at work.

One will find that constant practice of the *Gayatri* mantra itself – a mantra invoking Light, for illumination of the consciousness – develops precisely that kind of intuitive awareness required to enter into these higher dimensions of experience. This mantra is symbolised by the sun and is chanted all over India at dawn and sunrise with the eyes fixed on the sun's disc for the first five minutes of its appearance, and again during the last five minutes of the sun's setting. When chanted during the day, one visualises the sun internally with the eyes closed.

Next to the universal sound of *OM* the *Gayatri* is considered as the most sacred of all Vedic mantras and is propagated in the ancient *Manu Smrti (The Lawbook of Manu)* as *the* mantra for all Godward-going beings.

OM BHŪR BHUVAH SVAH
TAT SAVITUR VAREÑYAM
BHARGO DEVASYA DHĪMAHI
DHIYO YO NAḤ PRACHODAYĀT
OM – (SWAHA)

We contemplate upon that radiant Source of all Light, that our minds may merge as One with it, and Truth inspire our reflection.

Sensing the Inner Sound

Q. *Within the teachings of many faiths and practices leading the aspirant to higher fields of knowledge and well-being lie numerous references to sound. Many yogis advocate the use of special sounds to be intoned either silently or audibly. Most techniques of meditation with which I am acquainted in fact prescribe some object of sound by which to focus the mind.*

However, have we not missed one vital step? Those ancient sages heard those sounds for themselves. They were not instructed as to those sounds but heard them. I find this point of the utmost importance.

Do we ever hear inner sounds? The answer from many would be no. However, I would like then to suggest that they are hearing them, but are consciously avoiding them – Many, many times I have been aware of a high-pitched hum inside my head and ears. Sometimes more acutely than others; even, paradoxically, when circumstances were exceedingly noisy. The hum is apparently a very widespread experience. Since this sound can be heard within or without (it can still be heard with the fingers blocking the ears), and is common to many many people, perhaps all, then perhaps the answer to my former question is a resounding yes.

So what is this hum? Enough to say that no satisfactory explanation has been forthcoming ... [However] in point of fact, I am convinced of its usefulness. Meditating [by attention to this sound] has had an incredibly positive effect on my daily life.

A. Bravo! You have naturally found a secret sought by many a yogi striving in his cave. And I hope I shall be able to satisfactorily answer your question, having used and taught this form of meditative practice since my own initiation some twenty years ago.

This sound is spoken of in many traditions of the world as it is universally perceptible. It is frequently referred to in *Raja Yoga*, *Sikh* and *Tantric* texts, being variously known as *Nāda* (or *Nādam*); or *Sphotam* (the manifesting experience within on hearing sound); *Anahata* (the Unstruck Sound); *Shabd* (or *Shabda* the Word or Sound of the Creator), and also as *Omkara*, AUM or OM. This internal OM is generally known as the *Pranāva* (or 'ever-fresh' Sound of Brahman – the substratum of the universe). It is thus the subtle Eternal Sound of primal origin, which underlies the whole of creation and is therefore considered as the true 'Song of God'.

Its internally heard tuning-fork like tone is endlessly harmonising and holding together all the life forms of the universe. Should this sound change its pitch, the whole 'physical' structure of the universe could crumble into molecular fragments. And, according to the ancient cosmology of the Hindu sages, such is said to occur every umpteen billion millennia, when the universe dissolves and is then regenerated at the beginning of a new vast cycle of ages, with the recommencement of the *Word*.

But meanwhile (back at the earthly ranch), since this sound is postulated as the substratum and basic keynote of all structural harmony, it is evidently of inestimable value to tune in to it if we wish to become at one with ourselves and our environment. By the ancient method of listening to the *Nādam* or internal OM, we become effortlessly attuned to the universal *Om*-nipresence – the OM which is present everywhere. Yet it is often ignored for lack of acquaintance.

Many people tend to mistake it for *tinnitus,* a medical condition of 'ringing in the ears'. But that is a purely physical problem or defect in the ear itself and bears no relation to *Nādam*. Most people who believe they have something wrong with their hearing, and spend years going from one specialist to another, having all kinds of things done to their ears, are finally told to 'try and get along with it' as no amount of medication seems to help. The fact is, the sound is not occurring in the ears at all, but is resounding in the consciousness and can eventually be heard throughout the body.

Although many people are trying to get rid of this sound, there are a number of Eastern and Western esoteric schools and religious organisations who recognise its purpose and actively encourage its cultivation. Some of them are élitist and secretive, some more open, and some rather 'preciously' teach their methods for inducing the sound. But in general, the same thing is taught, even though each group gives the impression that only *they* have the 'real' mantric syllables to generate it, or the true techniques for awakening it.

However, the reality is that it is ever present, always sounding inside ourselves (the Omnipresence being eternally on the line, waiting for us to pick up on it), and no school has a monopoly on it. Those who smugly imagine that they alone have the 'Knowledge' (often an initiate's form of spiritual 'one-upmanship'), may be safely left to their own delusions, for the techniques involved can be found in several classical yoga texts.

Naturally it is always more helpful to have guidance from a trustworthy source, rather than blindly groping for the inner light. (The sound does in fact sometimes manifest as inner light in the consciousness, hence it is also called *ākāsha* – 'fully radiant or shining'.) There are many yogis from whom the method can be learned, quite freely and unostentatiously and without elaborate ritual. But if your nature inclines to instruction by a 'Great Guru' figure and more mysterious trimmings, then you can get the same thing from large-scale institutions or 'cult'-ivated groups, according to your taste.[1]

However, as the sound is self tappable, it is not absolutely vital to have the sound current so-called 'passed on' by the initiatory offices of a *guru,* whose teaching may be anything from good, bad, to indifferently misleading. (Do I hear screams of righteous indignation from the initiated faithful? Alas, inevitably I do. It is unfortunate, but I fear too many seekers succumb to the vested interest of spiritual self-esteem as one of an 'in-crowd' of initiates, who are unable to accept that they do not have the only 'true' and 'pure' teaching available.)

Of course, if you are convinced of the quality of a guru (by close rapport and experience, rather than by the highly embroidered tales of wide-eyed devotees), and he is more than a distant figurehead, then it is evidently invaluable to receive instructions from such a one. And a mantra given by one who understands its energy is of inestimable value in your practice. But such persons are few and far between. Not every guru who dispenses mantras is a mantra yogi. Even failing wise instruction, with or without the trappings of *mudra** or mantra, the resulting sound is still the same – even if it comes upon you by itself.

"One who has no manifestation of *nādam* should repeat *Om* vocally and mentally until it is manifested... As long as eternal *Om, nādam,* is not manifested [in your consciousness] one is not admitted [to be] a student of Yoga because he is not initiated by the Supreme."[2] So it is spoken of in many technical yoga texts and scriptures, thus explicitly emphasising that the sound *can* be self engendered, or comes as an acknowledgement of one's fitness for the Path as a gesture from 'Guru Omni the Divine'.

So what is this hum? The sound of *Nādam* is the effect of *shakti* (energy), the primal force which keeps all sub-atomic particles in a state of eternal vibration, creating what is known as the endless 'Dance of the Atoms'. This vibratory activity creates a peculiar resonance in the 'ether' which is heard in the head like a high-pitched electrical whine, or resembles the 'singing' tone of a bell after it has been struck. This 'after sound' effect is the result of molecular friction in the 'mind-stuff' (*chittam*) or that subtle energy which engenders the 'thought field' in which we think. Although this appears to be heard in the ears, it is actually apprehended first in the cerebellum, or hind part of the brain.

It is for this reason that it is also called *shruti* – or that which is innerly heard, or perceived *without* the use of auditory apparatus. And it is in this manner that the ancient sages internally heard and intuited the first mantras at the dawn of time. These same sounds are still available to anyone who is prepared to attune his mind to the highest levels of sensitivity as did the yogis of yore.

When *Nādam* occurs in ordinary people, it is the beginning of a call towards a contemplative consciousness. It can also strongly occur as a form of protection at times when external noise could otherwise be damaging, causing you to become aware of it to the exclusion of external sound. For the same reason it will become louder when you are in an agitated

*Yogic hand postures

mental condition. This is the Omnipresence 'singing' within you as an indication to tune in to it at these times for the sake of your equilibrium. Equally it will also come on strong when your head is free from thoughts (even for a few moments) as an encouragement for you to sink contemplatively into the sound.

One of the major purposes of *japa*-mantra (repetition of mantras) is to cultivate the interior conditions of consciousness which will bring about the intensification of one's perception of this 'Song of God'. Concentration on *Nādam* is known as one of the greatest methods for the evaporation of anxiety, restlessness and the racing mind, instability and depression. Peace and tranquillity are its by-products. Its practice is considered as the royal road to Cosmic Consciousness.

Making the Most of Your Mantra

Q. *I was given a mantra by a yogi in the Himalayas. He told me (severely) that I must only repeat it mentally. But I feel blocked by this and sometimes I just want to burst out singing it. And if I do, I feel it working better for me. But I am afraid I may be doing something wrong by not following his orders, although he was not my guru. I have heard of your mantra work (and listened to your tapes through a friend) and feel you could help me in this matter.*

A. You have absolutely nothing to fear from chanting the mantra aloud. And considering your natural inclination, in this case it is more advisable to do so. It is always the *feeling* you experience with a mantra which is all important. Make the most of your mantra by following through with whatever feelings may arise, rather than putting the brakes on your experience by adhering to the dry rules of technique or the nit-picking ways of traditional practice.

Just be careful to chant in private, or away from the ears of others if you are somewhere outside. Your own personal mantra should be for your ears alone. Not that mantras are generally secret in themselves, as a great majority can be found in yogic texts or looked up in any Sanskrit dictionary. But once a mantra has been given to you, if the teacher has transferred its energy to you in the giving, it should be kept personalised for your own protection.

The point is that your strength of *sadhana* – or drive to practise – can be weakened, or open to ridicule, when others know your own private vibration. Your energy can thus be undermined by others maintaining that *their* mantra is more powerful than yours, or that you have been given a negative mantra (according to their possibly inadequate understanding), or that their guru could give you a much better mantra. Demoralisation of this sort can undo all your previous work. And also unscrupulous occultists (if they had the skill) might use your mantra to negative purpose against you, in much the same way as practitioners of witchcraft and voodoo stick pins in images to destroy their enemies.

Therefore abusing your mantra by lightly revealing it to anyone (other than a trustworthy mantra yogi), or not using it sincerely, contravenes an inner law regarding its usage and its power can be taken away from you by the giver. But secrecy is mostly to assist you in generating and keeping up an inner intensity of mantric energy without any external dissipation.

In my experience, when one first begins to work with a mantra, it is preferable to chant aloud in order to fully saturate the whole body-mind complex with the quality of it. Then, once its resonance is ringing through all the cells, the vibration carries on by itself when you stop chanting. When the body-mind is thus already 'singing' of its own volition, it is then much easier to continue with the mental repetition. But even when chanting aloud, if there are others likely to overhear, your mantra can be verbally internalised. By this I mean that it can be intoned in such a way that most of the sound and vibration goes down into the body, allowing only a mumble to be heard externally. In this way you may be protectively secret, but not necessarily silent.

A fair number of yogis and traditionalists in India are unnecessarily tight and rigid in their way of doing things, being dogmatised by the particular school of philosophy they follow. Some schools insist that mental mantra is the most subtle and only 'pure' way. Yet others condemn silent mantra as a selfish practice, which benefits only one person, maintaining that audible mantra bestows blessings on all within earshot. In actuality both methods are equally effective in charging the surroundings with harmonious vibrations, provided that the mantra is chanted from the heart.

Your given mantra is (or should be) specific to your needs, and no matter how many others may happen to use it, or chant it audibly, it should remain personal to you. But this should not prevent you from chanting the same mantra loudly in a group, or from chanting other mantras when in company. Your own mantra is specific in its action, but other mantras can act as a general tonic to your whole being. Any mantra chanted wholly from the heart, audibly or silently, cannot but be beneficial.

Therefore chant on – and be blessed.

PSYCHOTHERAPY
AND BEYOND

(Or – does life exist outside psychotherapy?)

Healing the Hurts of Many Lifetimes

Q. *I am a bit hesitant about going into therapy, wondering if it is really helpful, or is it likely to be a dodgy and expensive mistake? I gather you have grown away from practising psychotherapy in recent years and am wondering if you have come to the conclusion that psychoanalysis is not worthwhile?*

I've seen a lot of adverts for hypnotherapists, all claiming to take you back not only to birth, but to previous lifetimes, to try and sort out your unconscious drives. Do you think this is a good idea? I'm curious to know about my past lives, but a bit frightened about digging into subconscious stuff. I mean, even accepting reincarnation as a probability, I'm not sure it is in the natural order of things to drag up the past like that. Are we supposed to? And if so, why don't we remember our previous lives normally?

Do you recommend any particular type of therapy?

A. I have to say I have not (totally) withdrawn from general practice because of a disenchantment with the methods or results of psychotherapy, but simply because my natural inclination is towards a more aspirational lifestyle, rather than to be endlessly delving into the darker regions of the psyche (whether my own or others). However, if something happens to come up spontaneously, I deal with it in a psychotherapeutic manner at the moment of its arising. I have no qualms about the value of psychotherapy, providing, of course, that it *is therapy,* and not merely a mental ball game between you and the therapist, as is generally the case with the old-style *analysis* in which you remain immobilised on the therapist's couch and ramble turgidly through your fears and fantasies.

With this kind of treatment you can quite easily stay out of touch with yourself forever, remaining totally in your head, without feeling all the subliminal organismal pains and seething biological life forces attempting to burgeon up to conscious experience. As we are psycho–physical organisms, we require a form of therapy which takes the complete body-mind complex into account. Therefore psycho-physiologic therapies such as *Primal, Neo-Reichian, Gestalt* (to a degree) and *Bioenergetics* are a great step forward in this respect. Otherwise, without a reactive and *connected* body-mind experience, in which the total organism takes part, very little of therapeutic value can occur.

My only reservation is that most 'advanced' philosophical attitudes of modern psychotherapy stop short at the 'new' body-mind concept and seem oblivious to the fact that man is not only a combined body and mind, but is also – and basically – *spirit.* And it is with spirit that my own interests lie. But it is here the average therapist leaves off. Fortunately there are a small but growing number of therapists who do take the spiritual dimension into account. It is possible nowadays to find a therapist who is sensitive to *all* aspects of being. Or you may simply work with what I would call a more mechanistic 'nuts and bolts' type of therapist for his or her knowledge of body-mind mechanisms, and seek out a spiritual mentor for further growth.

When the time is ripe, there is every reason for plunging into therapy. But I do not recommend anyone to begin something of the sort simply out of 'curiosity', as any kind of psycho-therapy acts as an agitative stirring-stick in the ants' nest of your mind. You have to be ready to work on what you uncover. However, if you feel near to a 'nervous breakdown' and are already beginning to crack up under the strain of trying to hold it off, then as your inner pains have arisen naturally, it is 'organically' the right time to work on them. If you cannot live with yourself a moment longer as you are, and something immediate is required, then there need be no hesitation about entering any of the more dynamic and 'speedier' forms of group therapy.

There is no doubt about the validity of re-experiencing traumatic events or repressed pains from one's infancy (in this life at least). One way or another, we have to 'unfreeze', the bodily tensions and mental-emotional attitudes locked into our system since childhood. A trauma or 'mental shock' is not actually in the causal event itself, but in the resulting mental or psycho–physical *reaction* and attempted avoidance of it. It may be in a shock to the organism which occurred before the thinking process developed, which continues to vibrate in the 'cellular memory' as indefinable tension. Or it can later be in the lack of ability in the infant mind to accept the implications of a situation, or even its own unreal projections of how it sees an event.

For example: if as a child you believed that, because your father or mother was blazingly angry with you, you could be killed or abandoned if you fought back or spoke your mind, then that thought would be too horrifying for your infant mind to handle without going insane. So the protective 'shutters' of the mind instantly slam down over the thought and the feeling, encapsulating it, and effectively numbing the memory and the senses. Although the body may feel like a 'dead thing' in later years, that very un-aliveness and sensation of emotionally-frozen feelings shows that the body has never forgotten the incident.

However, the *cause* of it is blocked out from conscious memory, and the residual tension of this 'unfinished business' of 'swallowed pain' somehow remains stored in the 'memory bank' of the organism for the rest of our days. As a result, a mental and bodily 'armouring' against life begins to occur. The organic 'factory' of our body begins a slow 'shut down' and we experience a gradual deadening of our feelings, especially if the original cause is compounded by other incidents of a similar nature. And this is almost inevitable. The more insecure and alienated we feel, the more agitated we become and the more noisy and upsetting things we do to gain attention, thus making ourselves all the more unbearable to our already exasperated parents, who are likely to have lashed out at us in desperation, only to confirm our sense of being 'unloved'.

Whether we are 'traumatised' by our own imaginings, or by the actual reality of a brutal, or love-starved relationship, the resulting effect is the same. As we grow we experience a mental and cellular 'constriction' of the life-force within us, which builds up a pressure like in any blocked artery, and causes us to act, and react, neurotically throughout adolescence and later 'adult' life. The majority of so-called adults are actually children 'frozen in time' at various stages of their growth, like mental-emotional 'snapshots' encapsulated in the psyche and circulating in the blood. Many put up a bold front behind a stiff ego-mask, desperately trying not to let the inner child show too much. Those who wish to be seen as 'respectable' conformists are perfect examples of repressed infants.

In psychotherapeutic practice it is now evident that these internal pressures from our 'frozen feelings' can be relieved by re-*living* the previously avoided experiences, or rather, by actually *living them through* for the first time, with all the attendant pain, or anger and misery which was not expressed at the time. Once the experience is fully felt, understood, and integrated, it no longer has a hold on the subconscious, because it is no longer *sub*-conscious. There are many valuable methods in the aforementioned modern release-therapies (and especially in group-work, which I recommend), which can help us to rediscover the original 'trigger-events' that caused us to close off in childhood, without any necessity for hypnotic induction.

Although hypnosis has been found an efficacious method for the *relief* of certain symptoms, it is not clear to me that it is a valid form of psyschotherapeutic *healing,* inasmuch as it would seem that some aspect of consciousness is being suppressed at the suggestion of an outside agency. If we are not in full possession of our faculties we cannot properly understand nor integrate an experience. Simply to be robotically stimulated by a subliminal suggestion from a hypnotist, even for our own good, is to remain under the control of subconscious forces. We are already in this position to begin with, being neurotically motivated by forgotten incidents from the past.

Even though we may be hypnotically induced to stop smoking or biting our fingernails, this does not free us from the reason *why* we were so agitatedly sucking and chewing in the first place. Not only have we not rectified anything by this subliminal modification of our behaviour, we have actually compounded the problem by smothering over our habitual emotional release outlets and adding to the burden of psychic repression. This is analagous to the allopathic medical treatment of illness by the suppression of the symptoms by drugs. The symptoms may well have disappeared, but that does not mean the disease is cured. It has simply retreated from the skin surface (where it was trying to expel itself from the toxicity of the body), only to be sucked back into the organs to come out in another form at a later date. If you keep on sweeping dirt under the carpet, eventually you will get a crick in the neck from bending to avoid the ceiling.

On the other hand, hypnotism as a method of diagnosis and investigation of hidden sources of mental aberration is evidently of great practical value. But whatever is found by this method has to be brought to the awareness of the fully alert mind to be consciously experienced and worked through. This means that one would need the services of a hypnotist who is also a capable psychotherapist of reputable integrity, who is capable of handling anything which might go wrong as a consequence of his or her investigations. Otherwise, trying to 'pull out' bits of past life experiences at random in the hands of a fly-by-night 'chancer' or 'backyard' hypnotist, could be a very risky business.

Although therapy is not to be taken lightly, it is not a frightening experience in itself. It is just that once you start delving into the subconscious regions of the mind in a psycho-therapeutic situation, you must be prepared for – at the very least – three years of (on and off) wallowing in miserable events and confusing, painful and fear surrounded memories. It is rarely the actual memories themselves which are frightening, it is more the fact that we become paralysed (often literally) by the approach of the *fear of the unfelt feeling,* which arises in us as we get close to *feeling* it. As the buried pain is coming up to conscious experience, the original fears which caused it to be shut down in the first place also rise and overwhelm us near to suffocation. This is because we are feeling them through the magnified memory of the frightened inner child.

When this happens, we tend to do all we can to hold back the fearful feelings and our imminent 'socially embarrassing' tears. At this point it is vital to give up the 'bottling' process we have indulged in all our lives. We have to stop fighting against the subliminal pressure. We have at last to allow ourselves to surrender to its volcanic force and let it rip like a champagne cork bursting out of a bottle. Once the feeling actually bursts forth and is felt in all its depth, it is a merciful release. The fear of the fearful feeling vanishes instantly. It becomes then almost a joy to cry out the pain of long buried feeling to the light.

This is obviously a very therapeutic process, and nothing else will do when internal pressures are making us near hysterical. But helpful though it is, one of the main problems I found with psychotherapy was knowing where to stop. *'Stop when you are cured,'* you might say. But since there never seems to come a time when we can pronounce ourselves truly 'cured', how long do we go on winkling out buried pains? Suppose we set aside several years for tracking down and unearthing all our 'historic' pains and problems. We work our way back through the ghastly emotive years of adolescence, and then through the sorrows of childhood and infancy to the pre-verbal years of babyhood. As the process becomes more subtle we may come to realise that although we are alleviating many pressures on the psyche, we are only patching up what seem to be the 'end products' of our pain and not the original causes of it.

We might pause to wonder *why* it is we reacted to certain experiences in our life in such a way as to 'encapsulate' moments of fear, instead of letting them go by? Another child in the same situation might have reacted differently, or not at all, and carried no psychological scar through life. And in some situations we ourselves are able to laugh at things which may cause someone else to cringe in fear. Therefore we are obliged to look further for the underlying reasons why we reacted in one way and not another.

The next thing we are given to understand is that our reactive attitudes to events in early childhood and later life were already predetermined, having been laid down genetically during our nine month gestation in the womb and in the following 'traumatic' experience of birth.[1] The process of birth is considered as being composed of four basic stages, each phase of which lays the foundation for the ways in which we are to react to external stimuli in future. This area of experience is the source of what we call *visceral* or 'gut-reaction' to things.

In the first phase of birth, known as the intra-uterine stage, when we are coddled in the womb, we are normally blissful and content, fed, protected and undisturbed. If this was our major experience of womb life we can easily find the same security in adult life in the arms of a lover, in music, attunement with nature, or in meditation and feelings of Oneness with the universe. But if our mother had a tense pregnancy, full of fears and wild emotions, fights with her husband, nervous insecurity and smoked and drank heavily, then all these influences would be impressed upon the cellular 'memory-banks' of the growing infant. In this way we can already be traumatised while still in the womb.

The second phase of birth is the breaking of the protective sac of waters and the onset of labour contractions. According to research it would appear that when a baby is biologically 'mature', it 'knows' when it is ready to come, and releases hormones which affect the lining of the uterus, thereby activating the mother's chemistry to begin contractions.[2] Evidently an induced birth must cause considerable traumatic stress to a baby whose organism is insufficiently prepared for the birth process. This primal 'unreadiness' is likely to be experienced in every eventuality throughout later life.

Even in a natural birth, this moment is fraught with potential psychological problems. Suddenly the *status quo* of nine months' security in the womb is threatened. Our established way of life is upset. If we are forced out of the womb precipitate, in later life we can react with emotional violence to any pressure to change our habitual way of living.

In the third phase of birth, we are pressurised into the birth canal and horrendously squeezed out of shape like toothpaste in a tube, emerging into what is often a vast and frightening, brilliantly-lit, loud-voiced and unpredictable new dimension. Those who had a hard time breaking out may suffer all their lives from the panicky 'no way out' feeling of fearful pressure and suffocation which is locked in the cellular memory. An adult suffering from this phase of the birth may have a continual fear of commitment to anything. Against his own wishes he may be unable to accept a binding job, or sign a contract with a time clause, or get married, or buy a house, and is often subject to recurrent feelings of being hemmed in, restricted, or pressurised at home and work. Indeed, he may even create these external pressures as an unconscious means of driving himself to break out of his internal pressure.

Babies born into softly lit and harmonious environments are later seen to be more easily adaptable and trusting in new environments and situations. A Caesarean birth, on the other hand, in which one is whisked out into the world before being ready for it, by-passing all the natural processes and being prevented from 'making it' alone, sows the seeds of many psychological problems. Caesarean children may have tendencies towards abjectivity in the face of life, a feeling of 'helplessness' and an inborn (unborn?) sense of lifelong resentment against everything. They can have a disinclination to enter easily into new ventures, or an inability to push themselves or struggle through difficult situations.

Finally in the fourth phase, the period following emergence, our fearful (or easeful) experience of birth could have been mollified or intensified, depending on how we were received into the world. If we were immediately up-ended and slapped, or the cord cut too soon (before all the blood we needed had been absorbed) – or we were taken away from our mother and left untouched, isolated in an incubator, or dumped in a cot in a room full of screaming babies for the night, then the sense of fear, shock, loss and abandonment would have compounded the traumatic experience of birth. Such eventualities colour our fundamental emotional attitudes for the rest of our lives.

Even so, such intense experiences are evidently not remembered by the conscious mind. If, under normal circumstances, we do not consciously recall the profound experience of our birth, is it any wonder that we are unable to remember our past lives? We are unable to remember most of this life. Almost all but snatches of our formative years have vanished from conscious memory. As an experiment, try to recall what you were doing at this time of day, on the same day of this month ten years ago. Or five years ago? Or last year – or even last week?

It is unlikely that you will remember.

We are unable to recall most of our life because we were 'not there' at the time. Our attention is almost never fully focussed on the present moment. We generally 'sleepwalk' our way through life, living internally in a mental fog of churning ideas and inexplicable feelings which cuts us off from the actuality of life and thus from conscious memory of it. We are only capable of consciously remembering those moments in life when we were fully 'there' in the moment, alert and absorbing everything.

Why then is it that we cannot consciously recall the moment of our birth, when we were obviously totally *present* and involved in it? Our earliest memories are normally inaccessible because the events occurred before we developed language in which to 'fix' them for recall. We think in words which evoke images; without words we have no concepts. We cannot 'picture' it. In the first couple of years of life it is the *feeling* centre of the brain which develops first. Whatever happened to us in this period was encapsulated in *wordless* feeling only. Hence we cannot understand our emotional drives because they arrived in the pre-verbal period before conceptual thinking developed. This thinking capacity occurs at a later stage, when the brain becomes fully operational between the ages of two and three.

However, as has been shown in neurological research, the memory of every second of existence remains intact, stored away in our incredible psycho-biologic system. Everything our body-mind has ever experienced is somehow miraculously retained by an internal etheric sound and film-like recording mechanism in the cells. By the implantation of electrodes and wires directly into the grey matter, the brain can be stimulated in certain places to evoke the same 'playback' memories over and over again. Yet the same thing may occur as the result of natural stimuli.

You may perhaps one day be eating an apple and suddenly the taste of it brings a flashback to the same experience of vividly tasting an apple at the age of six (as occurred to me) together with all the feelings, sounds, sights and even the smells of the scene at the time. So even the sense of *taste* can trigger off complete recall of an encapsulated moment of the past. This kind of thing is by no means an uncommon experience.

Similarly, the techniques of modern psychotherapy can bring to life the 'frozen' emotional experiences of early childhood and pre-verbal infancy. When the correct psychological 'trigger' is applied, the cellular body-mind can even play back the whole experience of your birth. Your adult body and mind actually goes through a total 'replay' of all the movements and feelings your baby 'body-mind' went through during the birthing process. During my own experience of reliving my birth, I was astounded to be able to observe with my adult consciousness, my body going through the birthing motions and then my voice crying with the voice of a new-born baby, and feeling its feelings, and *seeing* with a baby's eyes the magic of the movement of my fingers.

With other adults being 'reborn' in therapy, I have even witnessed the finger-marks and slap-marks of the obstetrician come up on their legs and backs, as the body 'remembered' every aspect of the process. This phenomenon has also been noted and documented by other therapists.[3] When the birth event is relived several times and is *completely* experienced (recognised for what it is) and integrated, it appears to free one from many of the neurotic and self-destructive attitudes which have been built into the system since that time.

One can realise that all this is a far cry from the more passive form of conventional psycho-analysis, which all too often remains as mere cerebral analysis on the mental level only. A participant in one therapy workshop told me, "I never knew this kind of therapy existed. I've learned more about myself in one weekend than in ten years of Jungian analysis." Unless one actually *feels,* relives and connects with 'historic' pains, one can go on analysing the reasons why one is acting neurotically until doomsday, to little effect. You may *understand* things better, but still remain as neurotic as ever.

So supposing we have tackled our birth traumas and overcome a major obstacle of life. Is this the end? Alas! There are still the hereditary problems inherited from our parents and the genes of their families, with probable fears and phobias and racial memories encapsulated as 'micro-computerised' information in their seed from way back down the line. And as if all that was not enough, we then have all the weight of previous lifetimes impinging on our subconscious, which sometimes surfaces to the conscious mind.

Some of our bizarre reactions to events can also be attributed to these non-conscious traumatic 'residues' carried over from what would appear to be a former life or lifetimes. A close friend confided to me that over the years, whenever she visited a castle, or castle ruins, she was overcome with fear and nausea and had to leave quickly. One day when I was wearing an old medieval-style tunic, she exclaimed, "Why, you look like a medieval lord!" At that very moment in a visionary flash, I 'saw' her dressed in a costume of the period, hair braided, and standing in the hall of a castle.

As I said, "I see you in a castle", I realised that she also was seeing something similar. She went white as a sheet and fell to the floor in a fit, clutching her throat, gagging, thrashing and screaming, like a spider burning in a candle flame. (She was a normal housewife to whom nothing of the sort had ever happened before.) This extraordinary and powerful reaction lasted for over two hours of uncontrollable body spasms and teeth-chattering terror. We came to realise that she was re-living an experience of being murdered in a medieval castle, where she had been locked up for many years.

In fact, she appeared to be re-living a compacted form of multiple lifetimes, in which she had her throat cut or belly ripped open (both as a man and as a woman) in successive lives. Also in this life she had undergone a Caesarean birth operation in order to save her child during labour contractions when the birth canal was blocked. It would appear that like attracts like in the psychological realm. All the experiences of one kind seem to accumulate in the same area of memory, as with the example of the apple-tasting experience, and are replayed in the consciousness with the requisite stimulus.

One of the positive and freeing aspects of my friend's experience was the realisation of why she had always adamantly refused to allow her husband to buy them a house of their own. Subconsciously a house had meant a 'castle' and thus 'confining walls'. But after this event the association had become clear and resolved in her and the owning of a house no longer remained a problem. However, the experience has returned to actual 'playback consciousness' several times and there are evidently many other aspects to be integrated and understood.

It can be seen that past life experiences can come to us unbidden in this way, when their time has come to be released and worked through, without the need for hypnotic search. I have the intuitive impression that cosmically we are all 'replaying' our past lives and entering into similar situations as in other incarnations (such as family strife, political strife and war), over and over again until we have learned the lessons they have to teach. Even in our present life we can observe how we fall into the same old habit patterns and relationship routines, doing the same damn-fool thing time and again, until we actually see what is happening and respond to the situation in a new way.

We learn nothing by experience, only by understanding and integrating it. Otherwise we return to the same old life-situations, dressed up in different clothes and different bodies, obliged to enter into the same old wars and sufferings, life after life, until we wake up and realise what is going on. Thus the 'patterns' of our past lives are still very much operational in the present one. Where then is the need to probe past lives when the essential factors from them are creating the daily conditions of our lives today?

Even if we have therapeutically worked our way through all our adolescent agonies, the traumas of childhood and then those of birth, we are obliged to go on and on, according to this way of perceiving things. What of the traumas of the dimension in which we existed *before* conception? And from there, the tribulations and death throes of the life we lived before that? And of the uncountable lives, births and deaths before that? And all the in-between times? How far do we want to go back? How can we hope to put right the miseries of so many lifetimes? Many people are unable even to bear the burden of *this* life, let alone that of others.

Eventually we may come to realise that the deep well of psychic pains is bottomless. I do not believe we can be completely cured by psychotherapy alone. Somewhere along the line we have to seek the *fundamental* cause of all our problems. At present there are boundaries beyond which psychotherapy cannot go. Our souls have to phase in to a recognition of the more spiritual aspects of existence. Life is not merely a matter of 'doctoring' the maladies of the 'mind', but of becoming aware of our place in this extraordinary existence, and discovering our relationship to 'whatever-it-is' that animates the universe.

Do we not have enough tensions, guilts and sorrows in this life that we should seek to load ourselves with the remembered agonies, angers and misdeeds of other lives? How great a load can we bear? If we are suffering in this life, it is partly on account of our misdeeds in other incarnations – or such is the affirmation of the great seers and sages, whose investigations into consciousness have taken them beyond the restrictions of time and mind. And if we knew worse things about ourselves, we might well go mad with remorse. It is truly a matter of grace that we normally do not remember our previous existences.

We are – more or less – allowed to begin again each time, with the slate wiped clean – of memory at least. I say more or less, because it would seem that we return again in our present life as the *sum total* of all that we were before. It appears as if all our good and bad deeds, our positives and negatives, everything that moulded us in our previous life, is somehow 'totted up' at the end of each earthly span and coalesces into the cosmic 'bill' (to pay off) or the 'credit' (to come back to us) which is carried on over into the next life. Thus we arrive once more in the world with certain preprogrammed propensities and potentials, and are deposited in favourable or unfavourable circumstances according to our 'Cosmic account' and needs for development.

Hence we get geniuses and infant prodigies who can compose sonatas at the age of four or five and the like, who have 'brought through' their creative capacities from the previous existence, perhaps intensified by the genetic traits of the family they have been 'attracted' to. Conversely, some are born with Downe's Syndrome or handicapped in some other way, that they may compensate for deeds and attitudes adopted in former lives. Some perhaps are needing to learn patience, dependence on others, trust or surrender. Some may even have *chosen* to come to specific parents in this way, so that certain characteristics may be developed in those who are to care for them.

There are also many remarkable cases of people who *do* naturally remember former lives. There have been instances of advanced yogis who were born with total recall from the moment of birth. And in every part of the world there have been many well-documented reports of people who have 'died' and their 'seed-essence' complete with memory has immediately been transposed into the womb of another mother. Souls who return so quickly to this plane of earthly existence tend to have complete recall of their previous life situation (often lasting for the first five to seven years of life). It usually happens that as soon as they are able to speak, they refuse to accept their new parents as their true parents.

Some cases investigated reported children leading their present parents (and scientific investigators) to the distant cities or villages where they claimed they used to live, finding their way through streets they had never been through before, to their former homes (one child even complaining that they had painted the front door a different colour), and confronting their previous 'wives' or 'husbands' who were still alive and living in the same place.[4] Often they were able to name most relatives (or nearby shopkeepers) accurately, and knew the name of the family dog and the names of their former dolls (if they had died as children). One child even led his investigators to the factory where he used to work and showed them how to operate the machinery.

It is becoming increasingly evident that this kind of 'far memory' is not such an isolated phenomenon as one might think. It happens equally among eskimos, American Indians, Africans, Chinese and Hindus as among the English, French, Scandinavian or Russian peoples. There are quirks in nature which allow such things to happen. Or perhaps it is a natural evolutionary event to awaken a soul to the reality of its true state of existence. It would seem that if there is reason enough, or we are psychically ripe, and have *need* to remember, then such memories, or an actually *experienced* psycho–physiological 'playback' of a former life situaton is given to us, commensurate with our requirements for inner unfoldment.

In many instances, it appears to occur as a consequence of the development of a meditative consciousness, which is beginning to pierce the veil of time and space. This is considered by yogis as the most natural and spontaneous form of 'psychotherapy' as part of the process of spiritual unfoldment. The inner work of spiritual development consists of plunging far beyond personality problems, and sensitising oneself to the 'Heart of the Universe', immersing oneself heart and soul in the sensation of the Omnipresence. Deep meditation acts as a refining fire on the psyche, purifying it of all mental dross.

In the process, yogis often undergo dramatic and bizarre experiences as the subconscious is purified and neurotic symptoms are worked out through the body. They may experience the effects of other lifetimes in their bodies, or blocked circuits suddenly becoming free, electric shock-like manifestations, limbs jumping and thrashing and weird blood-curdling cries arising from the soul. Some find themselves inexplicably running about on all fours, playing out vestiges of animal nature, howling like wolves or roaring with the true voice of a lion. Once all these hidden psychic manifestations have worked themselves out of the system, the yogi is cleansed of all subconscious impurities and afterwards radiates a deep sense of peace and contentment.

He has wrestled with the hydra-headed monster of his psychological deeps, known as the *sense-of-ego*. The yogi sees this 'beast' as *the* cause of all other 'causes', maintaining that as we are – in this moment – the distillation of all our deeds and thoughts of every previous incarnation, and all our *karma* (or mental and physical actions and reactions and resulting psychological problems) is encapsulated in this phantasmagorical creature. If we can subdue this sense-of-ego by seeking its origin, then all the ego-produced problems of this and every other lifetime will be cancelled out at one and the same time.

Is the Spiritual Quest Neurotic?

Q. *I have been involved in yoga now for fourteen years. I have studied formal academic psychology and yoga in parallel, and although yoga has little to do with the main body of psychology as taught today, there are some areas which overlap and have caused me some confusion over the years. My confusion is caused basically by one area of psychology and that is the work done by Art Janov.*

Although Janov is probably not taken at all seriously within formal psychology . . . he is the only serious challenge I have ever found to yoga philosophy, in that he explains ideas of spiritual search, or questions such as 'Who Am I?' etc., in terms of underlying neurosis. These explanations are often convincing, and throw down the gauntlet that if the underlying neurosis is cured, then the spiritual quest is over. To Janov, the person who asks 'Who am I?' is neurotic: to the yogi it may be a sign of the wakening individual. Now as an individual I can't deny the neurosis in myself, and I see it in many others I have met on the path.

Yoga . . . as a reliever of stress has great potential in attracting millions of people. My experience of yoga is such that if I practice meditation regularly, then I feel relaxed, etc. But if I let the practice slip, within a few weeks or days the old habits tend to return. So is meditation etc., an alternative to blocking the mind in the same way that tranquillisers are used nowadays? Obviously the Ancients did not have access to these drugs, but did they see the source of the problem as the mind and seek to control it?

The main question here then is: are we better off on a spiritual path or a psychological one? And is achieving bliss merely synonymous with becoming un-neurotic? If it is, then we must forget all about spirituality and concentrate on curing the neurosis if we are really interested in easing the suffering in the world and in ourselves.

Dr Arthur Janov became a prominent figure in the world of psychotherapy with the publication of his best-selling book The Primal Scream: The Cure for Neurosis *(Putnam, New York 1970, Abacus, London 1973)*

A. Your question echoes almost exactly my own sentiments and doubts when I first encountered Janov's work. I was extremely impressed with his contribution to the psycho-therapeutic model, having garnered little joy from the academic pontifications of fuddy-duddy old Freudians and other orthodox psychotherapists, and having become somewhat depressed by the seeming slowness of my own development on the spiritual path. I was therefore beguiled by Janov's persuasive promises of a speedy and permanent 'cure' for the neurotic condition of the personality.

What Janov defines as neurosis is basically the unreal responses we make to life, as evidenced by the wall of defences we put up against the world. These defences, which cut us off from life and feeling, are characterised by continual mental and bodily 'armouring', developed as a result of avoiding the pain of unmet needs in childhood. Needs such as a longing to be loved which was never adequately fulfilled, make us retreat inside ourselves for comfort and protection from the unstable and threatening world 'out there'. Thus our responses to it are neurotically defensive or manipulative. And when we are unable to receive love from our parents, we seek elsewhere for solace, transferring our affection to 'symbolic' sources of comfort.

As children we compensate for lack of love by seeking security in our toys and dolls, or in an imaginary 'friend' we can talk to. As we grow older we seek it in ever new objects, demanding roller-skates, bicycles or computers 'like the other kids have' (even if we never play with them). Although these things never seem to make us happy, we still find ourselves playing this same unsatisfactory game in later years. To fill that ever-present yearning for love unrequited, we can find ourselves always playing roles we don't believe in (for the sake of 'admiration' in place of love), forever actors, seeking applause in the theatre of life. We try to cajole the world into liking us by adopting unreal and devious attitudes. We push ourselves to achieve unfulfilling substitutes such as fame or riches, degrees, or a status symbol wife or husband, the latest car, or a bigger and better house like the 'So-and-So's' have, all for nothing more solid than the reflected results in the eyes of others. And still we remain empty whatever we do, because we are forever outwardly defending ourselves against the primal pain within and locking out the love life has to offer us.

Dr Janov's way out of this syndrome is forcefully to batter down the doors of our defences to get at the core problems as quickly as possible. For some people this method is precisely what they need in order to reach down into their feelings, but for others it can be too great a shock to the system. However, Janov maintains that only by working through our Primal (original, primary, causal) pain can we be released from the false associations and unreal self-justificatory attitudes our minds have devised and arrive at the non-defensive and real person underneath.

So far, so good. Although this may only be a partial picture of the complexity of neurosis, it is seen as a reasonable position from the psycho-therapeutic standpoint and few would quarrel with it. However, other therapists in similar practice maintain that not everyone needs 'blasting open' by what they consider Janov's 'mechanistic' formula, in which everyone is put through the same treatment regardless of where they are at (i.e. their level of being or sensitivity).

This is not a strictly accurate picture, however, as although sheer weight of numbers makes it unavoidable that there are sessions in which dozens of individuals lie isolated on their own mats in a large hall and receive the same suggestions for triggering the release of pain, the personnel trained in Primal Therapy are conscious of the delicacy of working only at the level the patient has reached and no deeper. Also psychotics are given a much more lenient and slower programme of treatment.

It is unfortunate that although Janov's system has evident validity, he has somewhat alienated himself from the therapeutic community by his assertions that his method is virtually the *only* viable form of therapy available, and claiming to be the 'discoverer' of primal therapy and therefore suing every other therapist who uses the word. This attitude has aroused a great deal of contention and animosity in psychotherapeutic circles and many critics have taken Janov to task for his somewhat messianic pretensions and pronouncements. Fellow therapist David Freundlich summarises the general opinion as follows:

Because Arthur Janov formulated the most basic concepts of primal therapy and has written more about it than anyone else, many people tend to idealise him and worship him – to become Janovian Witnesses (coined by Barbara Grinnell). This reverence is intensified by the promise of a cure for neurosis, the spectacular claims and case histories in his writings, his confident manner of presenting his work, and his denouncement of most other therapies as being almost totally ineffective. His 'warning' that primal therapy should not be practised by anyone who has not been trained at his Primal Institute and that it is dangerous in the hands of untrained personnel further adds an air of exclusivity to primal and the name Janov.[1]

Although Janov appears to deny the achievements of all those who have gone before him, in his actual practice he uses a blend of methods developed by his forerunners in the field, such as Fritz Perls and Wilhelm Reich, yet neglects to acknowledge their contributions to his findings. Despite his claim to be the originator of 'Primal' therapy, it is commonly known in therapeutic circles that Wilhelm Reich and others had previously developed methods whereby patients worked on the whole body-mind complex for the unblocking and release of childhood traumas by 'primal' screams and cryings.[2] And as for the word itself, even 'Grandfather' Freud speaks of 'primal feelings' in his writings.

As a personal aside, I might mention that during my own training in the primal-type therapy field, I worked with former associates of Janov (from the Primal Institute of Canada) and also with Dr Frank Lake, a charming and brilliant but unassuming spiritually-oriented therapist (and founder of the Christian Clinical Theology movement), who was achieving similar results some twenty years or so before Janov made his mark. Many other therapists in Europe have also been quietly working on similar lines for many years. Not to mention the masters of India, the Shamans of Asia and other cultures and the witch-doctors of Africa who have been doing virtually the same thing for centuries. Therefore to denounce others in the field as dangerous dabblers reduces the credibility of some of Janov's other assertions and causes critics to question his own undeniable contributions.

It is fair enough to be enamoured with one's own discoveries, (and Janov's findings are valuable enough in themselves), without needing to disparage the work of his contemporaries. In all fairness, when one first becomes involved in the 'primal-pain game' it really *does* seem to be the only way and the answer to mankind's problems, especially if one gets carried away by Janov's eloquence and enthusiasm. But when we look a little more closely at some of his assumptions and pronouncements, we may come to other conclusions.

To begin with, few other therapists would be rash enough to claim that Primal (or indeed any other kind of) therapy could really be the final 'cure for neurosis' as Janov proclaimed on the cover of his first book, *The Primal Scream*. At least his publishers have had second thoughts (after universal criticism from the therapeutic world) and it is noteworthy that in later printings this subtitle has been discreetly dropped from the cover of the English edition and only appears on the inside title-page.

According to Janov, neurosis is a 'disease of feeling' and essentially 'the suppression of feeling and its transformation into a wide range of neurotic behaviour'. Now whilst we may consider neurosis as a dis-*ease,* inasmuch as being a lack-of-ease in body and mind, do we have to see it as an *illness* that can only be 'cured' medically? Might we not see it as something amenable to other forms of approach as well? A good many people who enter into therapy (being unaware of other possibilities, or not yet ready for them) are averagely 'normal' people simply seeking inner growth. They are not pathologically neurotic or clinically 'schizophrenic' (at least not *before* they begin therapy). Of course, there are many levels of neurosis, but in general these are just people dissatisfied with the way they are, their petty irritabilities, irrationalities, outbursts of rage or suppression of feelings, and knowing things could be a lot better if they got rid of a few hang-ups. In the East such a person might be seen as an unquiet soul rather than suffering from a medical condition.

From the viewpoint of Fritz Perls' *Gestalt* therapy, a neurotic is defined as: "...a person who is unable to assume the full identity of mature behaviour. He will do anything to keep himself in the state of immaturity, even to playing the role of an adult – that is, his infantile concept of what an adult is like."[3] He also says: "The neurotic instead of mobilising his own resources, puts all his energy into manipulating the environment for support."[4] By this criterion it is evident that we are all neurotic to a degree, inasmuch as we knowingly or unconsciously manipulate the people around us for our own comfort and peace of mind. When we cease to manipulate, wheedle or cajole the world around us for our own ends, we can be considered to be free from this aspect of neurosis.

But even if we were brought up by the most evolved and well-meaning of parents, it appears impossible to reach maturity having been so sheltered from the knocks and disappointments of life, that we have accumulated no psychological scars along the way. That being so, we might conclude that a certain percentage of neurosis inevitably develops in everyone in the divine order of things. If it cannot be avoided, it would seem that personality problems are there for a purpose, that purpose being something in the nature of a goad to push us towards self-development and, ultimately, Self-realisation. Without such a spur in the flanks, we would be too lazy even to consider the need for working on ourselves. But if we are pressured by our inner quirks and imperfections, this acts as a constant reminder of the need for self-improvement.

One of the major spiritual injunctions of Jesus was, "Be ye perfect as thy Father in heaven is perfect." Just how we go about this task depends on our level of evolution and needs of the present. Despite the Janovian point of view, there *are* more ways than one. And although neurosis is a *disturbance* of our psycho-physical functioning – so also is the sense-of-ego, which is similarly a mode of consciousness which distorts and narrows our true perception of the world – but we do not necessarily need to regard ourselves as mentally sick on that account. Even though, as soon as we enter into therapy it certainly begins to look that way.

When we begin to therapeutically stir up the murky subconscious we agitate a fathomless ocean of fears and horrors and start to imagine "*My God!* I really *am* sick!" Unconsciously we begin to conform to the medical model of ourselves as presented by the therapeutic community environment. To clarify what is going on we avidly devour books on psychology and unwittingly apply its labels and terminology to ourselves. We find we are worse than we thought, since all the labels seem to apply to us – *manic, paranoiac, schizophrenic* and the like. In this way we colour our consciousness with psychological concepts, thereby reinforcing our self-image as a 'case suitable for treatment'. And before we know it, we have become a fully-fledged 'therapy-junkie' and need years before we can kick the habit.

Although Primal therapy is alleged to be a relatively speedy process, among the participants in my therapy workshops, I have encountered a number of 'primal-addicts' who have found a new way of life in kicking-and-screaming with no view of an end in sight. Many of them become 'hooked' on the group-therapy scene and wander forlornly from one group to another for the release of their weekly scream. This is not the fault of the therapy, but a lack of understanding and vision, having nothing more in life to look forward to if therapy comes to an end. Such people also have the impression of gaining some kind of social 'therapy-groupie' status by virtue of being old Primal veterans. A fair number of these unfortunates remain trapped in their 'historical' pains, even to the extent of holding off present pains and emotions for the sake of converting them into pressures which can be saved up and 'primalled out' at the next session. Thus they avoid the opportunities for dealing with their emotional problems in the here and now of their actual present life situation, preferring to remain as perennial patients instead.

'Patient' is a word I could never come to terms with in my own practice. I only saw *people* with problems. To me they were never 'medical cases' but individuals trying to understand themselves; in other words, *Students of Self* – SOS – or people in distress. I never cared to categorise them with any psychological label that they would later have to struggle to shrug off. I did not work according to a medical model for sick people, but rather encouraged the attitude of a 'transformational model' for the aspiring soul largely burdened by the coarsening mentality and insensitivity of the gross and worldly-minded environment all around. Thus my parallel adjunct to therapy was to assist in the cultivation of finer feelings, such as love and reverence for life, and an awareness of the importance of feeding the neglected soul-sick spiritual side of one's being. It is this aspect I now much prefer.

Although uncovering childhood traumas and reliving them is a valuable working method for the release of hidden tensions, it does not automatically mean that at the end of a long series of kicking-and-screaming sessions your life will be magically transformed – as you may have been led to believe by 'Psychotherapy Promotions Inc.' A new way of seeing and being has to be consciously worked for, both during the therapy and in one's everyday life. In any case, at the ordinary everyday level of consciousness, there is no final and decisive 'cure' or 'end' to therapy. One's duty as a therapist and guide is not to simply 'fix' a robotic 'patient' and send him back 'adjusted' to the kind of life-experience which was largely responsible for his mental-emotional perturbation in the first place. There has to be something more. One needs a deeper awakening of something from within, which makes of life an on-going enjoyable experience – a worthwhile adventure in which to participate.

Janov is aware of such a necessary 'goal-oriented' stimulus and in his later book, *Primal Man,* he offers his projected image of a 'Post-Primal Person'. This idealised 'Primal Man' is posited as a virtually new species of human being, who is totally cured of all his neurosis after Primal Therapy. Some see this conception as a megalomanic fantasy – a therapist's pipe-dream; while others take it simply as a psychological sales pitch – an alluring and tantalising carrot dangled before the wallets of the deluded. I have to admit it does give one the impression of being offered a pot of gold at the end of the rainbow. And as anyone will know who has tried to reach the end of a rainbow, the more you go towards it, the further away it gets.

Many therapists regard this post-Primal 'super person' as a more far-fetched fiction than the nature of the meditative and spiritual search for identity which Janov maintains is no more than an airy-fairy symptom of neurosis. He affirms categorically that after his therapy, the post-Primal person will no longer meditate, or become involved in such 'neurotic' pursuits as the spiritual quest. This may well be true for some. Those, for example, among his post-Primal patients whose 'toyings' with spiritual development were previously prompted by escapist fantasies in avoidance of the harsh or humdrum realities of their daily lives. Or those so awed by the therapeutic process that they have accepted Janov's down-to-earth philosophy hook, line and sinker. Certainly no one with any real experience of mystical consciousness would dream of giving up the inner quest as a result of losing his neurotic tendencies.

But to consider all enquiry into the spiritual nature of existence as 'neurosis' is to put the insights of the Primal therapist on a footing way above such 'neurotic' individuals as Moses, Buddha, Jesus, Baha'u'llah, Zarathustra, Dattatreya, Milarepa, Shankaracharya, Lao Tzu, and any number of other spiritual sages whose visionary teachings have given joy to mankind for hundreds or thousands of years. It would seem hardly necessary to labour the fact that the spiritual quest is a fundamental and inexorable urge in the evolution of every human individual. And it *is* a matter of evolution. Sooner or later it comes to everyone: even to those who most condemn it. (Saul on the road to Damascus is a perfect example.) And those who achieve the full realisation of this quest become a light of inspiration to the whole world.

Although Janov may be a master of the mind in his field, when he pronounces on matters beyond his spiritual apprehension, one becomes acutely aware of the lack of spiritual dimension in the understanding of his heart. It is for this reason his projected 'Primal Man' is someone who seems to be so well adjusted to his life in the world that once all his neurosis has gone, he has no interest in the profounder aspects of his own nature. He is a man who neither enquires where he comes from nor where he is going. Nor does he 'neurotically' consider his reason for being at all. But then – neither does a cabbage.

On the other hand, this condition – from the perception of an enlightened being – could be seen as extremely positive. To be able to live totally 'here and now' in the present moment, would be the condition of a natural mystic. But this does not appear to be a considered attribute of the Primal Man. We are given more a picture of a socially stabilised person, well grounded in himself, who will no longer stand in awe of the mystery of existence in this inexplicable cosmos. If this is so – how would it be to always experience life on a mundane level, without the capacity for wonder? Would we consider such a life worth living?

The new Primal Man or Woman is also presented as having many positive and admirable characteristics. A Primal person is said to be a wonderfully understanding parent, untroubled by demanding children; incapable of doing violence to another; having no ambition but to live in peace; disinterested in politics and dominion; he is healthier and more productive than his peers, being unplagued by irrational fears and phobias; he sleeps well, is untroubled by cancer, neither a smoker nor a compulsive drinker; a respecter of nature and life, he neither exploits nor pollutes and is conscious of the social good, but is sufficient unto himself. A Primal Person will also live much longer than others. Although Janov insists that this near-perfect being is not a Utopian dream, but is based on his clinical observations, it stretches credibility to accept that all these wonderful qualities are to be found in every post-Primal patient who has stayed the course.

After going on nearly two decades of this relatively 'speedy' form of therapy, one might begin to wonder where these shining examples of 'Primal Man' are to be found? If they are simply living quiet lives and bothering no one, as Janov intimates, then he has rendered an inestimable service to society in general. But even though these people may be living happier lives, it does not mean they are necessarily in a blissful condition. How many people do we know of who – having been 'cured' of *all* their neurosis in therapy – are now living in a state of unalloyed bliss? Even Janov does not maintain that the removal of neurosis equals inevitable bliss. (He might well consider mystical bliss only another form of metaphysical neurosis.)

In fact, Janov seems to equate everything 'mystical' with the common man in the street's notion of the word, which is something 'vague and misty' (with which it has no connection) and a somewhat fatuous and simple-minded spirituality. Therefore, when speaking of 'split-levels' of consciousness, whereby certain messages do not get through to the rational (left brain) thinking sector of the mind because of neurologic dysfunction, he can say: "...this helps explain the reason that someone can be a genius in his field and be totally irrational and *mystical* otherwise."

As an example of this 'misty-cal' attitude, he cites the example of a surgeon who, despite all he can do, sees his patient die on the operating table and then is 'irrational' enough to believe that "it was meant to be", or that some "higher force" was in control, or that the patient still "lives on in different form". There is not the remotest chance of any of these three possibilities having an actuality in Janov's stolid philosophy. Nor evidently, does he conceive of any *First Principle* behind the manifested universe. For he goes on to say: *"If you never had a parent who was a friend, and you make God a friend (the one you never had and need) then no one is going to convince you that there is no God."*

Strong stuff. If one is open to realising the validity of this statement, the shock of it can be a very persuasive and shattering argument for those whose faith is founded on *belief* (and hope) rather than on *experience*. From my observations I would estimate that Janov's premise is applicable to the vast majority of both sincere and middling 'believers' of any religion, and especially so among the 'Father'-followers of Christianity. And I do not say this unkindly or as any form of attack. If you are therefore one of those for whom the cap appears to fit – and feel your blood boiling at the very suggestion – I would ask you to please – PLEASE – first: stop (NOW), and look into your heart of hearts (at your fears and fabrications and self-justifications), and see if there is not more than a hint of truth in this statement, before you hurl your anger and abuse in my (or Janov's) direction, or dismiss the notion out of hand. These are the areas in which we fear to look. And it is *essential* that we look at them for the spiritual vitality of our otherwise generally complacent lives.

As it stands, Janov's assertion is a truism. People *do* use their *idea* of 'God' in this fashion. Unfortunately, it would seem he takes the *implication* of this statement as evidence of there being no *actual* Consciousness behind the manifested universe. Yet to look at the extraordinarily smooth-functioning complexity of this astounding and boundless cosmos and say, 'So what? There it is: there is nothing behind it. There's nothing that makes it tick,' seems sheer schoolboyish belligerence and short-sighted silliness. And even more so, when the most brilliant scientist of our epoch has stated:

The Cosmic religious experience is the strongest and oldest main-spring of scientific research. My religion consists of a humble admir-ation of the illimitable superior Spirit who reveals himself in the slight details we are able to perceive with our frail and feeble minds. The deeply emotional conviction of the presence of a superior reason-ing power, which is revealed in the incomprehensible universe, forms my idea of God ... The most beautiful and profound emotion we can experience is the sensation of the mystical. It is the sower of all true science. He to whom this emotion is a stranger, who can no longer wonder and stand rapt in awe, is as good as dead. To know what is impenetrable to us really exists, manifesting itself as the highest wisdom and the most radiant beauty which our dull faculties can comprehend only in the most primitive form – this knowledge, this feeling, is at the centre of all religiousness.

Doubtless these 'mystical ramblings' of Albert Einstein can be psychologically explained away as a 'neurological shut-down of Primal Pains', as opposed to his more 'rational' and scientific achievements, such as the invention of the atomic bomb (for which he was duly repentant). But what then of the great spiritual leaders of history? Here are beings who have also plumbed to the depths of their sorrows, and risen to the heights of bliss, eventually penetrating all superficial levels of consciousness in deep meditation, and arriving at the super-transcendental state of Unchanging Reality, beyond all appear-ances. In this condition they were cleansed of all mental im-purities and became consumed in the ecstatic joy of communion with the Omnipresent Consciousness.

Yet after having had actual *experience* of the True Nature of

Existence, they still persisted in teaching their followers how to achieve the selfsame mystical path to Self-(or God) realisation. A thoughtful person might pause to wonder why.

In spite of Janov's mystical incomprehension, he has made a major contribution to mankind's understanding of psychophysiological functioning, by his ability to plumb to the "primordial depths of man's subconscious" and make it accessible to the conscious mind. When the subconscious is brought to the light of awareness and the two are merged together, then one can for the first time, see things clearly as they are. This condition is what Janov calls 'full consciousness'. He says: "It is only consciousness which can stop the flow of unconscious activation, because consciousness means that the unconscious is now conscious – and that is the *only* meaning of consciousness for me."

It is unfortunate that he has taken this stand. Since he has so profoundly sounded the *depths* of the human mind, it is a pity we are to lose out on this same investigatory application to the *higher* levels of consciousness. But if, through lack of acquaintance, he denies their existence, then those of us who *have* experienced mystical awakenings to a higher level of consciousness, are perforce obliged to resort to those who *are* aware of their reality and who have spent lifetimes investigating them. I refer of course to the yogis.

In many Asian, Eastern and Far Eastern countries, there are those who – without the benefits of Western psychotherapy – have undergone spiritual training in yoga practices and meditation, and by these methods alone, have succeeded in eradicating not only all symptoms of neurosis, but have also dissolved the major stumbling-block of life – the *sense-of-ego*. This is a matter little considered within the psychotherapeutic model, and ego is often only regarded as something which needs *strengthening* in certain cases: and never as something which needs annihilating altogether! Yet ego is the arch-manipulator of the world, and the source of all psychological defensiveness.

Therefore where a vestige of ego still exists, there is still neurosis.

Those yoga 'graduates' who have succeeded in entirely

eliminating the sense-of-ego, incontestably become charismatic personalities, whose presence of being attracts, inspires and electrifies the spirits of thousands of people. Will the post-Primallers with such capacities please stand up and be counted?

The techniques of yoga have been tried and tested and perfected over thousands and thousands of years. If they did not work, they would have been rejected long before. And this science of the soul is an eternal form of spiritualised psychotherapy which has been available since the beginning of the world, and always will be while the world exists, because it is 'built-in' to Man's evolutionary drive. Such practices are also infinitely cheaper than modern psychotherapy (and, on that count alone, perhaps are condemnable as being bad for business!)

According to the sages, we have passed through many different incarnations before being born into this present problemmatical life. If we are to try to set about healing the hurts of many lifetimes, we might have to go on forever, pulling out deeper and deeper buried problems in psychotherapy – like countless rabbits from a conjurer's hat – and never see the end of it. Eventually we will have to go to the very Core of our Existence. There must come a time when we realise that it is only *Spirit* which can ultimately *transform* the quality of the psyche and illumine the dark contents of our consciousness, as is written in the spiritual psychology of the ancient yogic scriptures.

In these writings, the Ancients advise us to directly tackle the mind itself, rather than its endless products. By practice, they found that when the mental flow of flotsam we call 'thoughts' permanently ceases, then all the neurotic symptoms 'mind' has created evaporate along with it. This may be a long and arduous process, but its eventual results are unquestionably life transforming. The practice of 'mind control' is only a first step for the beginner. In fact, we are advised not to try and 'control' the mind (one might as well try to control the wind!), but first to try to steer it in the direction required, and then rather *withdraw* from the movement of mind altogether. This may be achieved by the practice of mantra and meditation. But we should seek out the type of meditative practice which most suits us.

One of the greatest yogis of medieval India, Svatmarama Swami, suggested this form of therapy: "Through continual concentration on the *nada* [the inner sound current] *accumulated personality problems are annihilated.* All movements of mental energies and mindstuff then merge in transcendental consciousness."[6] Note that he speaks here of *continual concentration* in one's practice rather than a wishy-washy twenty minutes a day, or now and again every few days. We have to be constant if we expect results. It is no use trying to dig a well for water and giving up after six feet, then trying another place, digging for two feet and then trying a week later at four feet somewhere else. One has to dig deep and continuously in the same place until the Source is reached. Otherwise old habits and downward-flowing thought patterns will naturally return.

The practice of *Nada Yoga,* or listening to the inner sound is universally recommended by the sages and can be done at any time. One need not listen only when sitting for meditation. The sound can be heard like the ringing in the ears you experience after an explosion (and this sound has been singing on since the 'Big Bang' at the beginning of the universe). You can listen to it as you make the beds, wash the pots, sweep the floor, chop the wood, fix the car, do the garden, go for walks, or whatever. By tuning into it, if only for a few minutes, every hour at your office desk you will experience its regenerative effects. Never feel you are wasting time with it. The sages well knew what they were about. Constant practice has a cumulative effect.

Another such practice is the method of Self-enquiry made known by the modern sage Bhagavan Sri Ramana Maharshi of Arunachala. His suggestion was that at all times one should live in the spirit of the question 'Who am I?' on the understanding that one day this bag of bones and skin I call a body is going to drop off from around me – so therefore *Who Am I* without it, beyond this temporary appearance? One only has to read the life-story of this remarkable being and recognise the flawless wisdom of his utterances to realise that (in spite of promoting the so-called 'neurotic' spirit of Self-inquiry) here was one of the most un-neurotic and radiant beings ever to grace this planet with his presence.

For those who are unable to hear the inner sound, or find themselves unready for Self-inquiry, the sages proposed a further method of counteracting the negativities of our thoughts by superimposing their opposites. Thus whenever thoughts of greed arose, they were quickly countermanded by thoughts, and acts, of generosity. Feelings of jealousy or hatred would be stifled by receiving the offending 'other' into your heart with loving amity; whilst gloom and misery succumbed to the cultivation of joyous thoughts, and so forth. Hard as this practice may appear to be, it is evident that for the most part, we experience what we *choose* to experience.

The yogis chose to phase out old attitudes of mind until they were no longer problems. Rather than dwelling in depression ("Getting into my heavy feelings, man, because they are there!") they *transformed* the situation by saturating themselves with divine thoughts. This practice might be considered akin to Behaviouristic therapy, in which a positive suggestion is superimposed over a negative thought pattern while the original problem still remains buried underneath. But immersion in divine thoughts, gradually dissolves negativities and develops a divine consciousness. No one is incapable of this practice. But how the sense of self-justification adores wallowing in righteous resentments and negativities! And those we fume against may suffer little from our thoughts, while we poison our whole system by carrying *them* constantly in our blood! It is our choice entirely.

In summary, we have seen that both psychotherapy and yoga can overcome the miseries of our subconscious: the former by bringing up every pain and releasing it, and the latter by 'burning up' all the hidden pains and problems and transcending them by the intensity of spiritual practice. However, although after psychotherapy we may be free (or at least, freer) from neurosis, and thus happier, our consciousness is not therefore automatically raised to a higher level. It is simply *clearer*. But then, to be relatively free from our pains and problems is doubtless all that most of us want, which would explain the frequency of post-Primal drop-outs from the spiritual quest. Without a goad we rarely go on.

It is almost certainly true that many of the spiritual greats of all time actually *did* suffer neurotically on their way towards emancipation. But the point is, having no other therapist than the 'Indwelling Spirit', they struggled on to the goal, until their suffering souls finally merged with the Supreme, becoming healed once and for all in the realisation of the *Self*. After such a momentous merging, they e-merged from the experience as transformed and God-like beings. Of such Masters, the Sufi leader Hazrat Inayat Khan said: "The God-realised person need not speak of God, or discuss the name of God; his presence will inspire the sense of God in every being and charge the atmosphere with it."

This atmosphere of softly dynamic presence, together with a penetrating and illuminating perception of life, an inexpressible grace of being, and the capacity for kindling love in the hearts of millions, should be ample evidence of the difference between a Spiritual Master and a post-Primal patient – or psychotherapy and the spiritual path.

Evolving Out of Ego

Q. *Everybody teaches that dissolution of the ego is a good thing. If that is so, why have we got an ego in the first place, and what is its purpose?*

A. In the *first* place, we do not have an ego. *An* ego is a psychological phantom. As with the fiction we call 'mind', ego is not a *thing,* but a kind of mental illness – or a socially acceptable form of mild schizophrenia. More than anything it is an unfortunate and shameful habit of mental functioning which, when persisted in, long past its usefulness, causes us untold suffering (such as endless rounds of births and deaths until the end of time).

Ever since the psychologists postulated their hypothetical concepts of *'ids'* and *'egos'* we have been stuck with them as if they actually existed as wilful entities in their own right. We have been beguiled into believing in them, although they are no more than spasmodic manifestations in consciousness. Ego is not a self-existent entity but a particular mode of mentation by which we habitually tend to function, at the expense of finer modes of feeling and expression. The ego-*sense* is the source of what we might call the 'Mundane Mind' or the normal 'earth-and-body-bound' mentality.

We have seen elsewhere that 'mind' is no more than a stream of thoughts. And that thoughts are like the rippling flow of muddy waters, clouded by accretions and past proclivities, swirling here and there in winds of change, and gathering flotsam along the way, often turning back in on themselves in turgid eddies. If we follow this thought-stream back to its source, we find it seeping from the sense-of-ego. There is nothing that we think which does not refer back to it. Although thoughts are the flowing movements of the 'mind' the sense-of-ego is the fontspring from which they arise.

So if it is not a parasitical entity over which we have no

control, then what is the essential characteristic of the sense-of-ego? It is the sense of separative self-ness. It is the feeling of existing as a separate being, isolated from the rest of creation. But as the actuality of existence is that we are intrinsically *spirit,* indivisible from Universal Spirit, this is therefore an illusory or unreal mental impression. The very word *individual* means 'that which cannot be divided' (*in*-dividual). Thus from the Absolute viewpoint, the sense of individual existence is evidently a false 'sense' (or *non*sense of ego) rather than the reality. But the reality is rarely perceived by the average human being.

We have become so habituated to referring to this sense-of-ego to deal with our every thought arising, that we have fallen under the delusion that it and 'me' are one and the same thing. And at this level of perception it would appear to be so. We are what we take ourselves to be. And we take ourselves to be the ego-centred personality we have acquired and built up over the years and refer to as 'I'. But this 'I' is an acquired assumption. This 'I' is as falsely assumed a character as the part played by an actor on the stage. If the actor is unable to dis-identify with his role when he leaves the theatre, he has a personality problem. Similarly, if we identify with the sense-of-ego and the sense of selfhood it generates, we also have a personality problem. The word personality derives from *persona* – a theatrical mask adopted to portray a particular character.

Our problem is that we are unaware we have assumed a mask of false *I*-dentity.

Nearly two thousand years ago, the great Indian Seer *(Rishi)* Patanjali, defined the problem in his *Yoga Sutras,* stating that " . . .egoism is the mistaken identification of the one who sees, with the *instruments* through which the world is seen . . ." that is: the senses, mind and body. When we take the body we look out of, to be the actual *being* who is looking out, it is equivalent to mistaking the spectacles for the person who looks through them. Patanjali further points out that for the body to function at all, it has to be infused with the power of the Omnipresence (Universal Consciousness) and in order to be aware, the local-ised concentration of energy known as 'mindstuff' (by which power we see) must be similarly suffused. He states: "The appearance of these two powers [Cosmic and individualised consciousness] as though they were identical, is the affliction known as *asmita* – egoism."[1]

In other words, the ego-sense is identification with the body and mind instead of with our Source – the Omnipresence. Identification with the Omnipresence expands one's being into the whole cosmos, whereas the ego-centric sense is like a centripetal force which sucks everything in towards itself, relating everything back to the localised 'I' experience. My sense of '*me*-ness' as a seemingly individual, embodied entity, is a life-and-soul shrinking condition which keeps my consciousness contracted to a minimal mode of functioning. In this respect, the sense-of-ego is our lifelong psychological prison-keeper. It confines us, like a fly in amber, to a fixed conception of ourselves as an 'I' forever qualified as a *something* or other.

The qualified 'I' is only capable of seeing the superimposed condition. It thinks – according to the accepted evaluations of consensus mentality – I am a man or a woman; I am a father or a mother; I am a respected businessman; I am a wonderful footballer; I am an ordained priest; I am a *swami;* I am a genius, I am an idiot, I am a loser, I am a poor man, I am unloved, I am useless, etc. I am always something qualitatively established, either positively or negatively, in relation to my over- or under-developed sense-of-ego. If I paint, or teach, I take on the role of an artist or a teacher, and identify with that. But that is *not* what I *am:* it is what I *do.* When my identificatory ego-sense is not operating, I may discover that I am not this or that – I simply *am.* Just as I am. I am then what I *really* am.

Such was the revelation of Moses on the mountain, when he experienced the profundity of the words: "I AM THAT I AM". This was not exactly the '*voice* of God' but the thundering reverberation of the Omnipresence making itself self-evident in his consciousness. He was given to understand that he was not merely a localised sense of *I am* – but that he was *One* with the unqualified, immeasurable, incomprehensible *I AM* which underlies the whole cosmos. This same knowledge is the ultimate heritage of everyone.

In which case, how come we do not know it? How did this shrunken state of mistaken identity come about in the first place? If we consider the mother's womb as the 'first place' (in this life at least), it would appear that *there* we had no sense of self-conscious ego. We had a certain capacity of auditory and sensory conscious-awareness, but no conception of individual selfhood. And even after being born, in the first few years of life, we existed in a state of undifferentiated consciousness. In other words, we were At-one-with-the-universe, having no sense of separate identity. We were unified with all the world around us, because it was not experienced as 'other' than ourselves. We just existed in a condition we might simply call – *'beingness'*.

While we remained in this condition, everything was as it should have been. We were omnipotent: we only had to cry out in hunger and a great breast would come out of the sky to suckle us. Yet it was not experienced as something separate, since it was one with the all-encompassing sensory continuum in which our 'beingness' had its expression. For almost the first three years of life, the growing child is amazed at everything, enchanted by everything, and lives in a magical world. It is in love with everything and is the expression of love itself. Who is not charmed by the open-hearted joy of an infant? It radiates an unselfconscious atmosphere of artless innocence which captivates the hearts of everyone around. This angelic radiance is the effect of the Omnipresence freely operating through a vehicle as yet unclouded by a sense-of-ego.

Alas, this happy condition cannot last. All too soon its sense of 'oceanic' existence is lost as waves from the worrisome world roll in. As soon as the rudiments of language are impressed upon it, the infant is forced to become aware of *difference*, of the separative sense of *you* and *me*. Its homogeneous and unitary sense of being slowly starts to fade away, and a growing (or shrinking) sense of separation from things 'out there' begins. Thus shyness is a sign that the sense of self-awareness has started to rise. The previously all-wise, all-warm, god-like world of adults now begins to bring on feelings of unease or alarm, as the child is exposed to incomprehensible emotional outbursts and prohibitions from its ego-centred environment. Its body and mind begin to contract in apprehension from a world that is 'not me' any more.

A bewildering anxiety develops as it feels the widening gulf between itself and the former 'oneness' it knew with its mother. It now no longer feels automatically enfolded in its mother's love and affection. She has become 'someone else', not wholly beneficent. Her changing moods are *seen* and *registered* as a source of fear, as the infant's perceptive faculties grow. If she is a harrassed mother and has no time to coerce the child, each of her busy intrusions into its magical inner play-world by force, is seen as attack and rejection. And the more upset and agitated the child becomes, the more it suffers from abusive shakes and slaps, or sudden changes in its situation. Its sense of outrage and injustice cannot be formulated in its mind, but a defensive form of consciousness begins to develop to safeguard itself from harm. Because it is so open and vulnerable, the infant must of necessity create some kind of mental 'space' or 'barrier' between itself and its unpredictable environment.

This is the first subtle contraction of consciousness we know as the *sense-of-ego*.

This can be seen as an inevitable and natural form of weaning. The unformulated feeling of the child is: "Okay then, if I'm not the centre of your world, if you don't have time for me, if I don't live in your love – I can look after myself!" With this newly-acquired 'I' (which feels unlovable) we begin to conceal and console ourselves. The sense-of-ego seems like an 'inner friend' we can now talk to inside our own heads. This somewhat schizophrenic activity acts as a kind of 'psychic shield' of protection between my adopted 'self' and the 'outside' world. By constant utilisation of this psychic shield, and putting it up against every threat, we begin to identify with it. Eventually we take this habitually compulsive barrier-reflex to be 'I'.

Thus in Western psychology, it is this defensive manoeuvre which was at first considered to be the 'entity' known as *the* 'ego'. However, on deeper investigation, it was later realised that the domain of ego-related mental functioning was much broader than previously imagined. It was found to operate in many areas unrelated to the 'fight or flight' reaction. For example, the ego-sense encompassed *drive* and *ambition*. The 'pushy-ness' of ego was seen to be a beneficial aspect of growth in a competitive society. A self-assertive capacity for 'standing on one's own feet' was a laudable progression towards self-expression and self-development – that is, development of the little *self*, or the individualised sense of *'I'-ness* – as acceptable to society. On the other hand, it became evident that an over-blown ego could do things in such an arrogant and over-confident manner that its effects were even contrary to personal (or national) safety.

Therefore the psychological concept of ego had to be expanded to encompass a wider-ranging complexity of functioning covering the whole spectrum of social interaction. Ego thus became the 'middleman' or *mediating principle* which sought a balance between inner desires and outer demands. One's inner desires, however, are already inevitably prompted by the ego-sense in relation to outside influence and the effects of the 'Social Ego'. The social sense-of-ego is a subtle form of cultural conditioning. It acts as a stabilising influence in society, by subliminally regulating everyone's attitudes and aims within one's social group.

No matter whether one lives among dukes or dustmen, the sensitive sense-of-ego monitors unspoken assumptions and reactions among one's peers. This elicits our correspondingly correct comportment according to our perception of *their* sense-of-ego. Or, alternatively, we flare up, do precisely the opposite, and 'kick against the pricks' and pressures of the mass mentality. But either way, by compliance or reaction, we are still under the influence of ego-motivated activity. Whilst we remain attuned to the ego-centric centre of consciousness, we will always feel the need to fight, to defend, or to hide ourselves, because we are not yet aligned with our true centre. For this reason we always have the impression of being 'off centre' and unstable. This makes us feel transparent and naked in the eyes of the world.

So we do whatever kind of 'cover up' job we can manage to camouflage ourselves with false fronts, imitative personalities, credentials, social status, fine clothes and other symbols of well-being. But ego is a garment with which we can never cover our emptiness. To live in ego is to live in constant fear of being 'found out'. It becomes impossible for us to find rest, always having to be on the alert in case we are 'seen' even in our intimate relationships. Therefore in many situations we may push ourselves beyond our physical and mental limits just to 'show them' we are really something, even though we may be unsure of it ourselves.

Yet we do not have to stay in bondage to our ego-prompted attitudes. At times our more rational selves may stand back and decide against a foolhardy idea proposed by the sense-of-ego. We might reason that if a more sensible centre of consciousness exists – which is able to stand back and observe the stupidity of ego – then this 'ego' is not 'me'. The one who witnesses the working of the mind is evidently of a higher, or deeper, level of being. It is therefore not a *function* of consciousness, like ego, but is the actual *seer*. To align oneself with *that* instead, would seem the wiser course. Those who have come realise this possibility in their lives, begin to probe beneath the surface of themselves to discover the *source* of this witnessing consciousness.

Meditators, mystics, monks and yogis, who are totally disinterested in the social scene, worldly ambition, or ego-prompted 'pleasurable' distractions, plunge themselves deeply into their own consciousness seeking the true centre of their beings. The most advanced yogis and meditators thereby enter into realms of consciousness beyond all movements of the 'mind' and in which no semblance of the ego-sense exists. Those who have found their true centre are thus no longer swayed hither and thither by the promptings of a non-existent ego. As in the pre-egoid condition of the infant, the yogis are similarly existing in a state of universal *at-one-ment*. But these two states are of differing degree, as the first occurs *before* the arising of the ego-conscious condition and the other *after* it.

However, although Western psychology is aware of these two seemingly similar conditions of undifferentiated consciousness, it has no adequate concept for them. It therefore tries to amalgamate them into its already established ego-concept, by unconvincingly stretching its operation to universal proportions. Thus Sigmund Freud maintained:

Originally [in infancy] ego includes everything; later it detaches itself from the external world. The ego-feeling we are aware of now is thus only a shrunken vestige of a far more extensive feeling which embraced the universe and expressed an inseparable connection of the ego with the external world.[2]

So near and yet so far. Freud is close to the intuitive feeling of the reality, but feels obliged to squeeze it to fit his intellectual theory of the all-embracing *actuality* of the ego. But, if in his terms ego is the awareness of 'I', then an infant without any sense of 'I' cannot be held to have a universally expanded sense-of-ego, when it does not even have the mental equipment for locally individualised ego-awareness. It simply has the sense of *being*. But without being *this* or *that*, or *I* or *me*. It is existing in the thought-free ocean of its Source – the Self (God-ness) – although remaining blissfully unaware of the fact.

The difference between the child and the yogi or meditative mystic, is that the yogi is in a *cognitive* state of beingness. He is *aware*, whereas the child is not. He *knows* that his sense of selfhood is merged into the Supreme. At least, he knows it in the early stages of fluctuating *samadhi*, as his experience of the Omnipresence deepens, and his sense of individualised consciousness comes and goes. Later when all possibility of further return to egoid consciousness is totally eliminated, there is only the Omniscient consciousness flowing through the filament of the yogi's body. This overflows from his eyes as radiance and love.

Unfortunately, since the whole of Western psychology is based on the erroneous assumption that the ego-sense is the natural and definitive state of consciousness, any other level or form of conscious experience is viewed as an *aberration,* or a quirk of nature. Yet the natural pre-ego condition of the infant belies that theory. And the yogis who enter into the final *effortless samadhi* state and remain in it for the rest of their lives, while serenely conducting their daily affairs, are living proof that the lack of an individualised sense-of-ego does not mean catatonic stupor.

Yet even Carl Jung, who dabbled his toes often enough in Eastern philosophy, falls disappointingly short in firmly stating: "No consciousness can exist without... an ego... We know of no other kind of consciousness, nor can we imagine a consciousness without an ego."[3] Thus Western psychology is evidently lacking in imagination and fixated in its own pet concept. Even the few advanced psychologists who *do* speak of states of consciousness transcending the ego, are pejoratively dismissed as 'obscure' or 'mystical', by their contemporaries firmly entrenched in the *status quo*. As Western psychotherapy is also oriented towards 'normality' (another fictitious condition) or gaining and maintaining the *status quo,* there is little chance of further progress until its proponents begin to break through this ego-barrier and awaken to the fact that entry into states of being beyond the local sense of 'I' is a natural on-going evolutionary process.

We have to remember that Western psychology is still very much in its infancy, whereas the *evolution-oriented* Eastern psychology has been developed and refined over thousands upon thousands of years, by the finest intellects this planet could produce. And their conclusions were not only based on intellectual analysis, but also on practical *experience.* Eastern psychology does not consider the notion of ego to be the centre of the psychological universe. However, although some schools of thought do posit the *Ahamkara* or Cosmic Ego – the sense of universal I AM-ness – there has to be one who is consciously aware of it in order to experience being one with it. The practice of attempting to expand one's sense-of-ego to unify oneself with Cosmic Ego is obviously fraught with danger and many become caught in megalomanic delusions of grandeur.

The localised *ahamkara* or individual sense-of-ego, is seen as only one among many differing functions or aspects of consciousness. It has its proper place in regulating thought processes during the years of development, but may be ultimately discarded when it has outlived its usefulness. Once its growth-protecting function is over and one has gained a certain measure of maturity, its main function is properly considered to be its own eventual annihilation. A popular yogic analogy for this is the image of a thorn being used to prick out another thorn head embedded in the skin; then both are thrown away.

Thus ego can be seen as an evolution-shaping tool which needs constantly refining. *Ahamkara* is not restricted to the concept of 'big-headed' egoism or selfish self-centredness, as in the popular Western sense, but is that agent of consciousness which is able to discriminate between what is good for the being and what is not. Therefore its ultimate purpose is to discard what is unnecessary for our growth and guide us on to our highest evolutionary potential. This it does by channelling our energies according to our disposition. Thus the *ahamkara* is seen to have three basic forms of expression:

(1) *tamasika ahamkara* in which egoism is expressed through indolence, indifference, ignorance and inertia. People such as those who are bored or boring, smug, self-satisfied, gross and vulgar, or beady-eyed and clutchingly covetous, are some who could be included in this category.

(2) *rajasika ahamkara* – is that kind of ego which is expressed through dynamic activity and derring-do, such as dare-devil riders, or conquerors pillaging other lands for fame and fortune, or sportsmen, actors and politicians seeking public acclaim to fill their lack of self-esteem. And finally:

(3) *sattvika ahamkara* – which is characterised by the positive aspects of the ego-sense: such as the attraction to goodness and the doing of good works in the world for the benefit of others – as in the case of animal welfare, and famine-relief workers, or ecological activists, doctors, healers and nurses, those who work in charitable institutions, or for philanthropic projects, spiritual teachers, and those in any occupation who work with spiritual care and understanding in the world.

Although these latter may still be subject to the dictatorial sense-of-ego, they are in the process of refining and modifying its effects by their inner attitude of giving and doing rightly; whereas the former are those who, even though they may conquer the world, are never in control of themselves, always remaining the driven slaves of their sense-of-ego. Adherence to the negative side of the ego-sense makes us subject to what

both Hindu and Christian sages call the ego-born 'diseases of
the heart', namely pride, passion, infatuation, fear, anger,
malice, conceit, vanity, envy, jealousy, greed, cupidity, lying,
artificiality, attachment and aversion, and fear of death.

Any of these ego-motivated afflictions will cause *karmic*
repercussion – or what might be called in English 'reboundage'
– the bouncing-back into our lives of the psychic negativity
we give out. Thoughts are like boomerangs. Whatever we
send out, comes back at us with double force. Thus the major
Cosmic Law is that the more we emanate harmful thought
waves, the more we receive a maelstrom of mental confusion
in return. We can observe this process in every second of our
lives. *As you sow, so shall you reap* is not merely a pretty
metaphor. It is *actual*. *All* ego-motivated thoughts or actions
cause reboundage. It is only the time-lag between the thought
and the result which makes us forgetful of the fact.

Minor mental transgressions bring on what is known as
'instant *karma*' – maybe within moments – such as knocking
your teacup over the tablecloth, cutting your finger, burning
your supper or missing your train. Think back and you will
see how uncentred your thoughts were just before. Greater
transgressions appear to take longer to mature, whether in this
lifetime or another. But return they will, with commensurate
severity – in mind, body or 'outward' circumstances. The only
escape from this syndrome is to accept with equanimity whatever self-made troubles come to you (without railing against
'unjust' fate or whining 'why me?': we *know* why), and to
withdraw altogether from identificatory association with the
sense-of-ego.

But how to go about it? How do we begin to kick the ego
habit? Firstly, (and lastly) the practice of meditation is of
paramount importance. This will help us to realise how the
sense-of-ego obscures and limits our experience of the universe. Yet even when (by constant practice) we begin to
expand our existential frontiers, and enter into states of consciousness beyond the perceptive level of egocentric experience, we are frustratingly thwarted. The ego-sense is experienced as 'going under' and immediately we are pulled back
into its centre of gravity and body-bound consciousness with a

jolt of fear. At this point it is on the threshold of being transcended – if only temporarily. But because we have identified ourselves with it for so long, we believe it is ourselves who are about to disappear. This is the great obstacle we have to overcome if we are to gain freedom from its seemingly addictive clutches.

But here the sense-of-ego warns us: "Better the devil you know than the one you don't! You might go mad you know, meditating like that. *Be careful!* You might never get back into the body," and other such beguiling advice. So, fearfully, we withdraw awhile from practice and remain in our cosy, yet uncomfortable, egoid condition. And time passes but we don't improve. Once more we ponder on the fact that the wisest sages in every part of the world have repeated down the ages that without removing the distorting lens of ego we can neither see anything clearly, nor can we fulfil our life's potential.

And our potential is the regaining of that 'Paradise Lost' of undifferentiated consciousness we vaguely knew as infants and have been un-consciously seeking ever since. To rest at last in Oneness with the Omnipresence – through ego-loss – is taught as a panacea for all human suffering, by every Spiritual Master who ever achieved it. Yet none may enter into this blissful state of Omnipresent Love while the sense-of-ego is still the centre of their consciousness.

Where ego is: love is not.

Thus the sense-of-ego prevents the full flowering of the heart. And it is through the heart-centre that the sense of Universal Love is felt and manifested. Here we have the basic answer to ego and all its afflictions – *the constant practice of abidance in the heart.* The heart-centre is the true *centre of consciousness* in the human body. We have been so accustomed to feel our sense of selfhood in the head, that we do not recognise the fact. Yet intuitively we know it. For example: if a stranger in the street shouts out, "Hey *you!*" – do we point to our heads and say, "Who *me?*" – which we might well do – considering our focus of attention? Not at all: we automatically point to the middle of our chests, where we instinctively feel the centre of our being to be.

Consciousness arises from the heart–centre and the brain is merely its reflector and organiser. As a first step towards freedom from top-heaviness we can withdraw from the head and relocate our sense-of-being in the central region, known as the *spiritual heart*. Or rather, we should re-cognise ourselves as having been there all along. We say, 'home is where the heart is' and this is no less true of our spiritual 'home'. In 'homing-in' to the heart–centre we purify ourselves of ego. Purity of heart is the pole-star for the seeker of the Self. Out of all the wealth of spiritual practices which exist, there is none so important or worthwhile as *the purification of the heart*. If one could *constantly* remember to feel oneself in the heart–centre, no other practice would be necessary. In fact, all practices should be realised as being done towards this end.

It is helpful to imagine the interior of one's head as trans-parent as a crystal and empty of everything except light. Or, when dark thoughts bring you down, or you catch yourself involved in ego, then simply pause, and drain your head like an hour-glass full of particles of crystal sand, and sink down into the loving sensation of the heart.

Since every arousal of ego casts shadow on one's heart, we should ask ourselves at every moment: "Does this purify my heart or darken it? Do I feel well, *truly* well within, as a result of my every word and deed? Or am I poisoning my own life? Have I darkened any other (human or animal) being's heart today? Will I sleep well tonight, knowing that my heart is clear?" By this practice you will never lose your way on the spiritual path.

The oftener and deeper we sink into the centre of ourselves, seeking the source from which all consciousness arises, the more we become aware of a subtly-growing sense of the Omnipresence. As we evolve, whilst remaining within the heart–centre, the ego–sense becomes less and less operative (although it is always ready to blaze up again like a forest fire given the slightest encouragement). Otherwise it gradually becomes quiescent, like the silent hour between the darkness and the dawn. As the sunlike sense of the true Self begins to rise, the dividing line between *inner* and *outer* experience disappears. If the defensive psychological barriers are removed, where is the need for a 'mediator'? The world within and the world without come to be experienced as one essence, one spiritual continuum and the manifestation of One Consciousness within *everything*. There no longer being a sense of differentiation, the localised sense-of-ego is automatically annihilated.

As for what then remains – it is the joyous purpose of our lives to *realise*.

MYSTICAL
MISCELLANY

(Spiritualism, Siddhis and Spiritual Practice)

'Blue-Rayism' or Seeing Through Spiritual Silliness

Q. *As I am writing, I might as well ask you a frivolous question. Can you tell me exactly what you mean by a 'Blue Ray' person? I've heard you use the expression and once or twice I've come across the phrase elsewhere, and recently with reference to a well-known New Age teacher who somebody described as "a very sweet person, but a bit too 'Blue-Ray' to be taken seriously". Perhaps you could clarify the meaning of this seemingly spiritual malady?*

A. Ask a frivolous question and you can expect a tongue-in-cheeky answer. So, my sins are finding me out! Actually we came up with this expression years ago in our *Gandalf's Garden* community in London, as a wryly humorous description of a certain type of wide-eyed spiritual seeker. I had no idea it had 'escaped' out into the world to become current coinage!

'Blue-ray' seekers are the kind of people who go in for a somewhat 'airy-fairy', wishy-washy, wishful-thinking kind of spirituality. The kind beloved by British and American genteel 'drawing-room' spiritualists and their attendants, who are always surrounded by spirit-guides and haloes, 'Ascended Masters', angelic hosts and 'rays' of clairvoyantly perceived light from etheric *son et lumière* spectaculars.

Now I am not trying to put down the practice of spiritualism itself here, which has many varying levels of validity and genuine usefulness. I am simply drawing attention to the 'lightweight', ungrounded and somewhat 'precious' atmosphere cultivated by some groups, as an example of the kind of vibration I mean. I get a similar sort of feeling at effusive poetry readings, where the sentimentalised tones of the readers are trying to put over bright-eyed aspirational ideas in an unreal and romanticised way. Their voices generally come across as cloying, rather than inspiring, even when the poems themselves are of good quality.

And so it is with those 'blue-ray' mediums lacking in spirit-

ual depth, who 'guide' select little circles and dole out very
'frothy' preachings and practices. But even so, we have to
realise that each can only give and receive according to his
capacity, and even these – if they are sincere – have their place
in giving heartwarming companionship to those who gather
round them. Not everyone is ready for or capable of
assimilating the deeper truths of the Spirit.

I do not wish to give the impression that spirit-guides and all
the rest have no actuality. But I rather incline to the conception
that such things belong to what I would more properly call a
'relative reality'. And all things are relative. For example: a
rainbow has a relative reality in relation to the position of the
person who sees it, the moisture particles in the air and the
position of the sun. Yet of itself, the rainbow has no tangible or
permanent reality.

It would appear to be similarly so with various aspects of
psychic phenomena, such as messages from 'higher beings'. It
is often the case that it is the inner 'climate' of the receiver
which normally determines the type of message or phenomenon coming through. And all phenomena, when we get
down to it, are no more than frequencies of consciousness. It is
these particularised 'frequencies' manifesting in the consciousness during meditative or mediumistic trance states which
form themselves into 'entities'. Phenomena such as these are
experienced at higher mental frequencies in all cultures of the
world. They are variously known as 'ascended beings', 'spirit-
guides' or 'spiritual helpers', 'angels' or 'nature elementals' (in
the West); or as *djinns* (among Muslims); *Muwakkals* (to Sufis);
devas and *dakinis* (to Hindus); 'allies' (to Yaqui indians);
khadomas (to Tibetans) and so on.

Such beings might be considered as 'spiritual quickenings'
or 'manifestations of gradual awakening' in consciousness,
which form according to the cultural conditioning of the
experiencer. My friend, the late Ogilvy 'Roc' Crombie, a
scientist known as the 'White Wizard of Edinburgh', used
frequently to hold conversations with the nature spirit Pan,
and the odd faun or two, in Edinburgh's Botanic Gardens.
When I questioned him on what he saw, he admitted that these
appearances could well relate to his classical upbringing and

that for someone else these same energies might manifest as, say – a clairvoyantly perceived, etheric flying saucer. A Christian becoming receptive at a similar frequency might have a vision of 'Mother Mary', while a Hindu yogi might see 'Lord Shiva' and a Tibetan monk any one of a whole pantheon of deities he has been nurtured to look for. Equally, a Westerner immersed in Eastern culture might come to experience the inner 'Buddha' of himself.

I find it interesting that the greatest Masters and Sages of the earth, never appear to have recourse to 'messages' coming through from such beings (unless it is to impress their words upon a simple-minded and childlike people who need such manifestations). But a real Master has no desire to impress. One only becomes a true Master after having transcended all one's cultural conditioning and its 'wayside entities'. A truly stabilised Master then becomes the 'message' in himself. He has no need for messages 'coming through'. Without him having to expressly say so, the spiritually sensitive can experience that 'God-ness' is automatically speaking through him. As was said of Jesus, "He taught as one having (inner) Authority, and not as the scribes." (*Matthew* 7:28)

However, it would appear that lesser illuminates who have a need to be useful, or thought well of, rather than developing their own spiritual understanding by inner work, prefer to gain credibility by the easier method of becoming 'channels' for 'Godly messages' of varying validity. Much of what is passed off as 'revealed wisdom' could be churned out in the normal state by anyone who has read a few 'Blue-ray' books, without the need of troubling the 'angelic hierarchy'. It is therefore necessary to have some sort of spiritual discrimination between the over serious and unctuous channels (or the gushing, starry-eyed sentimentality of the Blue-ray attitude) and the quiet, smiley joy of those who have actually experienced an inward grace, having become in the quality of their own lives, a visual expression of the 'message' of the Omnipresence.

The basic understanding of what are termed 'rays' in esoteric parlance, is that they are 'spiritual radiations' or transforming energies, which irradiate the whole universe and emanate from the Source of All – God, Self, or what you will. These so-called 'rays' are not the same as the measurable cosmic or light rays which bombard the earth from the 'external' universe. They are strictly the stuff of our inner psychic universe. In other words, they are 'frequencies of inner experience' which may manifest as colour, light, sound or feeling, according to one's level of psychic and spiritual development. And this kind of phenomenon usually occurs only to a certain class of people and may not necessarily manifest during the development of a different kind of seeker. In any case phenomenal experiences are only signposts along the way. But some become so fascinated by the signposts that they forget to continue the journey. Others may have no need of such things and prefer to 'cut across country', going directly towards the spiritual goal.

According to certain Western esoteric schools, these 'rays' or energies, are channelled through the 'spatial bodies' of vast cosmic beings who relay them to earth and into the souls who tune into them. These beings may be 'Nature Elementals' (bodiless entities of enormous dimensions assigned as guardian spirits over aspects of the natural world, or over continents, or whole planets), or sometimes 'Ascended Masters' or even the whole 'Angelic Hierarchy'. These beings are said to focalise 'rays' of certain colours in which the aspirant should seek to bathe himself, for his (or her) spiritual healing and evolution.

For example, as with the vibration of the colour blue, the 'Blue Ray' is said to have a spiritually 'quickening' effect and also has a calming influence on the mind and body. Hence, it is one of the most popular colours of the spiritual spectrum. A modern American group known as the Essenes Inc. (claiming to be 'Under the Guidance of the Angelic Host') have produced a booklet called *Spectrum of the Soul* (avowedly 'dictated' by the Cosmic Holy Spirit Himself!) It speaks of all the 'rays' in turn and has this to say about the blue-ray itself:

The blue ray of the Will of God is carried within the body of El Morya, whose body is a body of Light, encompassing the whole world. His Light flows with the love of God within the being of Lady Miriam, whose body is composed of the pink ray, which likewise encompasses the whole earth. All who truly desire to follow the Will of God must first surrender their own will to the Father-Mother God, by loving the pink ray of Lady Miriam within the blue ray of El Morya.

This is glorious stuff to some and a load of old codswallop to others. The wise walk gingerly in between the extremes. However, I have to frankly confess that blue-ray '*God*swallop' of any kind makes me squirm in my seat. Somehow all this specious speculation seems to be superfluous. Where is the need for all these intermediaries between me and God? Of course, on the ascending levels, there is no doubt that there are many inner dimensions and planes within planes. ("In my father's house are many mansions." *John* 14:2). But when we can open our hearts directly to the *Source,* need we be involved in them? With all such mediumistic 'messages' we need a careful assessment of exactly *who* is channelling *what* through *whom?*

I always wonder who but a megalomaniac, or a sincerely self-deluded seeker, could presume to write stuff claiming to be the revealed 'Word of God?' A great deal of what is passed off on the gullible as the 'direct' Word of God is so obviously tainted with the idiosyncratic brush of the medium's own devising. No doubt most are genuinely trying to uplift the world with their 'messages', but often their pronouncements smack of either a holier-than-thou condescension, or of a romanticised Blue-ray idealism. I have encountered countless creepy old mediums who have precociously tried to sound like their idea of how an 'Evolved Being' might speak. But there are always clues which give them away.

You will find many of their 'messages' are generously sprinkled with patronising phrases, such as: 'O My Dear Little Ones' or 'My Beloved Children' or 'If *only* you knew...' (coming from a wistful 'God' or various 'Ascended Beings'). These messages are invariably thickly spread with spiritual maiden aunt advice and inevitably larded with Biblical terminology. An evolved being is never treacly or condescending. And one who pontificates in the language of the Bible always makes a message extremely suspect to my sensibilities. Is 'God' so far out of touch and behind the times? Or is the 'Old Man' living in the past?

And when 'God' begins sending *me* pious directives through genteel blue-ray third-party channels, I show a clean pair of heels.

Yet on the other hand, when unpremeditated thoughts or events are projected at me (without being prepared in the ego-conscious 'scrambling mechanism' of the mind) I am always open to experiencing them as direct messages of the Omnipresence. Suppose, for example, some snotty-nosed kid on the street were to say something like, "Cor! You fancy yourself, don'tcha?" as I passed, it would be more in my nature to accept *that* statement as a directive from 'God', cautioning me to watch myself for any signs of mental or spiritual 'swagger' in future. Or if someone steals things from my car, I have to reassess my attachment to possessions, or come to realise that I have been too anxiously preoccupied with money-making matters for my livelihood, rather than tuning in to the Omnipresence which knows my needs.

In any kind of spiritual group where an atmosphere of 'preciousness', piety and 'hushed holiness' is created, you can bet your boots you are in for moonshine. An overly serious and long-faced 'virtuous' atmosphere is devoid of spiritual spontaneity. In the 'energy-field' or 'aura' of a true catalytic presence – or spiritual group leader – one can switch from laughter to spiritual awe in a moment. Unfortunately it is the attitudes of self-styled 'humble' channels who take themselves too seriously (or would have others take them seriously) which cast doubt and discredit on the genuine mediums. And there are many poseurs inflating their egos by playing at being 'humble channels' of 'God's Word'. You can be sure that anyone who actually *tells* you he is humble is lying. For humble, read *humbug*.

But in so saying, we must be careful not to tar everyone with the same brush. I simply caution against accepting all messages, hook, line and sinker, without discriminating the sane and sound from the merely specious. In the relative scheme of things, there *are* entities of various kinds, existing on relatively real planes, or inner dimensions.

When the Sage Sri Ramana Maharshi was asked if the Hindu gods and their different heavens were real or figments of the imagination, he replied: "They are as real as you and me." By this he intended to convey that you and me are only relatively real too. This world is our imagination. A dream world seems real when we are in it, but seems 'unreal' when we wake up. Yet it 'existed' while we were in it. Similarly this waking world 'exists' while we are in it, but seems as a dream when we wake up from it in the enlightened form of consciousness.

On the way to the enlightened state, there are yogis and genuine mediums who immerse themselves in 'higher worlds' or 'frequencies' of perception, tuning themselves into certain 'channels' like Cosmic television sets. The spiritual experience of these realms 'coalesces' to form 'entities' through which experiences or 'messages' are channelled, untainted by the earthbound personalities or ego-sense of the mediums themselves. It is the messages of such quality mediums which ring true being free of condescension, gimmickry of language, or constant reference to the Bible (as if that was the only holy scripture in existence).

On the other hand, lesser mediums have often only gained contact with the next level up of their own natures, where they may experience fleeting phenomena of sound, light, colour and occasional images. Some of these images may only be their own romantic reflections which they take to be attunement with 'angelic beings'. As their normal minds are still partially active in this phase, being so close to the next level, their messages are often filtered through the sense-of-ego under the name of some 'spiritual guide'. This is a not unusual and forgivable form of spiritual schizophrenia. It is most frequently found in those who sincerely need to feel helpful in the only way they feel their words will be accepted. But they may be considered 'a bit too blue-ray to be taken seriously'.

I have only been using mediumistic channels as an obvious example, but 'blue-ray' people are not confined to this section of spiritual society by any means. They are to be found at all levels of the spiritual spectrum. Such persons are basically seekers who are spiritually naive, although generally open and sincere, but somewhat 'stage-struck' with the ideas and atmosphere of the spiritual life. Thus they tend to play fancifully with the imagery of 'Love and Light' and cling to idealised mental utopias, rather than having their feet on the ground and getting down to the 'nitty-gritty' of real inner work.

Even more tongue-in-cheekily, one might consider those whose aspirations are theoretically heavenwards, but whose actual daily attitudes cast anger, gloom and despondency around them, as decidedly *'brown-ray'* people. Where do you see yourself in the spiritual spectrum? I feel my ray is decidedly spotty after this answer.

Opening the Inner Eye

Q. *Recently, whilst suffering the effects of an abscess, I became feverish and then delirious. Whilst delirious, I had visions of what was happening inside my body at the site of the abscess. The perception was telescopic and could not, I believe, have derived from my 'imagination'. I believe I may have inadvertently projected my astral body inwards.*

It seems to me that the ability to do this at will would be very useful and I would like to know if you can suggest a way to develop this ability, or if there are any books available which would help. I must also add that I had not taken any drugs when this incident occurred.

A. This was undoubtedly a genuine experience and not imagination. I have also undergone a similar involution of consciousness myself, in my early twenties, when my consciousness was precipitated into the cellular awareness of my body. I felt myself to be looking out of the 'eyes' of every individual cell at one and the same time. Thus I was made aware of the complexity of cellular 'sight and feeling' and of the conscious perception and limitation of biological intelligence. It also gave me insight into the intuitive understanding of the enigmatic description in the biblical *Revelation of John*, where he speaks of four mythical beasts (aspects of man) who had "eyes all over, inside and out". *Revelation 4:6 (New English Bible).*

This type of phenomenon is little known or spoken of in the West and is rarely mentioned in spiritual writings, although it can be found occasionally in Eastern technical yogic texts. It is something generally only experienced by adepts and *siddha* (accomplished) yogis as a by-product of their practices towards perfection. Yet it would seem to be a possibility attainable by all, as it occasionally occurs unlooked-for in advanced stages of meditation.

In his autobiography *Chitśakti Vilas*, the late Swami Muktananda of Ganeshpuri relates an experience of this nature during a period of intense spiritual practice. He describes the approach of a deep state of intensive meditation as accompanied by the awareness of a reddish aura which suffuses the vision and is apparent with the eyes open or closed. In this rosy radiance he often saw a moving point of blue light which he named the 'Blue Pearl'. Sometimes this 'pearl' shot out of his eye, to be seen externally, and sometimes shot back in again where he could see it inside his head. Eventually this point rose up inside him until it burst like a star in the *sahashrara* or crown *chakra* region at the top of his head.

He writes: "Inside the red aura thousands of sparks from the exploded star twinkled. By their light I could see within me all my nerves, my excretory system, my gall-bladder, and my internal organs."

This reminded me of something similar which occurred to me for a far less exalted reason. At a birthday gathering some years ago, I was given a slice of cake which, unknown to me, was spiced with hashish. Within a few minutes of eating it I was seized with an awful rushing sensation of acceleration, like the take-off pressure of a rocket-ship. I had the sudden urge to vomit. I was only able to stagger a few yards to my kitchen, before I fell unconscious. After a few moments I came round again. As I did so, I could somehow see the whole of the inside of my head in a brilliant light. (I thought the atomic bomb had been dropped!) It was as if I was looking from behind at a living, pulsing x-ray photograph of the contents of my own head.

Evidently spontaneous accidental experience such as this, can occur through sudden shock, fever, drugs, or intense emotion causing altered states of consciousness. In your case, it was obviously the delirium which withdrew your mind from the outside world, thereby allowing the 'mind's-eye' to focalise – to the exclusion of all else – on that part of the body causing the distress. Oblivious of all else but the pain, your consciousness was drawn to the spot, with that one-pointedness of mind we seek in meditative practice. To achieve this state, the yogic scriptures enjoin us to withdraw from the influence of the externally-oriented senses, as a tortoise withdraws its head and limbs into its shell. It is total absorption of consciousness which brings the capacity to 'see' internally and to roam within your own body.

As all our cells appear to be rudimentary 'eyes', we are naturally endowed with omniscient inner vision as our birth-right, but it will only operate automatically given favourable circumstances. Otherwise it has to be worked for. This '*in-sight*' is attributed to the functioning of the 'Third Eye' – the 'Eye of Divine Wisdom' – or *divya dristi* as it is technically known in Sanskrit. It is of course, not an 'eye' as such, but a mode of consciousness considered to operate in conjunction with the finer 'tuning' of the pineal gland by the practice of meditation. Its psychic force-field is said to be triangular in shape (somewhat like the gland itself). The base of the triangle rises vertically from a point between the two eyebrows to the centre of the forehead, and its apex points into the middle of the head.

Meditative withdrawal from the senses and conscious focal-isation on this area, stimulates the operation of the psychic capacities of the pineal gland. As the intuitive faculties develop, we become aware of knowledge beyond the range of the physical senses. We 'see the light', both literally and figura-tively, as the pineal gland appears to be a 'sensor' of inner and outer luminosity. Biological research has shown that although it has no direct connection with the surface of the body, the gland has indirect light-sensing capacities through connection with the optic nerve and through sensitivity to the radiations of ultraviolet rays emitted by the sun.

An interesting medical discovery is that lack of exposure to sunlight causes the pineal gland to inhibit its normal produc-tion of a hormone known as *seratonin* and to produce its opposite number, *melatonin*, which has the effect of diminish-ing sexual activity and fertility. Thus through the winter months, when little sun is available, we find ourselves less physical and more drawn towards inward practices. When the sun returns in greater strength, the pineal gland increases seratonin production, which actually stimulates sexual feeling and fertility. It is small wonder then that the 'mating season' occurs in spring, when – after a long 'winter of discontent' – all suddenly sun-struck creatures awaken to a joyful burst of song and sexual activity.

But I digress. Often on going to bed I am aware of a light inside my head, like soft sunshine in the region of the third eye. And I am obliged to open my eyes into total darkness, to see if I have switched off the light. This would appear to be a result of practising *Nada Yoga* – or 'mentemplation' upon inner sound and light (which has been described in an earlier Section, 'Sensing the Inner Sound'). One method of attuning to the inner light, is to press a finger firmly in the centre of the forehead, then fix your attention on the same spot on the *inside* of your forehead, where it may be seen as a tiny sun-like spot of dull colour. If the *nadam* or singing inner sound is also heard at the same time, so much the better.

For those to whom the concept of 'inner light' seems fanciful, I will here reveal the secret initiatory method of experiencing a similitude of the light which is described as 'brighter than a million suns'. One simply places two fingers over each closed eyelid and slowly and progressively pushes the eyeballs back inside the head. At first you will see bright flashes and spots of colour moving. As you press more deeply, this will give way to magnificent brilliantly white and dark geometric patterns of jewelled light, as you plunge into the spectacular star system of your inner universe. The effect is awesome. But this is purely to give an aspirant an inkling of the magical possibilities of delving into his own inner space.

One must be sure to release the pressure on the eyeballs gently and gradually. Do not open the eyes immediately afterwards, but keep them closed for a while until they have readjusted themselves and then open them slowly. This practice is not recommended to be done too frequently as it could be harmful in some cases. Certainly it should never be done by those with serious eye problems, nor while wearing contact lenses. Be warned. It is evidently preferable to find ways of entering the inner light naturally and progressively. One may safely follow the practices suggested in this book, or seek out a teacher in whom you perceive the light.

Obviously the training is long and arduous for gaining

proficiency in visionary inner experience. It means total dedication for life, not a half-hour's practice every day; although gaining minor *siddhis,* or occult powers, is relatively easy if one trains for that alone. As a basic step towards the cultivation of various powers (as well as for attuning themselves to the cosmos) many yogis begin with the mastery of the body and senses through the practice of *yoga nidra,* or 'yogic sleep'. This is a method which also brings many healing benefits to the body and spirit. It is a form of anaesthetisation by auto-suggestion, in which the body enters a profoundly deep 'sleep' beyond all normal relaxation, while the mind remains clear and calmly alert. [1]

This effect is brought about by the withdrawal of consciousness from the body, by the process known as *samyama* or (a) fixation of attention, (b) auto-suggestions and (c) absorption (of the suggestion). In the practice of *yoga nidra* one normally brings the mind to heel, by literally doing just that! One firstly fixes the attention on the feet, whilst lying stretched out on the ground in the 'prone pose', and then gradually moving up to the ankles, calves, knees, thighs, etc., one slowly withdraws the mind's energy out of each part of the body in turn. In each position one holds the mind at the site of attention for a while, while mentally repeating the *samyama* suggestions. Gradually the mind identifies with the experience of the suggestions given, becoming one with it and bringing about the state required.

These three aspects of fixation, suggestion and absorption are collectively known as *samyama* (in Sanskrit), but technically *samyama* does not properly occur until one is so proficient in the method that all three stages happen simultaneously. However, in general usage, the word *samyama* (which might be rendered 'mentemplation'* in English), is considered to be simply the fixation of mind on any specific object or image, idea or even an attribute or quality, such as compassion, joy, friendliness, warmth or light, etc.

Practising *samyama* on the inner light of consciousness, for example, is said to reveal knowledge of the subtle elements, such as atoms, and to give visionary access to things happen-

* See page 62

ing from afar. *Samyama* on the full moon gives knowledge of the star systems and their effects, and creates indirect communication with the Omnipresence. This practice is a preliminary step towards *samyama* on the sun. *Samyama* on the sun (at sunrise and sunset) gives direct communication between the individual mind and the Omnipresence, as well as knowledge of the universe and its workings. And *samyama* on the central nervous system brings one the knowledge of psycho-physiological forces, in the early stages, and then ultimately the experience of the unity of individual and cosmic forces.[2]

All such experiences, tersely treated in the *Yoga Sutras* of Patanjali and others, are not within the province of beginners, as they are dependent on entry into the *samadhi* state of meditation, when the mind is absorbed into the pure primal awareness of the Self. Nonetheless, the practices of *yoga-nidra* and *samyama* focalise the butterfly mind and prepare the way for inner experience.

One of the most popular and time-proven practices, which brings early results and benefits, is *samyama* on the flames of a fire. This method has been used in almost every culture since the beginning of the world, for easeful entry into heightened states of awareness. It is well known in Western traditions in its simplest form, as contemplation of a candle flame. And everyone is aware of the magical sense of reverie induced by gazing into their own hearth-fire. The famous chemist, Kekule, discovered the atomic structure of benzene in this fashion. While semi-dozing at his fireside, he suddenly saw the 'benzene-ring' form of atoms dancing in the flames. But when fire gazing is done with intent and contemplative clarity, the practice is rightly regarded as a doorway into other worlds.

There exists a mysterious relationship between the movement of the flames and our internal energies, which is considered to have correspondence with the flickering movement of the soul in the body. Many yogis devote years to the 'mentemplative' investigation of this phenomenon by identification with the fire and thereby enter into transcendental states of consciousness. Tantric yogis assert that the energies radiated from flickering firelight vibrate at specific frequencies, according to its colour and the substances which are burning, and one can attune to these frequencies when the process of *samyama* becomes profound. When one is precisely synchronised with these vibrations and they are mentally concentrated at the third-eye centre, then psychic powers occur and visionary entry into other dimensions becomes a reality.

It is for this reason a sacred ritual fire is carefully prepared with ingredients which produce the finest rate of vibration. These are basically *ghee* (or clarified butter) and dried cow-dung (being a pure and odourless substance), which are generally burned in a fire-pot of semi-pyramidal form of specific proportions, made of copper, silver or gold, as the radiations of these metals are also an important aspect in the generation of healing energies.

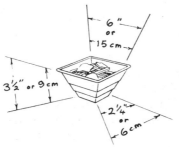

According to my own experience, one enhances harmonious attunement to the cosmos and generates divine love, tranquillity and energised well-being if the fire gazing is accompanied by the chanting of appropriate purificatory mantras,★ whilst feeling oneself in the *heart-centre* rather than in the third eye. In this way one is thereby safeguarded from possible negative occult forces, and one gains *spiritual* power, joy and healing energies instead of psychic phenomena. The superlative *Maha Mrtyunjaya* mantra is of the frequency of cosmic healing and is exceptionally beneficial for mental healing and the development of freedom from all fear.[3]

Another method of awakening *divya dristi*, or third eye energy, is the advanced practice of *vajroli mudra* (thunderbolt gesture). This is outlined by Swami Svatmarama in his *Hatha Yoga Pradipika* (v.82-89). Unfortunately he gives no clear indication of the method as this is a secret practice given only to advanced initiates. And one needs precise instruction from a competent yogi, as *vajroli mudra* is not simply a matter of contracting the vaginal, urinary and anal muscles, whilst sitting in the half-lotus posture, as given in popular books on yoga. That is all right to begin with; but in the advanced stages, the yogi continues by steadily inserting a foot-long, thin silver tube into the urethra, or urinary canal, an inch at a time. By means of this tube the yogi draws up substances such as water, milk, honey and eventually mercury, into the body, for purification and the acquisition of longevity. This practice is also preparatory to the conservation of, or re-absorption of sexual fluids which are used to nourish the 'sleeping' areas of the brain through which the intuitive faculties operate.

Mastery of this practice is said to bring about many *siddhis*. However, this shows that psychic powers of all kinds can be developed – and often are – by yogis who fail to achieve any corresponding spiritual elevation. They impress and overwhelm the people by their power rather than radiance from the heart. The display of powers does not necessarily indicate a master of any quality. There are those who manifest miraculous powers and merely mouth pious platitudes to impress the masses, but who are carried away by their own sense of glorification. On the other hand, there are those who simply

★ Details of mantras and method are available on cassette (see Reference 3).

follow the path of the heart, not looking for powers, but who quietly accept any which come their way without becoming unbalanced by them.

For those who are temperamentally 'go-getters', the safe and sure way to press on, is to develop both the spiritual (sunconscious) and technical aspects simultaneously. It is evident from the lives of the sages, that a combination of the spirit of reverence, constant meditative practice and attunement to the Divine Will, gradually evolves in the human spirit the perfect condition to receive whatever it is necessary for that soul to experience in this life. Many people in India have gained yogic powers simply by celibacy and eating a moderate amount of unadulterated pure foods for some years. But generally it is only by constancy in following through a steady sequence of yogic *asanas* (postures), *pranayamas* (breath regulation), *mantras* (purificatory sound-patterns), *pratyaharas* (sensory withdrawal practices), *dharanas* (fixations of consciousness), *dhyana* ('mentemplative' concentration) and *samadhi* (super-conscious meditation), which can allow the progressive blossoming of any really worthwhile powers.

Should any psychic powers begin to manifest prematurely, we are cautioned by accomplished gurus not to get caught up in them and lose our way in psychic side-alleys. When Swami Vivekananda went to his Master, Sri Ramakrishna, to tell him that psychic powers had begun to develop in him, he was then told to stop practising whatever he was practising until they went away again. When such *siddhis* come to us, there is a tremendous temptation to set up our bazaar by the wayside and display our powers as a spiritual side-show. We find ourselves immensely popular and forget we are walking the long way 'home'.

Even an adept as advanced as Jesus was several times tempted by his sense-of-ego in the desert and temple to deviate and stumble on the Path. So *siddhis* are an aspirant's severest test. It is as well not to wish for psychic powers until our sense-of-ego is well dissolved away, or we may never reach the final goal. Succumbing to the lure of 'supernatural' powers undoes the work already done in spirit and diminishes the energies required for completing the Quest.

UNDER THE CHURCH CARPET

(Or What Christians Prefer Not To Know)

Caution: The second article in this section, *The Unknown Journeyings of Jesus* contains a great deal of information which sensitive Christians really would prefer not to know about. If, therefore, you are one who does not wish to be disturbed, I counsel you to skip this section, rather than distress yourself.

On the Souls of Animals

Q. *For want of reading matter while on holiday this summer, I began browsing through a tome I came across called* The Catholic Dictionary *and was horrified to discover the following passage, regarding man's relationship to animals. About animals they say:*

As their souls operate through matter, so they spring from matter and perish with it. They are not created by God, but are derived with their bodies from their parents by natural generation. Without matter they are utterly incapable of operation, and therefore of existence; for nothing can exist unless it acts in some way or other. Hence their soul is extinguished with the dissolution of the body . . . These philosophic principles . . . determine the morality which regulates the conduct of man to the brutes. As the lower animals have no duties, since they are destitute of free will – without which the performance of duty is impossible – so they have no rights, for right and duty are co-relative terms. The brutes are made for man, who has the same right over them which he has over plants and stones. He may kill them for his food; and if it is lawful to destroy them for food, it must also be lawful to put them to death or to inflict pain on them, for any good or reasonable end, such as the promotion of man's knowledge, health, etc., or even for the purpose of recreation.

I could hardly believe such callous and primitive narrow-mindedness! With such sentiments, it is small wonder that our 'Christian'-based society supports such atrocities as whale and seal genocide, fox-hunting, battery-farming, animal experimentation and the Sunday shooting of almost anything that moves by groups of well-to-do-jolly-good-church-going-chaps.

What are your sentiments regarding the above? And have you any thoughts on the spiritual status of animals?

A. I am as astounded and dismayed as you are. This ignorant and ludicrous 'philosophising' reads like a concentration–camp inquisitor's manual for self-justification. How it got past the Dictionary's Board of Censors is a mystery. One can only assume that the ecclesiastical hierarchy is in accord with these sentiments. But if we are to consider all *that* as a 'Catholic' viewpoint, then it only confirms my observation that the only brute in creation is *Man*. However, I hardly think this passage could be considered as representative of anyone *truly* following Christian principles; even though it does appear to be representative of the kind of 'double-think' to which, in my experience, many so-called 'Christian' clergy and their flocks are prone.

I have to admit that this kind of attitude and the lack of vegetarian ethic in Christianity – as popularly practised – does in some measure contribute to the support of the institutions you mention, as well as the unthinking perpetration of such horrors as slaughter-houses and factory farming. Yet this is a strange state of affairs, when we consider that most Christians accept on face value the King James' translation of *Genesis*, in which God is held to have stated: "Behold I have given you every herb-bearing seed which is upon the face of all the earth, and every tree, in the which is the fruit of a tree yielding seed: *to you it shall be for meat.*" (*Genesis* 1:29). Thus at the very beginning of the Bible, according to the Jewish-Christian conception of 'God's Word', it was ordained that herbs (the vegetable kingdom) and fruits were given as the proper food for mankind. At that time, the word 'meat' was the common term of the day for a meal, or food in general.

Also in *Genesis* it is written: "And God *created* great whales, and *every living creature that moveth,* which the waters brought forth abundantly, after their kind, and every winged fowl after his kind." (*Genesis* 1:21). And also: "God *made* the beast of the earth after his kind, and cattle after their kind, and everything that creepeth on the earth after his kind: and God saw that it was good." (*Genesis* 1:25). Unless the Catholic Bible is vastly different from any other Bible, it would seem that our 'philosophiser' has not been too particular in his reading with due regard to the theological interpretation of the origin of species.

It would seem that the average Christian attitude on this matter was a sore point as early as AD 400. In the compendium of writings of the Desert Fathers, *The Philokalia,* St Neilos the Ascetic, taking unnatural appetites to task, also quotes these same passages as a Divine Ordinance, stating: "Thus we have been given a common diet with the animals; but if we use our powers of invention to turn this into something extravagant, shall we not rightly be judged more unintelligent than they? The animals remain within the boundaries of nature, not altering in any way what God has ordained; but we, who have been honoured with the power of intelligence, have completely abandoned His original ordinance." (AD 400)[1].

Although *Genesis* also states that God gave man "dominion over the fish of the sea, and over the fowl of the air, and over the cattle, and over all the earth, and over every creeping thing that creepeth upon the earth" (1:26), this indicates his *intellectual* superiority and *not* despotic domination. In times of old, 'dominion' meant the right of governing, or 'mastery', thereby giving man a kind of natural stewardship over the earth. It was not said anywhere, "You may slaughter without need, torture, or eat everything over which you have intellectual domination."

Yet this is doubtless the prevalent attitude of mankind towards its fellow-creatures in the world today. We have no 'God-given' *right* over anything, animal, plant or stone. At best, we may be good 'gardeners' of the world which sustains us, for the duration of our brief stay in it. Where there is no feeling of 'stewardship' or reverence for the earth and growing things, we find exploitation and rape of the planet. Where there is environmental destruction without regard for man's own habitat, then the consequential ecological repercussion on all other life-forms is equally ill considered.

Unfortunately Western civilisation lost its sense of the sacredness of everything in the natural world with the advent of Christianity. The inherent spirituality in country people (the original meaning of 'pagan' was 'rustic' or 'country dweller') caused them to see 'godliness' in springs and rivers, rocks and trees, which were all experienced as sacred and treated with reverence. But all this 'superstitious' spirituality was overridden when the citified Christian religion gained ground.

The loss of the sacred and irreverence for all 'God's creatures' has culminated in a society which allows diabolical experiments on animals and breeds the kind of clinical scientific mind which progresses to diabolical and equally unfeeling experiments on man. What we allow to be done to others will ultimately rub off on us. With a daily diet of brutally sadistic television and cinema shows, we encourage the concept that living beings are simply *things* to exploit, experiment upon, or kill, without a second thought. As Jesus taught, "As you sow, so shall you reap." What we do to our earth and all on it, we do to ourselves. The law is inexorable. When a man reaches a level of spiritual evolution where this is an *experienced* reality, he becomes unwilling to harm even a gnat.

Man is not something so far apart from the natural world as he fondly imagines. All the forces of the cosmos – suns, moons and stars affect his bodily systems. Intrinsically he lives in a spiritual continuum and thus everything he thinks and does has its effects on the whole. In a similar way as fish exist in the ocean, so man exists in the cosmic 'Ocean of *Being*'. This all-encompassing 'ocean' is expressed by Christian mystics as the *Presence of God*. I try to stimulate this understanding with a question which is answered by a counter question:

Where does the soul go when the body dies?
Where does the sea go when the fish dies?

As all sea-creatures are made from the sea, interpenetrated by the sea, and again become sea in dissolution, never having been anything else but the sea – so it is with Man *in* God. The Universal Spirit, true Self or Omni-*presence* interpenetrates all beings – *and* all *things,* which are only emanations or mani-festations of that selfsame spiritual substratum. For simplicity of illustration, if we see all sea-creatures as complex coagula-tions of 'oceanic energies', so the localised 'condensations' of Universal Spirit may be understood as each individual 'force-field' we call 'soul'. Without such a 'field' there is no move-ment of life in any body, human or animal.

If the nature of that which we call 'God' is truly Omnipotent, Omniscient and *Omnipresent,* then 'God-ness' is inherent in everything, including animal, plant and stone. Therefore, when we inflict pain on animals for 'reasonable purposes' or for our 'recreation' we are inadmissibly inflicting pain on God through the visible manifestation. Not that God in itself is susceptible to pain, but inasmuch as God's 'quickening' exists *as* each and every soul, so we are guilty of spiritual transgression when we harm another being. "Whatsoever you do unto these little ones, you do unto me," said Jesus.

What is the difference between a dead body and a live one? When you look into the eyes of a dead person or animal, there is no longer anyone there looking out. The animating essence, or 'soul' has departed. What we are left with is a corpse. All animated beings, in order to manifest at all, are *ensouled,* be they ants or elephants. So to say that animals have souls but merely 'spring from matter and perish with it' is as absurd as saying the sea 'perishes' when a fish dies. If such were the case then it would equally apply to mankind. Both human and animal bodies perish, but souls are the very 'substance' of God and appear to go through a continuous recycling and refining process for as many lifetimes as needful before the final purificatory dissolution in the Source.

Why should we surmise that one type of soul (or spiritual force-field) be suddenly generated for a term of 'enfleshment in the body' and then cease to exist forever after, and another – human type soul – go on to paradise? Surely the same 'substances' should follow the same laws? Neither humans nor animals 'spring from matter', as it is soul which is the continuous element and matter which 'springs alive' when suffused by it, or disintegrates without it.

As for the thin-lipped argument that to have no 'duties' means to have no rights to emancipation, compassion or humane treatment, we could consider that our children have no duties, and therefore it is reasonable for us to slaughter or inflict pain on them for our 'recreation'. Even if there was the slightest validity to this inhuman and ridiculous argument, there could be no justifiable application of this 'philosophy' to the animal kingdom. The very idea indicates a completely dry-brained citified ignorance of the interpenetrative and wondrous workings of nature.

Just to cite a few examples: without the pollinating 'duties' of the bees and other insects, we would have no fertilisation of flowers and blossoms, and consequently no development of fruit to eat. Without the birds keeping down the pests, our crops would be overwhelmed with bugs. And without the 'dutiful' singing of birds to touch our hearts, we would be mightily impoverished in spirit. Without the plants and trees 'dutifully' creating oxygen, we would have no air to breathe (especially at the rate we are destroying the atmosphere). Without the falling of leaves and the manure of animals, our lands would be laid waste (as intense chemical farming has shown in America, for example, where the fertile farmlands were changed into the famous 'dust-bowls' in a few generations). The life cycles and dutiful deeds of all the billions of creatures on this earth, from the micro-organisms to the great whales are our ecological life-support system, and we alter them at our peril.

When the Australian cattlemen imported a special strain of very hardy Indian cows into their grasslands, they found that the dung of these cows was unable to break down by itself and remained solid on the surface, encrusting the earth rather than manuring it. Very soon the great grassy plains began to turn into deserts. After intensive research, it was discovered that in India there lived a special kind of indigenous dung-beetle, which worked to break down the cow-pats into the soil. Thus the cattlemen were obliged to also import millions of these beetles to restore the balance of nature and their grasslands. Although what the ecological repercussions of these mass importations may lead to, we have yet to discover!

But one could give innumerable examples of this kind, regarding the 'duties' that the animal world is unwittingly performing for us without our generally being aware of it. Another of these taken-for-granted qualities (or perhaps 'God-given duties') of animals is the tremendous joy and companion-ship they bring to humankind. Can you imagine the dreariness of a world without animals? With only locked-in-his-head Man for company? The love and adoration many animals have for humans is something to be wondered at. The unconditional love and faithfulness of a dog, for example, extends far beyond the mere 'cupboard-love' we generate by feeding it. It may pine to death for want of the human contact it loves. Through animals we see God's love in action. They are a constant reminder of the qualities of the heart.

Why should animals be so attracted to us? And to what in us

do they respond? Many times, when I have looked deeply into the eyes of a dog, or a cat (and on occasion, a horse, an elephant, or a monkey), I have been moved to see a great soul imprisoned there. And I am certain that something of indefinable importance passed between us in that contact. We were able to communicate directly, soul to soul. We understood, without knowing it, each other's deep need for loving contact. And this is the secret of our relationship with the animal kingdom (as well as the human) – the succouring by reciprocal love.

As humans we have one of the greatest possibilities for evolutionary advancement, by coming into contact with souls more spiritually evolved than ourselves. For creatures without a capacity for self-awareness, there is the possibility for their evolution through the experiences they undergo in association with human beings. Animals absorb something of a higher frequency of being through such relationships. And it has often been remarked how animals and their owners come to resemble each other and grow to have similar characteristic temperaments. For better or worse, our inner qualities rub off on our pets (as also on our environment, plants, children and everyone else around us).

It cannot be otherwise. We exist in each other's auric or radiational fields in the spiritual continuum. Thus as 'earth-stewards' we have a responsibility towards all of creature-kind. That is, to give out to them what we in turn would appreciate being given to us from a 'Higher Presence'. Animals are evidently stimulated by the quality of 'God-ness' we are able to generate in our relations with them, just as our hearts are awed and opened when we find ourselves before a holy being or suddenly experience ourselves as being in the 'Presence of God'. Many a time, when in a deeply loving or meditative mood, I have directed my gaze at a previously unknown passing dog, it has suddenly pricked up its ears and made a bee-line for me, running over to greet me with great joy as if I was an old friend. And even mice and rats have, on occasion, come to scramble over me during meditation, obviously attracted by something in the vibration or 'radiational field'.

(I hope I don't put off prospective meditators. Perhaps it was just that my clothes smelled of cheese.)

One of my treasured memories of my time in India, is of when I was living in a little house at the foot of Arunachala mountain in Tamil Nadu. One day, on opening my eyes as I came out of deep meditation, I was astonished to see a whole tribe of monkeys surrounding the house, all staring through the screen doors and windows. They were all unnaturally still and silently watching me. I rose slowly and walked over to them, gently opening the screen doors wide and sat down in front of them. Only one monkey at the front hopped back a fraction. Normally they would have all fled screaming, or the larger aggressive apes might have attacked or ransacked the house (as one had done the month before). But the meditative condition was still upon me, and feeling no sense of selfhood there was 'nobody there' in me, to frighten or disturb them, and so they all remained immobile.

I put out my hand slowly and the leading monkey placed his paw in it. The gesture filled me with a great love. For a few moments we gazed deeply into each other's eyes. The contact was profound. Then I looked up and around into the enquiring eyes of all the still and silent monkeys, some still clinging to the window bars, and felt the wonder of this fear-free relationship. Just then someone came down the garden path and they all scampered off quietly into the palm grove.

I understood this to be a lesser example of the kind of phenomenon which accounted for the safety of Daniel in the lions' den. Obviously his level of spiritual development had reached a degree in which his absorption into the *Presence* was so profound that his beatitude and resulting radiation was sufficient to overcome the instincts of a pride of hungry lions. There are many other authenticated accounts of advanced souls who have remained unmolested in the presence of savage creatures. Yogis and spiritual masters in India have been known to sit meditating in the jungle, protected by their lack of a sense-of-human-ego, while tigers or other predators walked around them without fear or aggression.

Sages such as Bhagavan Sri Ramana Maharshi of Arunachala have been observed on many occasions, to act like magnets to the creatures of the wild. When going out for his daily walk, sometimes birds would come to him from the sky, animals from the jungle, cows from their stalls and some said even snakes from the grass would come to his feet. No doubt St Francis of Assisi achieved this same kind of rapport with animals and birds and even insects, by ego-lessly steeping himself in the Presence. Even 'ordinary' people who have a way with animals, are often unconsciously manifesting the same atmosphere to a lesser degree, as they are generally quiet and unassuming persons, naturally adept at stilling their own personalities and remaining in the background. Therefore this special and wondrous relationship with the animal world is possible to us all.

It would seem that there are no warm-blooded so-called 'wild beasts' which are not susceptible to the Omni*presence* as operating through man. Many wild creatures of which man is afraid, have learned to be aggressive towards man because of man's aggression towards them. The scent of fear and ego-aggression in humans provokes the same reaction in animals, in the same way that someone else's ego rising makes us also raise our hackles. But on solitary islands where man has rarely trod, explorers and naturalists report their amazement and joy at having all kinds of what would elsewhere be 'wild' creatures walk all over and around them without any concern whatso-ever. Obviously the whole earth was once a 'Garden of Eden' and man's own attitude has set him apart from it.

But when mutual trust is gained, a bond of love can develop between man and the most bizarre of creatures: dolphins, whales, seals, rhinos, lions, elephants, orang-utans and the like. If brought up from an early age in the presence of man, the most savage of animals seems willing to be 'tamed' by him. This is our true 'dominion': a dominion of love. And most animals seem to revel in the 'aura' of such relationships, becoming suffused with the qualities and intelligence and subtle essences of a higher evolutionary life-form. I believe that in this rapport, the animal soul develops and perhaps eventually achieves human incarnation through these emo-tionally transforming influences on its state of being.

Bhagavan Sri Ramana maintained that animals are even

capable of directly attaining liberation. There was a cow at his *ashram* named Lakshmi, who even as a calf, would daily go from the cowshed of our own accord and lay her head in prostration at Bhagavan's feet. On many occasions she would go and collect the sage at the precise moment he was required to go and perform some ceremony or other, and altogether acted in an extraordinarily intelligent manner. Bhagavan tended her during her last hours of life and afterwards declared that she had been 'liberated' at the end, achieving union with the Absolute. This did not appear to be euphemistically spoken, for he saw to it that she had a *samadhi* or tomb, erected over her remains – which was a right usually reserved for Self-realised beings – and a plaque was affixed to it attesting to her liberation.

Another time a very old crow arrived at the *ashram*, and remained where it alighted, not budging from its perch on a tree stump for three days, even though many people came and hung on the tree stump whilst hauling water from a well. When Sri Bhagavan heard about it, he went immediately to see the crow and enquired, "What is the matter?" The crow very slowly opened its eyes to regard him. Then taking it in one hand, Bhagavan tipped a few drops of water into the crow's beak. A few seconds later the bird died in his hand. Later someone remarked that the crow must have been some great soul awaiting Bhagavan's touch before it could depart. "Yes, it appears so," said Bhagavan, and another *samadhi* was erected for the crow.

We have no way of knowing who or what kind of soul there may be inhabiting any of the creatures around us. But we can be sure that the way we respond to them, will have its effect both on them and on our own inner development.

There is no higher religion than that of sympathy for all that lives.
Rabindranath Tagore

The Unknown Journeyings of Jesus

Caution: This chapter contains a large proportion of information which many sensitive Christians may prefer not to know. If therefore, you are one who does not wish to be disturbed, then I counsel you to pass over the following section rather than distress yourself. If however, you are prepared to grow on through altered perspectives and accept other possibilities, then – read on.

Q. *In a recent issue of* Yoga Today *a Christian yoga teacher wrote complaining that the magazine was too Hindu-biased, so that he/she couldn't recommend it to his/her pupils. I wonder why he/she is practising yoga? Aren't most of us involved in yoga because it seems to offer a more practical approach to life and spirituality than does Christianity? And as yoga comes from India, how can a yoga magazine help having a Hindu bias? But what I'd like to ask is: do you think there is such a great dissimilarity (in essence I mean) between the teachings of Jesus and the teachings of the Hindu sages? And I have heard that Jesus studied in India. Do you know anything about this?*

A. Well, I am most grateful that crucifixions have gone out of style, for when I first published my response to this question, I began with the words: "You are going to get me into trouble in answering this," – and so it came to pass. Inevitably I came under fire from well-meaning but indignant reverends and lay Christians, who castigated me for my temerity in trying to extend the knowledge given in the 'authenticated' (though meagre) account of the life of Jesus as fragmentarily propounded in the Bible.

I was given to understand that I could not possibly understand Christianity because I did not 'stand-under' it. Now whilst I can appreciate a modicum of plausibility in this sentiment, my inability to understand 'Christianity' as so divergently followed today, does not preclude the possibility of understanding its scriptural teachings and historical validity. On the other hand, one might consider that it is possible to be so conditioned by traditional form and religious trappings that one can no longer see the scriptural wood for the trees. And from my unworthy position outside the canonically concep-tualised version of Christianity, it is my observation that many followers have been so moulded from childhood by ecclesiastical *Churchian* dogma and interpretation that they tend to misapprehend the underlying mystical teachings which are the kernel of the Christian religion.

It must always be remembered that Jesus was one of the world's greatest mystics and those who later organised and codified 'Christianity' were not. That it is possible for other mystics to understand the words of Christ without losing themselves in the obfuscations of 'Churchianity' (rather than *Christ*-ianity) should be self-evident; except, it would seem, for those who are accustomed to 'standing-under' it. However, I have encountered advanced sages in various traditions, who are able to perceive and clarify the essential spiritual import of *any* scripture of the world by direct perception (that is, God-suffused intuitive consciousness); just as Jesus was able to illumine the ancient teachings of the Hebrew prophets, without 'standing-under' the Jewish religion.

A great many people who adhere tightly to an established religion – be it Christianity, Judaism, Islam, Hinduism or whatever – are often those who have more of a childlike inner need of stability and security than others. And this is especially so among the orthodox. Whatever they have chosen to fol-low, *has* to be *the* unalterable truth – whether right or wrong. In my days as a psychotherapy student – in a milieu specifically treating Christian ministers, nuns, and the laity – I have seen that in the face of a bewildering world and an unlimited universe, there was often an unspoken relief and gratitude in finding that the limits, direction and goal of spiritual life had been defined and delineated by an 'authoritative' body of tradition.

The average believer is therefore able, to a certain extent, to spiritually relax in the comfortable confines of an undemanding doctrine and the socially supportive 'herd warmth' of like-minded religious fellowship. Simple acceptance of the scriptures as shown by a generally non-mystic minded priesthood, safeguards many from the actual effort of practical Self-enquiry. However, this does nothing to dissipate the inner disquiet of the Christian soul. During my Christian therapy work, it was my feeling that much of the inner anguish could have been alleviated if there had been some specific practices and definitive spiritual purpose, which would give them the stability they sought in the here and now – such as are to be found in yoga.

Of course, it can be spiritually disquieting to discover that one's accepted authorities have been 'covering up' and keeping the facts from the laity for the sake of ecclesiastical expediency. It is evidently far preferable to attack sincere researchers than to investigate the findings for oneself. I find it astounding that so many prefer the 'safety' of their doctrine to the discoveries which may open their minds and hearts. The refusal to open-mindedly look at one's beliefs in the light of new revelations, which may widen one's angle of vision, belongs to what I would call 'spiritual adolescence'. It is not the attitude of a mature seeker – one who is sincerely questioning his spiritual and physical existence – and the teachings by which he lives. A mature seeker is flexible enough to accept new possibilities, at any cost to his illusions, and be prepared to grow by them.

However, after the first publication of this article, a very devout woman came up to me at the end of one of my workshops and told me, "I came prepared to hate you for what you said about our Lord – but I find I can't." At least she tried. Even though I had said nothing unkind about Jesus. But this is an attitude I have found not uncommon among those who purport to follow the teachings of the Christ: "Touch my cherished beliefs and fantasies and I will hate you." Yet I do not recall that Jesus said to hate anyone for trying to 'cast the scales from one's eyes' and open them to the truth. Especially since he was condemned by the orthodoxy of his own day for doing precisely the same thing.

At the end of the article, I had previously written: "Only

those of little faith can have it shaken by hearing something other than they have been told to believe". Therefore the lady concluded defiantly "Anyway, you haven't shaken *my* faith!" If this was so, I wondered, then from whence came this fear-engendered feeling of hate? For hatred is a cover-up which, in this case, masks an existential fear: a fear which none but the spiritually brave will dare to face. 'My religion' is often the lid which covers that fear. If the lid is shaken, the fear of exposure to that fear is paramount. Thus fear provokes hatred.

"Let man overcome anger by love . . . hatred does not cease by hatred at any time; hatred ceases by love – this is an old rule." Gautama the Buddha, *Dhammapada v.5.*

"Love your enemies, bless them that curse you, do good to them that hate you, and pray for them that despitefully use you and persecute you . . . Do unto others as ye would have them do unto you." Jesus the Christ (approx AD 30)

"You must so adjust your heart that you long for the welfare of all beings, including the happiness of your enemies . . . Among men who hate us, let us dwell free from hatred . . . With pure thoughts and fullness of love, I will do towards others what I would do for myself." Gautama the Buddha (approx BC 500).

Let me make it plain at the outset: I feel obliged to state that it is *not* my intention to 'shake' anyone's faith, but to encourage intelligent faith in the meaningful things rather than in the doubtful interpolations and ecclesiastical embellishments. I can only caution sensitive Christian readers once again, that if you feel susceptible to distress regarding revelations contrary to your beliefs, then, please, do not read on. I am merely responding to the question as honestly as I am inwardly impelled to do, in the light of my findings over the years.

These discoveries have cleared away some of the Churchified cobwebs and encrustations which have nearly ossified Christianity into its grave – for me, at any rate – and has given it a new life and interest which its evangelical dogma had previously stifled. And it is noticeable that even when more enlightened Christian ministers have attempted in all honesty to speak out, or write of their similar findings in these matters, they also have been swiftly condemned by their superiors and the faithful (if ill-informed) Christian rank and file. It is evidently left to those who do not 'stand-under' the Canonical Law, to make available that which those within the fold who *do* 'understand', are not allowed to reveal.

SEEKING THE REAL JESUS

In order to cover properly all the finer points and enumerate the evidences relating to this subject, I would have to write a whole book. But in the space of this (ever-growing) article, I will try to give a few brief indications of what is an extremely vast field of study (on which uncountable researchers have been engaged for nigh on the last two thousand years). Many of their discoveries have not been allowed to see the light of day, having vanished without trace into the 'archival swamps' of the Vatican. Thus we are obliged to go on the scraps of information garnered in our own haphazard researches and accidental finds.

I might add that after my own Christian 'education' at the hands of 'blue-ray' Sunday school Bible pushers, it was many a long year before I could come to accept Jesus in any shape or form. But during my wanderings in many lands, I came across references which made me perk up and begin to take an interest again, and search for something of the *real* story of his life. What I discovered has made him more believable a character than the white-washed, 'gentle Jesus, meek and mild' of my school-days. And I have found that my inner and outer research on answering this question has allowed me to break some barriers of reserve around my soul and brought me closer to the Christ within.

Many of my 'findings' have long been known to Christian historians and theological researchers (although not widely publicised, for fear of upsetting the doctrinal apple-cart). Some of my other more 'obscure' discoveries are common knowledge among Muslim theologians and other non-Christian scholars in the Middle East and India, who have no vested interest in the matter, and therefore have nothing to hide. Nor have they anything against Jesus, as he is extolled and venerated as a great prophet by Mohammed in the *Holy Koran,* and is also revered by the sages of India.

Many works of scholarly merit are often exceedingly boring, and therefore unread by the masses. Many new discoveries are known only to the researchers and savants of the scholastic world, and the information generally takes years, and even decades, to filter down to the man in the street (or the man in the Church). This is especially so if the new findings are not palatable to the ecclesiastical powers that be, when they are played down, or swept under the carpet and discouraged as far as possible.

GOING GODWARD

In answering this question, one of the things which strikes me first, is that in the true all-embracing nature of Hinduism, there is no élitism and always a willingness to honour the sages and scriptures of other lands and religions. Naturally there are always strait-laced élitists and dividers among the protagonists of any set of teachings, but I speak here of the general attitude, and the injunctions implicit in the Hindu teachings themselves. And in my travels I have found that the masters of India, or of any other land, are always delighted to find anyone who is inwardly travelling the spiritual path, no matter what religious route they happen to have chosen. And (Muslims apart) even the laity of those countries often recognised that one was 'Going Godward' and that was enough.

Whereas among a remarkable number of Christians (except for those spiritually at rest in their faith), I am always being asked, somewhat apprehensively: "Are you a Christian?" – as if they might catch something unpleasant if I am not. If I answer anything other than in the affirmative, in innumerable instances I have experienced a rather prim barrier of reserve come down between us – even though I may be feeling the spirit of the Christ resounding deeply in my heart. Such tight attitudes unfortunately drive away many from appreciating the teachings of Jesus.

I have as much reverence for Jesus, as for Dattatreya (the Christ of the Yogis), Buddha or Milarepa, Hui Hai or Lao Tzu, Ramana Maharshi or any other of the Great Sages of this earth, who bring light to my heart and mind. But as for practice, I do find that Hinduism offers a far wider variety of practical methods for the spiritual unfoldment of aspirants at all levels of development, than does Christianity. Even though there has always been a practical approach in Christian devotions also, this has been developed mainly among the Christian mystics and desert hermits, who fled from the 'Churchian' organisation of their faith to practice their devotions in the wilderness.

Although their philosophies have profoundly affected serious Christians, their practices have usually been of a contemplative nature, and considered too 'mystical' to find favour with the majority, even within the church or cloister itself. Most Christians seem to prefer to concentrate on 'good works' or *karma-yoga* as the equivalent concept is known in the Hindu faith. But the contemplative monks who became ecstatic visionaries and transcended the confines of their doctrine, always found that their experience had to be made to fit in with the existing theological canon, lest they be excommunicated and branded as heretics. There was no place for further evolution in the Churchly creed. And a living saint was mostly an embarrassment to the Churchian fraternity until after his or her death, when they could then be safely canonised (and their writings expurgated) being no longer in a position to rock the doctrinal boat.

THE WAKENING CHURCH

It was this kind of narrow pressure which prompted the celebrated Cistercian monk, Thomas Merton, to wryly remark (albeit with a twinkle in his eye): "The way the Christian faith is lived is so schizophrenic that it is a wonder that one can be at the same time a Christian and sane, that is, a Christian according to the approved pattern and forms."[1]

Happily, with the newly awakening spiritual forces in the world today, even the Church is removing its blinkers and opening its eyes to wider possibilities. It has begun to wonder why its churches are closing down at an alarming rate and to investigate what people are turning to as a more valid alternative. It will take a long time for this movement to filter down through the hard core conservative ranks. But at least it has begun, thanks to a few emerging 'New Age' Christian ministers with one foot in the Nave and the other outside in the fresh light of a newly dawning day. (And the sunrise is in the *East*).

Thus the Church is reviving older practices and 'new' ones are being adapted from Eastern sources. We begin to hear of seminars for 'Christian Yoga' and 'Zen and Christianity'. And as for Merton's 'schizophrenic' element, even Pastoral Counselling is undergoing a revolution. This is mainly due to the work of the late Dr Frank Lake and his associates, of the Clinical Theology Association in Nottingham, England (with whom I was privileged to work as a trainee therapist). This progressive group is bringing a Christianised form of psychotherapy to both the clergy and the laity. So from now on it will only be the most hidebound of Christians who will resist the tide of outside influences, encroaching upon what they mistakenly imagine to be the insular 'purity' of the religion they have adopted, or into which they just happen to have been born.

It always amuses (or saddens) me – according to my mood – when I come across the type of staunch Christian who has a horror of being contaminated by anything so 'pagan and primitive' as Eastern philosophy. Or – for that matter – by any other kind of religious thought from anywhere else in the world. This seems to me all the more short-sighted and extraordinary when – even after a cursory study of the scriptures of other lands – one can discover that the Bible is saturated with philosophical concepts from all over the East. It also contains quotations from many other earlier Middle Eastern scriptures and spiritual cults; the fertile soil from which the flower of Christianity grew. Innumerable scholars have noted a wealth of parallel ideas and teachings from Hindu and Buddhist sources, too numerous to go into here.

But in the *Gospel of John* for example, there appears to be at least one direct quotation from the ancient *Vedas* of India, which pre-date the Bible by – at the very least – a thousand years, and by many thousands more according to some authorities. In the famous opening lines of the Gospel According to John we read:

"In the beginning was the Word, and the Word was with God, and the Word was God.' (*John* 1:1).

Then in the Vedic scripture we find:

"In the beginning was Prajapati the Brahman (God the Creator), with whom was the Word, and the Word was verily the Supreme Brahman."

The construction of this phrase and the identical mystical concept can hardly have been a coincidence in the latter-day Bible. So John at least, had knowledge of the Hindu scriptures, as is evident from a close study of the rest of the mystical writings accredited to him. These arc totally different in tone to the rest of the Bible and expound Eastern mystical knowledge with a decidedly Gnostic flavour. Most authorities acknowledge that John's gospel is based on a far more solid and ancient mystical tradition than the other gospels. And if it is not taken directly from Eastern sources, *The Revelation of John* may have been based on mystical Egyptian or Greek cosmologies, such as *The Book of the Divine Pymander* (a Western 'Upanishad'), which combined Eastern and Egyptian thought with Greek wisdom.

As the numerous parallels between the essential Hindu and Buddhist scriptures and the teachings of the Bible have been so well elucidated and documented by other writers, let us look at some of the so-called 'alien' concepts which are anathema in the eyes of those devoted to the codified doctrine. Perhaps we may find that the seeming divergences are not so divergent after all, and that it is possible to bridge the gap so carefully widened by the Church Fathers.

GOD BY ANY OTHER NAME

But first I must confess that I am still a little chary of using the word 'God' as it has such an emotional charge for many people who have suffered at the hands of bigotted and die-hard religionists. And also because of the overtones of ownership of 'God' by Fundamentalists and other overly orthodox 'Keepers of the Faith'. I am reminded of a totally insensitive American Bible-thumper I encountered on a train in Iran. He was a loud-talking preacher from the southern States, who was all set to evangelise the superstitious 'heathen'. I asked him why he did not just leave them alone to worship in their own way, as they were already doing that in any case, getting off the train at every desert stop to do their ritual prostrations. He remonstrated heatedly with me, stating: "*Naw!* They are not worshipping *Gahd!*" (his accent was strong) – "They're worshipping *Allah!*"

"Oh come on!" I replied. "What is *Allah* except God by another name?"

"No, no!" he insisted, "Only *Gaahd* is Gaahd!"

I smiled: "Then unfortunately you and I must agree to differ; since I am trying to relate to 'God' and you worship *Gaahd,* which – according to your conception – evidently must be something else altogether." He got up and departed in a fit of Fundamentalist pique.

If the gentleman had taken the trouble to read the scriptures of the 'heathens' he was ready to convert – if only to understand their spiritual nature – he would have found, in the words of the Prophet Mohammed: "Do not argue with the people of The Book (the Bible) . . . and say, we believe in what was sent down to us and to you, and our God and your God is the same – is One." (*Koran,* Surat Al'Ankabut 46).

Those who so easily mouth the word 'God' are often those who have no inner relationship to that of which they speak. If they had, they would not speak so blithely, for real experience of the 'Glory' engenders a humbling awe in the soul. As a former Bishop of Woolwich, John Robinson, said in his book *Honest to God:* "I can at least understand what those mean who urge that we should do well to give up using the word 'God' for a generation, so impregnated has it become with a way of thinking we may have to discard if the Gospel is to signify anything."[2] I, too, feel apologetic in speaking of 'God' in mixed company, as the word seems to be specifically trade-marked *Christian*. I personally prefer to use the term *Omni-presence,* for that has been my experience of the nature of this wondrous mystery. However, when I am immersed in a Christian theme, I am perforce obliged to speak of *God,* just as I would speak of *Allah* among Muslims, *Brahman* among Hindus, or the *Great Spirit* among the Red Man.

THE DIVERGENT DOCTRINES

Perhaps the greatest doctrinal divergence between 'Christi-anity' and virtually all other spiritual traditions, is the 'Churchian' insistence that Man and God *are eternally separate entities*. Whereas in every other culture, in which people have not lost their roots in sophisticated civilisation, the knowledge that Man and the Absolute are One and indivisible is the underlying experience and teaching of the Sages, be they Sufi saints of the desert, Hindu gurus, Zen monks, or African witch-doctors. And I would include the Christian mystics among these. Their's also was the same unificatory experience. How could it be otherwise? And they too, taught that purifi-cation and perfection of the soul resulted in the spiritual fusion known as *At-one-ment,* or 'Oneness with God'.

But according to the canonical interpretation of the scrip-tures, this possibility is not conceptually available to the ortho-dox Christian, unless he or she transgresses the limits of doc-trinal understanding as so delineated. Without a doubt, it is this unfortunate misconception of the teachings – more than anything else – which has created the downhill slide in the credibility and the impoverishment of the Christian Church. Bringing the true teachings of the Christ back into Christianity could be its saving grace.

In the first three hundred years after Jesus, when the faith was propagated in many circles, more from heart to heart, than by the Church, the search for union with God was held to be the very basis of the practices of the diverse sects of Christian hermits who thronged to the desert communities throughout

Asia Minor and Egypt. In various ancient texts which have been unearthed in recent years, dating from this period, we can see that most ascetic Christians accepted that striving for this ideal was originally an integral part of the teachings. Just as the life of Jesus indicated. Why otherwise would he have suffered all the earthly trials and temptations just like any other man, if not to prove that it could be done?

In the Coptic Christian tractate known as *The Sentences of Sextius,* which was popular throughout the Middle East in Christian circles (being known in Latin, Armenian, Syrian and Georgian translations★), we have the assertion that: "A man who is worthy of God, he is a God among men, and he is the Son of God."[3] Thereby indicating that all worthy men should aspire to the same status.

MAKING LOVE WITH GOD

The mystical writings of the desert hermits reveal that this idea was current among them for at least a thousand years. And like all mystics of earlier times, they used the symbolic language of the mystery schools in their writings, speaking allegorically – as did Jesus – of the 'Bridegroom', which signified either 'God' or the 'prepared initiate'. The mystical term the 'Bridal Chamber' meant the 'Love of God in the Soul', and 'to have intercourse with the Bridegroom' meant 'to be in ecstatic union with God'. From this we can understand that there was no diffidence among the early Christians in attempting to achieve Oneness with God (which term is also synonymous with the real meaning of the Sanskrit word *yoga*).

In the ancient work, *The Divine Pymander* by Hermes Trismegistus, an Egyptian Priest-King, Arch-Magus and Alchemist (whose writings were engraved in the pyramids around 3,000 BC) we find the same vision:

"Man is a mighty wonder, for he passes into God's Nature, as though he himself were Divine. How happy is the blend of human nature. Joined to God by his resemblance to the Divinity . . .

Trismegistus: "But why does he who knows himself, pass into God?"

★ The oldest and most authentic version was found at Nag Hammadi in Egypt in 1945 and published in 1978.

Pymander: "Because the All-Father is Light and Life, whereof Man is made."

"If, then, thou learnest and believest thyself to be of Light and Life, thou shalt pass into (God's) Life.

"Thus spake the Shepherd of Men." (1.21).

"The Essential Man is the Cosmic or Universal Man, Who, because of Nous, [Supernal Reason, *Buddhi*, or Sunconsciousness] is one with the Supreme Lord. When man has overcome all that is below, he unfolds his latent powers and consciously enters the Universal Life."[4]

The author of these inspired words was deified as the Great God Thoth in Egypt and in Greece as the Greek God Hermes. His writings were enormously popular with practising Christians and the Founding Fathers of the Church, who liberally quoted from them for centuries. I would emphasise here the word *practising* Christians, as opposed to the merely intellectualising dry theologians of the city, who were those who later dogmatically asserted the 'impossibility' of such a union, and propounded its denial as canon law.

Yet every Christian mystic, from the beginning until the present day, who has enriched and deepened the faith with his or her writings, has always maintained to the contrary. The great German mystic, Meister Eckhart (AD 1260-1327) was a Christian preacher who boldly declared:

"God must be very I, I very God, so consummately one, that this he and this I are one 'is', in this is-ness working one work eternally; but so long as this he and this I, to wit, God and the soul, are not one single here, one single now, the I cannot work with, nor be one with that he."[5]

Naturally his experience and expression of the soul's Oneness with God was condemned by the Christian Inquisition. And things had not improved any a couple of centuries later. Some of the writings of the celebrated Spanish mystic, St John of the Cross (AD 1542-1591) were also suppressed by the Church because he based his whole teaching on the 'heretical' concept of gaining *experiential* union with God.

The intelligent person will realise, that whenever the Church suppresses something, or declares a mystic's writings to be heretical, we can be certain that they are extremely worth-while reading for the development of the soul. All through its sorry history, the Church has been known for its intolerance and persecution of many of the world's most noble souls and worthy philosophers. The attitude of Jesus seems not to have registered in the ecclesiastic consciousness. Even the persecution of the disciples and the early Church, seems to have left no impression among the business-mongering Bishops, regarding the injustice of religious persecution.

Even in our own day, although it is still doctrinally unacceptable, Christian contemplatives continue unobtrusively to seek that same mystical union, which constitutes the deepest craving of the human soul. In a posthumous work, the Cistercian contemplative, Thomas Merton expressed: "I have only one desire . . . to disappear into God, to disappear into his peace."[6] Perhaps it is for this reason, that towards the untimely end of his life he was veering towards Buddhism, and a milieu in which this was a supported and acceptable goal. Notwithstanding the fact that the word 'God' does not enter into Buddhist terminology (probably for Bishop John Robinson's reason), their concept of the 'Great Void' may – in its profoundest sense – be ultimately considered as 'God' by another 'no name'.

CHRISTIAN BHAKTI YOGA

But what is the need to look elsewhere, when the Way is expressly given in the Bible itself? The Apostle John says: "If we love one another, God dwelleth in us, and His love is perfected in us. Hereby know that we dwell in Him and He in us, because he hath given us of His Spirit . . . God is love and he who abides in love abides in Him." (*I John* 4:12-16). It could not be clearer. Only a nit-picking scribe with no spiritual experience, could fail to understand the obvious implication of unity here. Unless the human spirit is of one substance with God, this loving Oneness could not be possible. But in selfless love we are suffused with the Nature of God.

This practice John implores us to follow is equivalent to the pure *Bhakti Yoga* (or way of Loving Devotion to the Lord) of

Hinduism. By this method the devotee becomes so immersed in the love of the Divinity – as seen in everything and everyone – that ultimately this love merges into the Divine Love: thereby becoming One with that Love-which-*IS*-God.

The authority-dominated believer, however, is obliged to interpret such scripture as essentially implying separation, in spite of all the mystical testimony to the contrary. Whereas a mystic (or even layman) of any other tradition would immediately recognise it as true of that union which may be experienced by anyone who sufficiently stills his mind and penetrates to the deeps of his heart. And this is precisely what Christianity constantly exhorts us to do. The major command of the Old Testament is to "Be still, and know that I am God." We are enjoined to meditatively seek within, on the asssurance that we can come to know God: not with the mind but with the heart. Only in this way are we of the same essence. St Paul confirms the fact, stating: "He that is joined unto the Lord is One Spirit." (*Corinthians* 6:17).

Why then, should we be asked to make the effort, if it was considered impossible to become one with God? Of course, it never was. Even in the Old Testament we have accounts of the sages who achieved this union. We are told: "And Enoch walked with God, and he was not; for God took him." This does not mean that he died (or 'ascended') as some imagine, but that he was so transported, so totally God-identified that his own personality no longer existed. He had become *One with God*. Such a condition was expressed by the ancient writers as 'walking with God'. Noah was also exalted in this way, for we find: "Noah found grace in the eyes of the Lord . . . and Noah walked with God." (*Genesis* 6:8-9).

The pursuit of this capacity is also the essence of the Hindu scriptural teachings, which emphasise the fact that, in any case, we are already 'One with the Lord', if we did but know it. Yet it is only by the practical meditative methods of stripping away the veils of ignorance from the mind (or by *Bhakti Yoga*) that the experiential recognition of mystical union can be achieved. And it *has* been achieved by many sages – both *before* and *after* Jesus – since the beginning of the world. And it is still being attained by sincere seekers of every persuasion throughout the earth. This process is a natural law and will continue until the end of time.

The *Real*-isation of being One with God or Self, is the ultimate purpose of every individual existence.

Considering all the foregoing evidence, it would appear that the 'Churchian' interpretation of this experience, does not represent the actual *Christ*-ian standpoint. Jesus himself declares in the New Testament: "The Father is in me and I in the Father", and "The Father and I are One." (*I John* 10:30-38). Although the Church accepts this possibility for Jesus alone, it is heresy for anyone else to lay claim to it. Even though Jesus stated that anyone who really had faith could be equal to him in spiritual stature, saying: "He that believeth in me, the works that I do shall he do also; and greater works than these shall he do". (*I John* 14:12)

To be capable of doing 'greater works' than Jesus was able to do, implies that an aspirant must of necessity reach a level where he also 'walks with God' if he is to manifest equal, or greater, spiritual power. This is a point the Church Fathers tended to overlook in their deliberations, when they insisted on the uniqueness of Jesus as being the 'One and Only' Son of God for the rest of eternity. And one cannot help thinking that this is hard luck on the billions of souls who lived in the millennia before the birth of Christ, who had no chance to be 'saved', if reincarnation does not exist. It seems a pretty unfair kind of arrangement, or bad management on the part of the Almighty. However, according to his promises, Jesus evidently considered the way open for every other aspiring soul.

Perhaps when the theologians find this passage too discomforting, it will discreetly disappear from the Bible, as has been the fate of many other portions in the past which did not fit neatly into the canonical doctrine. Which brings us to that other notable old bogey – reincarnation.

REVISING REFERENCES TO REINCARNATION

Here is another spiritual concept which appears to be accepted by every other religion in the world, except Christianity. But this is only apparently so. For any Biblical historian with half an eye open, knows full well that Christianity *did* originally embrace the concept and that there were several references to it in the early compilations of the Bible. Reincarnation did not become a taboo subject until over three hundred years after the birth of Christianity. It was only then that the machinations of organised 'Churchianity' attempted to have all relevant passages excised from the scriptures and from the annals of Church history. The Books of Enoch, the Epistles of Barnabas, the Gospels of Thomas and Mark and many others became the so-called 'lost' books of the Bible. Fortunately certain other biblical passages were overlooked, which did not disappear into the hands of the Bishops or into the impenetrable archives of the Vatican. Nevertheless, the obvious references to reincarnation which still remain in the Bible are either glossed over, or even nowadays, being altered, and the historical evidences are assiduously ignored.

THE SLEEPING PROPHET

But before we investigate the more factual data, let us look at some of the extraordinary assertions of one of the most astounding clairvoyants of modern times – Edgar Cayce (1877-1945) of Virginia Beach, USA, whose biblical revelations are relevant to our inquiry. As a child Cayce began to realise his psychic capabilities when he discovered that by sleeping for a few minutes over his school books, he could 'photographically' remember every last word of his lessons. As he grew into a young man, he became mysteriously ill and was unable to speak in more than a whisper for a year or so. Eventually he lost his voice altogether and the doctors could do nothing.

At the suggestion of a hypnotist he put himself into an unconscious state, and was told that he could look inside himself. Responding to this suggestion, to the astonishment of his parents, in a clear voice he gave an exact medical diagnosis of his condition. He told them that it was a psychological state which could be cured by suggestion while in the unconscious condition. On awakening he knew that he could speak again.

This newly discovered ability ultimately led to many other people coming to him for psychic medical 'readings' as this phenomenon came to be known. Cayce would put himself into a 'sleep' and he would then be questioned as to the problem and cure of those who came to him. In the waking state he was a photographer, with no medical knowledge whatsoever. But clairvoyantly he was able to see into each person's problem, clinically describe it and prescribe a wide variety of remedies from nature cure to the very latest tongue-twisting name of a drug known only to the most up to date of doctors. Considering the fact that he was able to diagnose countless numbers of mysterious illnesses, and give accurate medical instruction for the ultimate cure of those cases given up by the doctors, we may afford his other more mind-stretching readings some measure of credibility.

After some twenty years of these medical readings, one Arthur Lammers, a student of philosophy and comparative religion, decided to ask him some out of the routine questions. The result was something of a calamitous shock to Cayce on awakening. He was told that he had given information relating to the questioner's previous lifetimes. As Cayce was brought up as a staunch Protestant Christian Fundamentalist (and remained one all his life) one can appreciate his horror at being the mouthpiece for such a 'non-Christian' heresy as reincarnation.

He was also a devout Sunday-school teacher, with no knowledge of anything metaphysical outside his fundamentalist beliefs. He feared that this new information must be the 'work of the devil'. It was therefore with great reluctance that he continued his psychic readings (for the sake of people in distress) and found that he became ill if he refused to help anyone. From hereon he entered a new phase of investigation, known as 'Life Readings', which considered the psychological problems of the questioner's present lifetime, as a result of events which occurred in previous lives.

In his role as the 'Sleeping Prophet' Cayce was able to give details of the previous incarnations of thousands of people, from any point in the earth's history, and on any part of the globe, including that of vanished continents such as Atlantis and Lemuria. Over the next twenty-two years, an impressive and corroborative body of information built up of insights into other lifetimes, the best part of which correlated and dovetailed into each other, no matter how many years had elapsed between questions on the same subject.

It was found that many people who came to Cayce in this period had previously had some contact with each other, in and around the time of Christ's ministry in the Holy Lands. The Readings on this particular subject have been gathered together in a remarkable book entitled, *Edgar Cayce's Story of Jesus*. The book is very hard going, as the language of the various 'sources' or 'entities' who speak through Cayce, is often archaic, and many replies to the questions are obscure. This would appear to be because of the difficulty of beings of another dimension and time-sense, to transpose these concepts easily into language which is understandable to the modern mind. However, other entities, perhaps closer to our time, come across clearly.

Because of such problems, when I first read this book sixteen years ago, it signified very little to me. But now, on re-reading it in the present – having walked in Galilee and studied the life of Jesus – it produced at times such a plunging of my being into the awesome mysteries of time and space, that I knew I was in the presence of something authentic. I still had certain reservations, however, as I perceived that the tone of many of the Readings was that of a committed Christian, as contrasted with that of a more universal source.

The reason for this became clear towards the end of the book, when we are told that Cayce himself had previously incarnated as one Lucius, of Greek-Roman parentage, who became Bishop of Laodicea (in what is now Turkey) during the first century after Christ. He was an associate of the disciple Peter, and also of Barnabas and of the apostle Paul, with whom he later strongly disagreed. This information was apparently withheld from Cayce for fourteen years after his first Life Reading, because – as one discarnate spokesman put it, through Cayce's own mouth – "*this lowly, weak, and unworthy channel*" might have become too 'puffed-up' as a consequence. But this declaration clarified the 'committed Christian' aspect for me, of many of the Readings. It would also explain his vast knowledge of the relationships between people of the period he had known – if what was happening was that Cayce was tapping the memories 'encapsulated' in his own 'soul-field'.

THE INCARNATIONS OF JESUS

At times, it is evident that Cayce was taken over by other far higher, and more forceful entities with different voices (although still of a distinctly Christian persuasion), who vouchsafed unthinkable revelations concerning the Christ, which were far beyond his own possible knowledge or imagining – even as Lucius. When one questioner asked the sleeping Cayce if he could gain perfection in one lifetime, so as not to return to this painful round of birth and death, he was sternly admonished: "Why should you expect to do in one lifetime what it took the Master thirty lives to attain?"[7]

This stunning remark was only a corroboration of many other hints and constant references in the readings, which attested to the fact that 'Jesus' had many former incarnations before his appearance as Jesus the Christ. Several of these incarnations had been referred to almost as casual asides, during the Life Readings of certain people over a twenty-year period. When pointedly asked which were the most important incarnations of Jesus in the world's history, the 'source' through Cayce replied, without hesitation:

"In the beginning, as Amilius, as Adam, as Melchizedek, as Zend, as Ur, as Asaph, as Jeshua–Joseph–(Joshua)–Jesus."[7]

At a later date, to the query as to whether Jesus had *actually* been the original *Adam,* the source responded:

Study the book which tells of Him, JESUS, born of the Virgin Mary; [Then] know this is the soul entity [Jeshua] who reasoned with those who returned from captivity, in those days when Nehemiah, Ezra, Zerubbabel, were factors in the attempts to re-establish the worship of God; and that [as] JESHUA, the scribe, translated the rest of his books written up to that time.

Then realise [also] that is the same entity who, as JOSHUA, was the mouthpiece of Moses, who gave the law; and was the same soul-entity who was born in Bethlehem. The same soul-entity who, in those periods of the strength and yet the weakness of Jacob in his love for Rachel, was their first-born, JOSEPH. As ZEND [father of Zoroaster] – this is the same entity. And this entity was that one who had manifested to Father Abraham as the prince, as Melchizedek, the priest of Salem, without father or mother, without days or years, but a living human being in flesh, made manifest in the earth from the desire of Father-God to prepare an escape for man; as was warned by the same entity, as ENOCH; or, as in those days of ASAPHA, or AFFA, in those periods when those of the Egyptian land were giving those counsels to the many nations, when there would be those saved of the physical from their own making [or doing] in the physical. Or, as the first begotten of the Father, who came as AMILIUS in the Atlantean land and allowed himself to be led into the ways of selfishness... And this was also the entity ADAM – and this was the Spirit of Light."[7]

Shocking as these revelations may be to some, as one continues to delve into their possible plausibility, many loose ends begin to tie up, which would otherwise have remained obscure. For example, in the light of this Reading, the assertion of Jesus that he existed before Abraham, now makes evident sense.

When the incredulous crowd was heckling Jesus for appearing to put himself above their Father Abraham, he told them: "Yet ye have not known him; but I know him, and keep his saying. Your Father Abraham rejoiced to see my day: and he saw it, and was glad." (*I John* 8:55-56) If it is a reality that Jesus once incarnated as the mysterious Melchizedek, as the Cayce oracle affirms, then this otherwise difficult-to-explain passage becomes immediately comprehensible.

It is extraordinary that orthodox Christians in the present day are equally incensed at the suggestion, as were the orthodox Jewry of the time, who were ready to stone Jesus for this 'blasphemy', saying: "Thou art not yet fifty years old and thou hast seen Abraham?" And Jesus replied to them: "Verily, verily, I say unto you, before Abraham was – I AM." (*I John* 8:58) In using the term 'I AM' of the Mosaic revelation, it is evident that he is here speaking mystically of his cosmic or everlasting existence, and not merely of a passing incarnation as at first.

This is perhaps clearer when we remember that 'Christ' is

not the *name* of Jesus, but a *title,* meaning 'the Anointed One' – which is endowed upon a soul which has become sufficiently purified to 'Walk with God' as a spiritual Son (or Daughter). *Christ* is not even an Aramaic or Hebrew word, but an Anglicisation of the Greek word *kristos.* The original Hebrew term is *maschiaX* ('Messiah') or more fully, *m'shia* x *yaweh* ('the Lord's Anointed'). It also has the subsidiary meaning of 'measured'. Thus one who is so 'Christed' has been 'measured' or tested and not found wanting, having attained to identificatory nature with God as the Universal I AM. And it is to this inner experience which Jesus refers. This understanding seems to have manifested in his soul – at least, to a certain extent – all down the ages. And Cayce is not the only oracle to have noted it.

THE AQUARIAN GOSPEL

Another American psychic, known as Levi,* who was born thirty-three years before Cayce, appears to have anticipated him by tuning in to the same 'universal' sources, when Cayce was still an infant. By 'cosmic coincidence' Levi was also a mediumistic Christian Sunday-school teacher, who later became renowned as the 'channel' for the New Age Bible known as *The Aquarian Gospel of Jesus the Christ.* Although this book seems to have been transcribed when Cayce must have been around seven years old, it appears not to have been published until after his death. Yet strangely enough, it covers some of the same ground as the Cayce Readings on Jesus, and confirms in advance the assertions that Cayce was later to make, regarding the former lives of the coming Christ.

In the words of the *Aquarian Gospel* Levi was given the command to: "Write the full story of the Christ . . . the Christ who men have known as Enoch the Initiate.

"And you may write the story of Melchizedek, the Christ who lived when Abram lived . . . who gave his life a willing sacrifice for men."[8]

It is remarkable that two mediums, unknown to each other, both within a similar time period, became channels for vir-

*Levi H. Dowling (1844-1911)

tually the same message, concerning the previous incarnations of Jesus. It seems that somebody 'upstairs' had deemed the time ripe for these ideas to begin filtering into the world consciousness. Naturally such slender evidences as these 'mystical speculations' cannot be expected to have any validity with hard-nosed critics (in which category I am obliged to include myself, as I do not accept easily the mouthings of mediums). But when their pronouncements overlap, and accord with reason and deep spiritual intuition, and corroborate other sources, without the possibility of deceit or trickery, then one has to begin to take them into more serious consideration.

Another source which identifies Jesus with Melchizidek is the Gnostic Christian tractate entitled *Melchizidek* (dating from around the early second century), which was unearthed at Nag Hammadi in Egypt, after the deaths of Cayce and Levi. In a revelatory discourse, Melchizidek inspirationally and almost ecstatically speaks of his crucifixion and disappearance from the tomb, apparently as Melchizidek-Jesus, High Priest of God. This same notion and similar references are to be found in many other early Christian documents, especially from Egypt. The association is even echoed in the Bible, where it is said of Jesus: "Thou art a priest forever, after the order of Melchizidek." (*Hebrews* 5:6, 10)

A STAR OUT OF JACOB

In the Old Testament we find a cryptic prophecy by Balaam the Seer, who had the vision of a mighty prophet and king of Israel, saying: "I see him but not now; I behold him but not near. A star shall come out of Jacob and a sceptre shall rise out of Israel." (*Numbers* 24:17) This was a favourite prophecy of the Messiah-seeking sect of Essenes, with whom Jesus is linked in the Cayce Readings. In the symbolic language of the seers, a 'star' meant prophet and 'sceptre' meant king. As these two symbols are linked, it appears to have indicated that Jacob would sire a 'kingly-prophet' or a 'prophet-king' as of old. In the event, he fathered the godly Joseph, of the 'coat of many colours' whose jealous brothers sold him into slavery in Egypt.

Joseph seems to have been a righteous and radiant being, of whom it was prophesied: "From thence is the Shepherd, the Stone of Israel." (*Genesis* 49:24) This famous image of the stone – the cornerstone which the builders rejected – as also the shepherd, star and sceptre, has always been esoterically applied to the Christ. Although Joseph did become a visionary prophet and counsellor to the Pharaoh, he did not reach 'Prophet-King' status. What then of the prophecy? All falls into place if we accept the Cayce Reading that Joseph was one of the incarnations of Jesus. Several modern researchers now concur that Jesus may well have been in the royal line of David, and thus would legitimately have had claim to the throne of Israel. Therefore the 'Prophet-King' may indeed have come through Jacob after all, if the future Jesus-to-be already existed in the developing soul of Joseph. And thus the prophecies all fuse together in one being.

REINCARNATION IN THE BIBLE

But there are more explicit references to reincarnation and reboundage (*karma*) in the Bible. That the concepts were commonly accepted by Jesus and the disciples is made evident in the passage concering the man who had been blind since birth. "And the disciples asked him, saying: 'Master, who did sin, this man, or his parents, that he was born blind?'" (*John* 9:2) It can be assumed that they were not thinking of him as sinning in the intermediary period before his conception, but were referring to his former life, as was natural to the spiritually inclined people of the time. This question could not have arisen if reincarnation had not been common knowledge.

Even among the general populace, it was a current notion. For after the beheading of John the Baptist, Herod the tetrarch became worried on hearing the rumours about Jesus: "...because it was said of some that John was risen from the dead; and of some that Elias had appeared; and of others that one of the old prophets was risen again." (*Luke* 9: 7-8) Such was the expectation of the times that people were anticipating the rebirth among them of the prophet Elijah (otherwise known as Elias), as was prophesied by Malachi the seer, in the Old Testament "Behold! I will send you Elijah the prophet before the great and dreadful day of the Lord! (*Malachi* 4:5).

The common word for the reincarnation, or 'rising' of a prophet in those days, was 'resurrection' – a concept condemned by the Sadducees,★ who tried to convince the people that there was no such thing as 'resurrection' (or reincarnation). As the Gospels consistently hammer the Sadducees, why else would they have included their antipathy to reincarnation, unless to pointedly hold them up to ridicule? And in any case, few believed the Sadducees since the more popular 'people's party' of religious sectarianism – the Pharisees – strongly upheld the teaching of reincarnation, in which the old scriptures had given them reason to believe.

As Job says in the Old Testament: "Naked came I out of my mother's womb and naked shall I return thither". (*Job* 1:21) Evidently he is not like Nicodemus – imagining himself as performing this feat as an old man. He is undoubtedly referring to the fact of entering the womb of his future mother in the next incarnation, as he has been proven unworthy of 'walking with God' and thus gaining freedom from the round of birth and death in this lifetime. Any other explanation is unsatisfactory.

In the gospel of Matthew, Jesus is found speaking to the crowd about John the Baptist. He is telling them that John is much more than a run of the mill prophet and emphasises the fact that he is the one of whom was written in the scriptures: "Behold, I send my messenger before thy face, who shall prepare thy way before thee." He further declares: "Verily I say unto you, among them that are born of women, there hath not risen a greater than John the Baptist . . . for all the prophets and the Law prophesied until John. And, if ye will receive it, this *is* Elias, which was for to come.

"He that hath ears to hear, let him hear!" (*Matthew* 11:10-15)

The implicit reference to reincarnation in this passage has caused much embarrassment to the propounders of the present doctrine. Therefore we find that modern revisionists, such as in the *New English Bible* and the *Phillips Bible,* for example, have modified this clear-cut statement of Jesus, to try and avoid its implication. Its original sense has been completely

★See *Matthew* 22:23.

altered by the insertion of single quotation marks around the name of 'Elijah'. Thus the current version now reads: " . . . and – if you can believe it – John himself is the 'Elijah' who must come before the kingdom." With this interpolation, it now gives the impression that Jesus only meant a prophet 'like' Elijah and not Elijah himself as originally stated. One can understand from this blatant modern example, how the rest of the Bible has been tampered with down the centuries.

But this pussy-footing around the issue is to little avail. For only a few passages later, Jesus reiterates the same pointed statement once again for the benefit of the disciples, who were not with him when he spoke to the people in the market-place. Just after they have witnessed his transfiguration on the mountainside, the disciples see a vision of Jesus standing with Moses and Elijah (Elias) as they appeared of old. To them this evidently meant the fulfilment of the Old Testament prophecy. Thus they were all agog; but Jesus warns them not to speak of this vision until after he has risen from the dead. And they are disappointed, saying:

"Why then say the scribes that Elias must first come? And Jesus answered and said unto them, Elias shall truly first come, and restore all things. But I say unto you, that Elias is come already, and they knew him not, but have done unto him whatever they listed. Likewise shall also the Son of Man suffer of them. Then the disciples understood that he spoke unto them of John the Baptist." (*Matthew* 17:10–13)

REINCARNATION AMONG THE EARLY CHRISTIANS

Another allusion to the acceptance of reincarnation among early Christians – this time from a non-biblical source – is the *Apocryphon of John,* which dates from the first or second century AD. This Gnostic treatise presents the teachings of the risen Christ (or is so written) in which Jesus gives a revelatory discourse to John the son of Zebedee on the development of souls. Giving the gist of the text, the biblical historian and translator, Frederik Wisse (of the Institute for Antiquity and Christianity) states: "Finally Christ is sent down to save humanity by reminding people of their heavenly origin. Only those who possess this knowledge and have lived ascetic lives can return to the realm of light; the others are reincarnated until they also come to saving knowledge."[2]

According to other contemporary historical documents, and the letters of early Christian Bishops, it is evident that this important scripture was a familiar reference work in the libraries of many of the Church Fathers. It is small wonder then that the Sadducees had a hard time of it in denouncing reincarnation, when it was so much a part and parcel of the consciousness of the Church Fathers, the Coptic and Gnostic Christians, the Pharisees, the Essenes, the Greeks, Persians, Egyptians and peoples of all the lands from Asia Minor to China.

In the *Encyclopaedia of World Religions,* we find the following:

St Jerome (340-420) said that reincarnation in a special sense was taught among the early Christians and was given an esoteric interpretation that was communicated to a select few. Origen (186-253) thought that only in the light of reincarnation could certain scriptural passages be explained. But it was condemned by the Second Council of Constantinople, convened by the Emperor Justinian in 553, and became for a time a heretical doctrine. "If anyone assert the fabulous pre-existence of souls," decreed the Council, "and shall submit to the monstrous doctrine that follows from it, let him be an anathema."[9]

The 'monstrous doctine' was of course, *karma* – or the Law of Cause and Effect – as taught by Jesus: "As ye sow, so shall ye reap." Reincarnation as the result of the rebound back into the 'soul-sphere' – of every negative thought, word or deed of its originator – was a concept accepted right through from Rome to the Far East, long before Christianity came along. And we have seen that it was acceptable to Jesus and the disciples and to the various groups of early Christians. It is also known that Jesus had a large core group of initiates to whom he gave the secret teachings. Some of these teachings must have been written down, but where have they disappeared to? The Vatican only knows.

It appears that the Emperor Justinian and the Empress Theodora were not at all pleased at the thought of having to pay for their sins in another lifetime and were the prime movers behind the Church Council of Constantinople, which resulted in having all references to reincarnation removed from the scriptures, five hundred and fifty-three years after Christ. Fortunately they overlooked the few scattered references which still remain as evidence for the perceptive reader. For the same reasons, the great Greek theologian, Origen, had also fallen foul of the authorities by this time, and his reincarnationist writings – which had been Christian holy writ for nigh on three hundred years – were denounced and removed from Churchly affiliations.

It is therefore evident that most of the 'foreign' Eastern concepts objected to by Christians are already extant in their own scriptures. And even if there were no traces of Indian thought left in the Bible, then Western Christians must realise they have still adopted something which is – at the very least – a 'foreign' *Middle Eastern* neo-Jewish religion. And one which was basically cultivated and structurally developed by Armenians, Arabs, Jews, Egyptians, Syrians, Turks, Greeks and Romans, long before it ever arrived in Britain. Why therefore, the fear of foreign teachings?

THE PAGAN SOURCES OF THE BIBLE

Anyone who has done a little research, is aware that the Bible is not a homogenous 'revelation of God', but an amalgam of Middle Eastern writings and Jewish scriptures compiled by a savant named Ezra and a large body of theological scholars. Many passages of course, *are* divinely inspired, but not necessarily from Christian sources. A complete chapter of the *Book of Proverbs*, for example, was copied word for word from the writings of the Egyptian sage Amenope. The whole of *Genesis* was taken from the mystical Jewish *Qabbalah* (as were many other portions of the Bible). Several books of the Old Testament are said to have been copied by Moses from Egyptian temple records.

Even the Ten Commandments were not original to him, and the whole thing was evidently set up to impress the unruly Hebrew tribes. It is now known that the Commandments come from the Code of King Hammurabi of Mesapotamia, who lived four hundred years earlier than Moses, and whose engraved stone has been found, showing the King receiving direct from the hand of God, the tablets on which the Commandments were inscribed. Many other portions of the Bible were garnered from non-Christian anchorites, latter-day Christian laymen and various spiritual cults from all over Egypt and Asia.

It was put together in Aramaic, and mainly in the Greek-based hybrid language of the Mediterranean, the lingua franca of that period, known as *koine* (pronounced *koy-nay:* the 'Common Tongue'). It was said to be poorly translated into Hebrew and thence from one language to another, being later transposed into Greek and then Latin. In every language it inevitably lost nuance and exactitude according to the translator's lack of acquaintance with the mystical and symbolic language used by the original seers. And eventually we find it today in a multitude of differing 'authorised' versions in English, each interpreted according to the particular branch of Christianity which publishes it.

Taking all these factors into account, the orthodox Christian has no reason whatsoever for his disdain of 'foreign thoughts' and his attitude of '*my* religion is purer and holier than thine'. On the contrary, like many more aware and intelligent Christians today, he would do well to study the history of Christianity and the original scriptures of the East and Middle East from which much of the material was derived. Even the greatly revered Christian theologians, such as St Augustine and St Thomas Aquinas, openly acknowledged that much of their insightful and presumed 'Christian' writings, were actually plundered from the thoughts of the 'pagan' Greek philosophers such as Plato, Aristotle, Plotinus and the neo-Platonists.

All of these exceptional God-inspired philosophers were believers in reincarnation. And they in turn, had been mightily inspired and influenced by Eastern philosophy. Any thinking person might pause to wonder why it is that the greatest intellects this planet can boast, throughout history have all embraced reincarnation as the only plausible explanation of the mystery of life and death. The great *rishis,* or seers, of

India, were renowned for experiencing past incarnations in deep meditation. Thus it was the aspiration of many a Greek seeker and philosopher to go and study in India, which was considered as the fontspring of spiritual philosophy. There was a constant coming and going of pilgrims along the famous trade route from Byzantium to Benares. And it was not unusual for Hindu traders, scholars and priests to travel from India to Greece, at the invitation of their Greek hosts.

ST BUDDHA OF CHRISTIANITY

It is also recorded history that in 250 BC, the Buddhist Emperor Ashoka sent streams of missionary monks (known as 'Officers of Righteousness') through Afghanistan, Persia, Macedonia, Syria and the Holy Lands, and even to the Pythagoreans in Greece.[10] They also taught their tenets in the Courts of Egypt. And these Buddhists are believed to have been the first to develop monastic communities in the Holy Lands, having founded a monastery in Judea on the west bank of the Dead Sea. This is considered by some to be the same site as the later community of the breakaway Jewish sect, the *Sons of Zadok,* better known to others as the *Essenes of Qumran.* It is interesting to note that the mysterious and unknown founder of the Essenes was known by the Buddhist term 'The Teacher of Righteousness'. As Buddhist influence permeated the Mediterranean area long before the birth of Jesus, this could be a contributory factor to the Buddhist parallels found in Christian scriptures.

But evidently there were closer links, which Church history has erased from the common mind. For it is a remarkable and little-known fact, that Saint Gautama the Buddha was listed in the *Martyrologium* (the Register of Christian Saints), and was thus revered as a Christian Saint, right up until the twelfth century! Why was this? What was the connection between Jesus and the Buddha? We have yet to uncover the hidden details. But we can understand that there has always been a great deal of interplay between the great religions and, where possible, the mystic Masters of those faiths.

The Truth is always the same, but comes dressed in different garb and speaks through different bodies in words to suit the times. It is only the priesthood and the dry theologians and their equally dry followers, who have ever sought to destroy spiritual freedom and the openness to other faiths, and to fix the interpretive limits of their own scriptures, according to their lack of mystical comprehension.

THE LOST YEARS

Now we come to the mystery of the so-called 'Lost Years' of Jesus's life, which would seem to be deliberately missing from the Bible. We have the account of his miraculous birth, the flight from Palestine, and the years spent in Egypt as an infant; his return to Galilee and the later enlightening oratory in the Temple of Jerusalem, at the age of thirteen, when he so astounded the priests and elders with his wisdom. This child prodigy would have been the talk of the town. But suddenly – from here on – nothing. There is a total blank and mysterious silence in the Bible, regarding the next eighteen years of his life. We hear no more of him until the age of thirty, or thirty-one. Where was he all this time? What was he doing? And why this conspiracy of silence?

Some suggest that Jesus was 'just working with his father as a carpenter' all that time. But this is an untenable supposition in the face of the spiritual power he was manifesting at such an early age, and considering the portentous events surrounding his birth. If we are to accept that he was conceived of a virgin, and that an angel spoke to Mary and then to Joseph, at the conception of Jesus, telling them that their future son was destined to become the Saviour of Mankind; can we believe that they would just have left things at that and have allowed him to spend the next eighteen years simply doing carpentry on building sites?

Evidently all kinds of seers, priests and astrologers would have been consulted to clarify these events. Jesus would have had to undergo training to prepare him for his coming ministry, as foretold. And was it just by sheer chance that Mary (or, more correctly, *Miriam*) was chosen as a worthy mother for the conception of the Lord? Again the mediums

Cayce and Levi both concur (as do some modern historians) that Joseph and Mary were members of the sect of Essenes – the Sons of Zadok (the high priest of the House of David). The spiritually purist and ascetic Essenes were imminently expecting the coming of the Messiah into their midst. Miriam is said to have been one among twelve other temple girls, who were specifically trained in purity so as to become fit vehicles for the coming Christ.

Then, just after his birth, there are said to have been kings and wise men from the East, who came to worship the infant Jesus (*Jehoshua* – or *Jeshua ben Joseph,* as he was more properly known in the Hebraic language). Yet it is only in the gospel according to Matthew where a visit from an unspecified number of 'wise men' is mentioned, without further particulars. But in the popular imagination these travellers have developed into either three *Magi* (the Magians were occultist-astrologers of the Persian priesthood), or the three *kings* as named in modern Christmas carols; or confusedly, as both. As one of the kings is popularly supposed to have been black, he could not have come from the East (unless he was a particularly dark Dravidian from India).

Most modern scholars do not give much credibility to this story. Considering the fact that a great many earlier prominent figures in Eastern history were also held to have had their births attended by moving stars, virginal conceptions and visits by kings – in the myth-making tradition of the times – many now see the visit of the 'three wise men' as a wholly fictitious event. However, if the Essene intention of cultivating a Messiah from scratch is shown to be valid – as scriptural (via the Dead Sea Scrolls) and psychic evidence seems to indicate – then the propagators of this possibility would doubtless not have passed up the chance to let their influential sympathisers in high circles know of the advent of the chosen birth.

If this was so, once the word was out, there could well have been wise men coming from near and far. If we can give credence to either story, then obviously these princely contacts would not have been easily lost, and it would appear that royal patronage was available to the family of the 'Prophet' from many lands. Given the sincere interest in the child's welfare, invitations to visit their domains would naturally have been extended to Jesus and his parents. The community of Essenes would also have done their utmost to create and maintain a supportive network among such a high-ranking following.

THE MYSTERY SCHOOLS OF EGYPT

According to the Cayce Readings, when Miriam and Joseph were obliged to flee from the edict of Herod,★ they fled to Egypt with an entourage of Essenes, on the advice of the Prophetess Judy – one of the leaders of the Essenes at the time – from whom Jesus was later to learn the prophecies and the schema of his life. The Essenes were naturally anxious to protect the Messiah they had so ardently planned and prepared for, and the family was evidently taken to their sister community near Alexandria. "The period of sojourn in Egypt was in and about, or close to, what was then Alexandria,"[7] said the Cayce oracle. It has since been discovered that an Essene community was in actual existence near Alexandria at that time.

During my own sojourn in Egypt (in 1964), I came across references to Jesus as an adolescent having spent time in the mystery schools, notably at the Temple of Heliopolis in the Valley of the Nile. As Egypt was the central cradle of the sacred secrets of the world, it would have been natural for him to have returned to continue his studies there, after his childhood instruction under the Essenes. As his parents had lived there for several years they would have had many friends and contacts in that land.

Many years later, I was very moved when I found that the Cayce Readings corroborated my findings in the Egyptian documents. Both he and Levi maintain that Jesus *and* John the Baptist both studied in the mystery schools there. Cayce says they were both at Heliopolis (but in different classes) and Levi also mentions that John was at the Temple of Sakara (Saqquarah) – which was only a few miles away, on the opposite

★ There is no historical evidence whatsoever for this popular Bible story, although all the other unpleasant exploits of Herod have been judiciously chronicled.

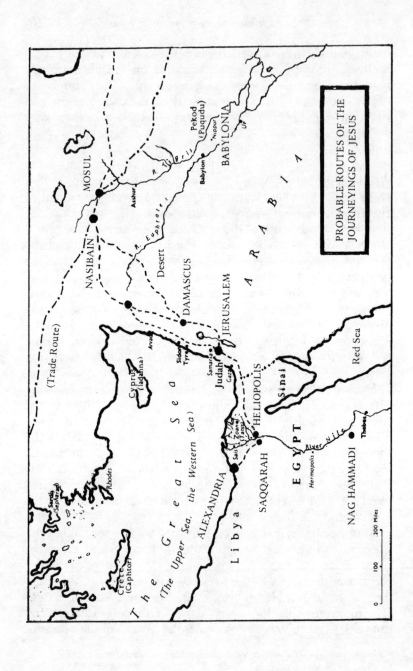

PROBABLE ROUTES OF THE
JOURNEYINGS OF JESUS

bank of the Nile – and that Jesus studied at *Heliopolis*. The 'cosmic coincidences' abound!

In his spiritual studies in Egypt, Jesus was undoubtedly preparing himself for his future journeys, learning the secret code words and teachings which would gain him acceptance into other esoteric circles of the East. As it was then, so it is still today, that masters send their students to various mystery schools or specific teachers, throughout the Middle East, for the development of different inner and outer skills. I have experienced this practice myself. After being accepted by the Head of the Whirling Dervishes in Turkey, I was sent along a chain of Sufi teachers (one of whom was a Prince and another a High Court Judge) until I reached Afghanistan. And there, evidently my merit ran out, as no further contacts were forthcoming.

After a year or two in Egypt, Jesus is said to have returned to Palestine when still in his early teens. He stayed only for a short time with his family, before he was sent on further travels by Judy the Seer, so that he might perfect himself in many ways and come to know the scriptures and the hearts of men in many lands. Cayce says: "His studies in Persia, India and Egypt covered much greater periods" (than those in Palestine). Another Reading says he was sent out to learn the secrets "related to those cleansings of the body in preparation for the strength of the physical as well as in the mental man."[7] These practices would be those internal cleansing processes known as *kriyas* or *śatkarmas,* known only to the advanced yogis of India; some of which practices were done preparatory to entering into a state of suspended animation.

PREACHING IN PERSIA

When first setting off on his journey to the East, it seems that Jesus travelled northwards through Syria, towards Nasibain (Nusaybin) and Mosul, on the edge of Persia, where the road joined the southern trade route to India. His passage there was recorded in the well-known Persian history book, the *Rauzat-us-Safa,* from which the following translation has been extracted:

Jesus (on whom be peace) was named the 'Messiah' because he was a great traveller . . . he used to wander from country to country and from city to city. At nightfall he would stay where he was. He ate jungle vegetables and drank jungle water; and he went on his travels on foot. His companions, on one of his travels, once bought a horse for him; he rode the horse for one day, but as he could not make any provision for the feeding of the horse, he returned it.

Journeying from his country, he arrived at Nasibain, which was at a distance of several hundred miles from his home. With him were a few of his disciples whom he sent into the city to preach. In the city, however, there were current wrong and unfounded rumours about Jesus (on whom be peace) and his mother. The governor of the city, therefore arrested the disciples and then summoned Jesus. Jesus miraculously healed some persons and exhibited other miracles. The king of the territory of Nasibain, therefore, with all his armies and his people, became a follower of his.

This is evidently not a contemporary work, but based on hearsay, for the author goes on to ascribe some unbelievable miracles to Jesus, which properly belong to the realm of oriental fantasy. But the kernel of the story rings true. There are doubtless many other Arabic works recording the travels of Jesus which have yet to come to light. One of the meanings of 'Messiah' or *Masshi* in Arabic, is 'traveller' from the root *Siahat* – travelling. The great Arabic lexicon, *Lisanul-Arab*, states: "*Isa* (Jesus) has been named 'Masih' because he was a traveller. He would not settle at any place." It is for this reason that many Middle Eastern histories and books of antiquity, refer to Jesus in passing, as *Isa* – Chief of Travellers.'[11]

The Cayce Readings state that wherever Jesus went, he was registered under the name of *Jeshua*. As this was pronounced *Yeshua* in Hebrew, it can readily be seen how in other tongues, this became Yesu, Yasu, Yusuf, Iesus, Issa and Isa. Not to mention *Jesus* as a Westernisation of his Jewish name; perhaps to avoid the impression of worshipping a Jewish prophet?

It would seem that Jesus the Traveller was always accompanied by a small entourage of stalwart disciples (and probably Essene guardians) so that despite the rigours of the road – the fly-blown, flea-bitten camel caravans and dusty, desert trade route to the East – travelling under the patronage and hospitality of kings and other influential contacts, may not have made the journey to India as arduous as supposed.

TESTIMONY OF TODAY

Many sages, mystics and visionary masters of India still speak of Jesus having spent time in the Himalayas to pursue his inner studies. A modern 'Man of Miracles', the remarkable Satya Sai Baba of Putthaparthi, in southern India, who has been compared with Christ himself, and who has been seen to perform miracles (such as healing the sick and producing objects from thin air) in front of thousands of people, says of Jesus:

Like most seekers, he searched for the Divine in the objective world, in nature, but he soon realised that nature is a kaleidoscopic picture, created by one's own imagination, and sought God within himself. Here, his stay in the Himalayan monasteries, in Kashmir and other centres of Eastern asceticism and philosophical enquiry, brought him greater success. From the attitude of being a Messenger of God, he declared that he was the Son of God, after returning from the East. [12]

HIS JOURNEYS IN THE EAST

The *Aquarian Gospel* asserts that Jesus was invited to the state of Orissa, in India, by one Prince Ravanna, who had visited his family in Nazareth. There Jesus was received into the Temple of Jagannath, where, for four years, he studied the *Vedic* scriptures and the *Laws of Manu*. Because of his popularity in teaching the lower caste Hindus, he aroused the animosity of the Brahmin priesthood, who hired an assassin to murder him. But he was forewarned and made his escape by night to Benares. There he remained under a master for a while, before going on to Nepal, and eventually journeying to Lhasa in Tibet, where he studied the ancient Buddhist texts. He is said not to have taught there, but returned to the kingdom of Ladakh (or Little Tibet) on the border of India, where he lived in the Himis monastery of Leh for some time, and there taught and ministered to the people of the town below.

According to my perceptual sensibilities, I find certain parts of the *Aquarian Gospel* to be somewhat artificial and contrived, and therefore I do not accord it the same authenticity as I find in most of the Cayce Readings. However, though some of the minor details do not ring true at times, the bare bones of the narrative appear to hold veracity.

Probable routes of the journeys of Jesus in India, Nepal and Tibet, according to the **Issa Manuscript** and other sources.

THE MANUSCRIPT OF LEH

For example, in 1887, a Russian traveller by the name of Nicholas Notovich, who had heard of a rumour about the existence of a manuscript in the monastery of Leh, pertaining to Jesus, spent the night there with a party of travellers. But the monks, like the people of those regions, were extremely touchy about revealing their history or sacred scriptures to foreigners, and so he let the matter lie.

But the hand of God decided otherwise. Next morning, as

the party left, Notovich's horse stumbled and threw him off. The fall fractured his leg and he was obliged to be carried back to the monastery to convalesce. The fracture brought on a fever and he was forced to remain at Himis (or Hemis) monastery for some time. As he recovered, he gained the confidence of the Buddhist monks and was able to broach the subject of the manuscript. A monk who could speak French, obligingly ferreted out the ancient text, and Notovich transcribed the whole of it as the Tibetan lama translated. One section of the manuscript gave a brief account of Moses (as *Mossa*) and the Exodus from Egypt, and the rest gave a piecemeal account of the life and travels of Jesus (written as *Issa*), but without any order to the text.

Notovich rearranged the writings in sequential order, from birth to death, without altering any of the textual facts. The story thus unfolded, gave new knowledge regarding the life and 'Lost Years' of Jesus. It also gives another logical explanation as to the timing of his leaving home and family at such an early age. The text states:

When Issa was thirteen years old, the age at which an Israelite is expected to marry, the modest house of his industrious parents became a meeting-place of the rich and illustrious, who were anxious to have as a son-in-law the young Issa, who was already celebrated for the edifying discourses he made in the name of the All-Powerful.

Then Issa secretly absented himself from his father's house; left Jerusalem, and, in a train of merchants, journeyed towards the Sindh.

In his fourteenth year, young Issa, the Blessed One, came this side of the Sindh and settled among the Aryas, in the country beloved by God. [13]

The manuscript goes on to say that the name and fame of Jesus spread far and wide in India. At first he stayed awhile among the *'Djaines'* (Jains) in Radjipoutan (Rajasthan: just inside India's present north-west border), before travelling on across the plains to *Orissa,* where he spent the next six years at the *Temple of Djagguernat* (Jaggernath), studying the *Vedas* with the *Brahmins,* and learning to cure people of physical and spiritual ills. But the jealous priests there 'resolved upon his death' and he 'left by night Djaggernat' and fled to Napaul

(Nepal) where he learned the *Pali* language and studied the Buddhist *Sutras*.

"After six years of study, Issa, whom the Buddha had elected to spread his holy word, could perfectly expound the sacred scrolls."

This would doubtless explain the many similarities which scholars have found in the teachings of Jesus and the Buddha. But Jesus was a Hebrew through and through. As he was so profoundly trained in the Hebrew scriptures as a child, and was so well versed in the books of the prophets, although he may have appreciated the Buddhist teachings, he was not to be swayed by them. He knew his role and purpose as the Messiah of Israel. Therefore his teachings may have become only lightly coloured by immersion in the Buddhist way of thought; as the similarities seem to show. And conversely, Buddhism may also have gained from the exchange, as it appears to contain many elements of what might be considered Christian ways and thoughts; although parallel teachings may be seen in any scriptures declaring the same truths.

In ancient Buddhist texts, it was given that the Buddha prophesied the coming of a 'Messiah' among his people, known as *Bhagwa Metteya (Maitreya)*. Some read *Bhagwa* as meaning 'Godly' or 'white' (or signifying 'fair-skinned', as was Jesus to the Tibetans). And *'Mettya'* again is taken to be 'traveller' among Sufis. When pronounced with a soft *'t'* or a lisped *'th'*, as in those regions, *'Metthaya'* becomes strikingly like *'Messiah'*. It would seem that the whole of the Eastern world was also awaiting the advent of another Master Soul. Small wonder, then, that 'wise men from afar' converged upon the Holy Lands at an astrologically predicted time. If so it was, and we can credit the signs and wonders of the birth.

CHRISTIAN-BUDDHIST CONFLUENCE

Some of the first Christian evangelists to penetrate into Tibet, were Friar Oderic in AD 1328, who reported seeing Buddhist priests performing miracles like those of Christ; and later, in AD 1661, the Jesuit Fathers, Greuber and Dorville, who were forcibly struck by the similarity to Christianity of the doctrine and ritual among Buddhists. They observed that the disciplines and dress of the different orders of monasticism bore a marked resemblance to that of the Romish Church; that the notion of an incarnation and a virgin birth was common to both, as also was the belief in paradise and purgatory; that the almsgiving, penance, vows and giving of absolution and use of holy water by the priests, was the same; and that the Superior Lamas wore costumes in perfect similarity to the different orders of the Romish hierarchy.

"These early missionaries further were led to conclude from what they saw and heard, that the ancient books of the Lamas contained traces of Christian religion, which must, they thought, have been preached in Tibet in the time of the Apostles."[14]

There are also Buddhist manuscripts of antiquity from China, which make mention of *Mi-Shi-Hu* (or Messiah) having been in Tibet,[15] according to the accounts of Chinese travellers; which adds a little more credence to the valuable discovery of Nicholas Notovich in Little Tibet. About the *Issa Manuscript* itself, Notovich wrote:

The two manuscripts, from which the lama of the monastery at Himis read to me all that had bearing upon Jesus, are compilations from divers copies written in the Tibetan language, translations of scrolls belonging to the library at Lhasa and brought, about two hundred years after Christ, from India, Nepal and Magadha, to a convent on Mount Marbour, near the city of Lhasa.

These scrolls were written in Pali . . . The manuscripts relate to us, first of all, according to the accounts given by merchants arriving from Judea in the same year when the death of Jesus occurred; that a just man, by the name of Issa, an Israelite, in spite of his being acquitted twice by the judges as being a man of God, was nevertheless put to death by the order of the Pagan Governor Pilate, who feared that he might take advantage of his great popularity to re-establish the kingdom of Israel and expel from the country its conquerors.[13]

A CONSPIRACY OF SILENCE

The then Governor of Ladakh, Pandit Surajbla Manphal, and various British dignitaries encouraged Notovich to publicise his findings. But when he returned to Europe and approached Christian authorities with his discovery, he was met with a stony wall of indifference or sheer disbelief. He writes: "I offered to return to Tibet in the company of recognised Orientalists to verify the authenticity of these passages on the spot. No one responded to the proposal." Therefore, in 1888, he went specifically to Rome and showed the manuscript to a Cardinal close to the Pope, who told him:

"What would be the good of publicising this? No one will attach much importance to it, and you will make yourself a crowd of enemies. However, you are very young! If it be a question of money which interests you, I might ask that a reward be made to you for your notes . . ."

After this rebuff, Notovich went to Paris, to see a Cardinal Rotelli, who responded in a like manner, saying:

"The Church already suffers too much from the new wave of atheistical thought; you will only give fresh pastures to the detractors and calumnators of the evangelical doctrine. I tell you this is in the interest of all the Christian Churches."

But Notovich was not to be bought off, or put off, by this ecclesiastical obstructiveness. Eventually he published the complete text of the *Issa Manuscript* and the details of its discovery, both in French and in English in 1894. He concluded:

"*The Unknown Life of Jesus Christ* is no novelty to the Roman Church, in that the Vatican library possesses sixty-three complete, or incomplete manuscripts in oriental languages referring to this matter, which have been brought to Rome by missionaries from India, China, Egypt and Arabia."[13]

The Christian archivist and scholar, Edmund Szekely, who worked in the Vatican has published *The Secret Gospel of Thomas,* which he discovered in his researches there. He also asserts that the Vatican archives contain a great deal of unpublished information pertaining to the true story of Jesus; information which – if it were known – some scholars consider, might well destroy Christianity as presently conceived and believed. Even the all-seeing eye of the Cayce oracle states in the Readings, that the true records of the Gospels "may be determined by investigations of the records related to the same . . . in the Vatican's own libraries."[7]

Thus it was that despite his sincere efforts to authenticate his discovery, Notovich was believed by very few and his book caused but little stir. Many Christians doubted that the manuscript ever existed, otherwise, surely it would have been verified by others? In fact, it was. After reading *The Unknown Life,* one Swami Abhedananda, of the Ramakrishna Mission in Calcutta (and a colleague of Thomas Edison, Max Müller and William James), set off for Himis monastery from Calcutta in 1922, to see for himself, being very sceptical of Notovich's claims. To his surprise, he found the scrolls in question, and, being fluent in the Pali language, was able to make his own direct translation. He later published his findings in his Bengali book of travels, *Kashmiri O Tibetti.*[12]

Another Russian professor and artist, Nicholas Roerich, also visited the monastery in 1925 and published his account of the manuscript, which was no better received than that of Notovich, for the common mind was still unripe for such an awakening.

THE JESUS DOCUMENT ON REINCARNATION

Colonel James Churchward, an English anthropographist, who spent his whole life combing the world for details of lost continents, seems to have independently come across the *Issa Manuscript* at Leh, somewhere around the same time as Notovich, either before or not long after him. He wrote:

A record in the Hemis monastery at Leh, Kashmir, written in Pali, is without question not an original, but a copy and not many hundreds of years old. This one states that "when Jesus left his home country, he first went to Egypt, and there for two years studied the ancient Osirian religion. From Egypt he went to India and in many cities, including Benares and Lahore, he studied the teachings of Gautama Buddha. After this he entered a Himalayan monastery, where for twelve years he studied the Sacred Inspired Writings of *Mu,* the Motherland, and her Cosmic Sciences. At the end of twelve years he became a master.

In another monastery I find a record stating that: "Jesus became the most proficient master that has ever been on earth." Today the name of Jesus is more revered in this monastery than by any sect of Christian priesthood, simply because these old monks knew him better. In addition to this record I found that they had a legend about

Jesus. The head of the monastery told me that for a long time this legend was oral only. Then to prevent it being forgotten or altered, it was written down about 1800 or 1900 years ago. This writing now runs:

"When Jesus was about to leave the monastery, a controversy arose between him and the masters on the subject of reincarnation. Jesus maintained that the Sacred Inspired Writings of the Motherland stated: 'that it was *not* the *material* body of man that was reincarnated out of the original atoms that formed his previous material body, but the *Soul* or *Spirit only* that was reincarnated.' The masters maintained that it was *both* the soul *and* the previous material body that was reincarnated, and that the identical atoms of the old body were used over again in the new (succeeding one)."

Through the courtesy of the head of the monastery, and as a special favour and compliment, I was allowed to see and examine the tablets over which the controversy arose. I deciphered and translated them. They read: "The material body returns to mother earth from whence it came. The elements are then used to form other bodies."[16]

MYSTERIOUS DISAPPEARANCE

It had been my intention, during my three years' pilgrimage in India, to go to the Himis monastery myself. But at that time (1972-5) Ladakh was forbidden to foreigners. The order to open up the area again was actually given in 1974, but written authority did not reach the District Commissioners until 1975, just after I had left the country. However, I sent friends and students there on my behalf, to verify the facts. But they were told that the manuscript had long since disappeared, and no one knows – or will say – whether it was purposely removed, sold or stolen. Sometimes the monks deny all knowledge of it, being no doubt tired of the streams of curious modern enquirers.

But it is reported that there are many rooms crammed full from floor to ceiling with ancient musty old manuscripts, the contents of which "even the monks don't know". However, in 1975, the Head Lama proposed that if any dedicated scholar is prepared to spend several years at the monastery, learning classical Tibetan, then the archives will be made available to him.[12]

JESUS RETURNS TO ISRAEL

When Jesus turned again towards his homeland, the *Aquarian Gospel* states that he joined a caravan of merchantmen in Kashmir Vale, to whom he had preached while at the monastery of Leh. With them he travelled back to Persia, where again he stayed and studied (as Cayce also confirms) and taught; and harangued the priesthood for preaching falsities to the people. And once again, the priests conspired against him, but instead of putting him to death, they had him hustled out of town in the dead of night and sent upon the desert road.

The Cayce Readings say that Jesus was recalled from Persia on the death of his father, Joseph, (although Levi says he heard of it in India). But either way, it would appear that contact was fairly constant with his home, and his abiding places stable enough for messengers to come and go.

The *Issa Manuscript* maintains that: *"Issa . . . was twenty-nine years old when he arrived in the land of Israel."* But after visiting his family (and doubtless the Essenes) he journeyed on again to Egypt (as Cayce and Levi both affirm), there to be assessed by the Egyptian hierophants and initiatory masters of his youth. He was also to complete his knowledge of: *"the after actions of the crucifying of self in relationship to ideals, and (which) made for the abilities of carrying on that called to be done."*[7]

This would bring us to the thirty years of age at which Jesus is popularly supposed to have begun his ministry in his native land. Levi maintains that Jesus also first went to Greece (in a highly suspect chapter to my sensibilities). But when the sleeping Cayce was asked if Jesus ever went to Greece when he was rejected by his own people, the answer came: *"We do not find such. Jesus – as Jesus, never appealed to the worldly wise."*[7] Which prompts us to wonder, if not as *Jesus –* then Jesus as *who? –* in which incarnation, did he appeal to intellectuals? Was he one of the great Greek philosophers?

THE CRUCIFIXION CONTROVERSY

Although we are unable to further validate our findings – no more than it is possible to verify the confusingly disparate testimonies of the so-called 'synoptic' Gospels – I feel we have assembled a reasonable reconstruction of the movements of Jesus during the years about which the Bible is silent. And now we come to the most controversial consideration of all – the crucifixion. Throughout the Middle East and further East, it is widely believed that the life of Jesus did not end on the cross, nor at the supposed 'Ascension'.

It is commonly accepted among many of the Masters of India and in Oriental scholastic circles that Jesus survived the ordeal of the crucifixion and made his way quietly back to India, where he lived peacefully until the end of his very long life. The renowned spiritual philosopher, Swami Rama Thirtha wrote:

You know, Christ did not die when he was crucified. This is a fact which may be proved. He was in a state called *samadhi,* a state where all the life functions stop, where the pulse beats not, where the blood apparently leaves the veins, where all signs of life are no more; when the body is, as it were, crucified. Christ threw himself into that state for three days, and like a *yogi,* came to life again and made his escape and came back to live in Kashmir. Rama [he is here speaking of himself] had been there and found many signs of Christ having lived there . . .

There are many places called by his name, places where Christians never came, and many cities called by the same name as the cities of Jerusalem [Palestine] through which Christ passed. There is a grave there of 2,000 years' standing. It is held very sacred and called the grave of *Esah,* which is the name of Christ in Hindustani language, and *Esah* means prince, so there are many reasons to prove that he came to India, the same India where he learned his teachings.

Again the people of India have a kind of magic ointment, which is called the Christ Ointment, and the story which the people who prepare this ointment tell, is that this ointment Christ used to heal his wounds with after he came back to life; and that ointment really heals all sorts of wounds miraculously." [17]

I will not go here into all the details of the crucifixion, of which I am aware, which can support these assertions of the Swami, but in essence, I believe them to be true. The practices which Jesus learned among the yogis would have well fitted him to enter into a state of suspended animation, simulating death upon the cross; although some modern researchers [18] [19] are now of the opinion that the proffered 'vinegar-wine' on a stick which was pushed into the face of Jesus, was drugged, thereby allowing him to fall into an unconscious state immediately afterwards: whereas normally such a pungent odour served to revive a flagging prisoner.

Normally it took a week or even longer to die by crucifixion and Jesus was only suspended for a couple of hours or so. Contemporary evidence from the Shroud of Turin – the holy cloth which covered Jesus in the tomb – appears to confirm the fact that Jesus was not dead, but still bleeding gently when his body was arranged for 'burial'. In a dead body blood coagulates very quickly; it does not flow or 'spurt' (as when poked by the Roman soldier's spear).

The evidence of the Shroud – which now appears to have been well authenticated by intensive scientific research – would indicate that Jesus in his deep *samadhi* state, had undergone a mightly metamorphosing force of energy, the charge of which had so irradiated the cloth which covered him, that his image was 'photographically' impressed upon it. The scientists cannot imagine how it was done, nor find any method by which it could have been faked. It must therefore have been another form of transfiguration as when light was emitted from the cells of Jesus on the mountain. If indeed, it *was* the Christ, whose portrait is thus borne upon the fabric.

For the impression shown is that of one who seems far older than a man of thirty-three years of age. Although some historians now conclude he may have been nearer forty-five. But if it was not Jesus, then it needs must have been some other sage of near or equal power.

In the *Holy Koran,* the Prophet Mohammed states: *"They did not kill him, nor did they crucify him, but they thought they did."* The *Koran* does not elaborate on this mysterious statement, but numerous Islamic commentators do. According to many of them, there was a substitute 'Jesus-like twin' who switched roles with Jesus at the last minute, and was crucified instead of him. This manoeuvre is attested to in many ancient documents of the Middle East. The substitute is generally named as one Simon of Cyrene, who appears to have been of close resemblance to Jesus, and ready to sacrifice himself for the Saviour.

Extraordinary as this assertion is, it is not unknown to the Church, as researchers have pointed out such references all down the ages. An Alexandrian scholar named Basilides (approx AD 120) who had written numerous commentaries on the Gospels, uncovered evidence of a substitution and wrote about it, much to the fury of the Bishop Irenaeus of Lyons, who repudiated it in his *Five Books Against Heresies (Libros Quinque Adversus Haereses)*.

But if in fact there *had* been a Jesus 'twin' among his followers, this would explain something which has always been a mystery to me; as Jesus was so well acquainted with the temple priests and the *Sanhedrin* (the Council of Jewish Elders), and was evidently instantly recognisable by all and sundry – why was it necessary for Judas to point him out to the authorities, as if he was someone totally unknown: unless there was a Jesus 'look-alike' among his entourage for whom he could be mistaken?

Among the finds of the Gnostic Christian community library at Nag Hammadi, was a document named *The Second Treatise of the Great Seth,* which tells a very different story of the crucifixion to the orthodox version. The Gnostic Christians were opposed to the development of the organised Church, and its immediate commencement of tampering with the truth for the promotion of the new faith and creation of the Christian myth. They considered themselves to be the only true practising Christians and guardians of the real teachings. This may well have been so, for Jesus taught the deep esoteric secrets to a closed circle of followers and only spoke in parables to the crowds.

In spite of the fact that the Gnostics were persecuted by the developing Orthodox Church, they were venerated by the ascetics of the wilderness and spoken of with great respect – as ones who *know* – by the Desert Fathers for many centuries.

Many Muslim researchers speak of documents which tell of Jesus having hidden in a niche in the wall and having watched the crucifixion from his hiding place. Western scholars now have corroborative evidence in the finding of the *Seth Treatise,* in which Jesus is presented as saying:

I did not succumb to them as they had planned. But I was not afflicted at all. Those who were there punished me. And I did not die in reality, but in appearance, lest I be put to shame by them, because these are my kinsfolk . . . and I did not become fainthearted in the face of what happened to me at their hands. I was about to succumb to fear, and I [suffered] according to their sight and thought, in order that they may never find any word to speak about them. For my death, which they think happened, [happened] to them in their error and blindness, since they nailed their man unto death. For their Ennoias did not see me, for they were deaf and blind. But in doing these things, they condemn themselves . . . It was another, their father who drank the gall and the vinegar; it was not I. They struck me with the reed; it was another, Simon, who bore the cross on his shoulder. It was another upon whom they placed the crown of thorns. But I was rejoicing in . . . the offspring of their error, of their empty glory. And I was laughing at their ignorance.[3]

This is, perhaps, the only account we have ever had in which Jesus is said to have laughed; although it is not the kind of laugh we like to ascribe to our conception of the Christ. I for one, would prefer to think of this sentence at least, as a fabrication. But what if the whole thing is the truth? This treatise of course, was not actually *written* by Jesus – just as there is not one passage in the whole Bible which was actually written by him. So everything we have to go on is only hearsay, as reported by later chroniclers. As the *Seth* manuscript appears to have been written about the same time as the Gospels, we cannot determine if it is any more, or any less, accurate than any other of the words which have been put into the mouth of Jesus. We only know that it is an early Christian (albeit Gnostic) document, written by those who venerated Jesus, and which has come down to us in its original form (preserved for nearly two thousand years) without ever having been tampered with by the interpolating religion-builders of the Church.

Until further evidences are uncovered, we can only attempt to feel its validity, or otherwise, with our hearts, rather than with our prejudices. Either the version propounded by the Church is a fabrication, or the Gnostics and many other Middle Eastern authorities have been following a red herring.

But whether he was saved by a substitute or not, the evidences seem to be accumulating which indicate that if it actually *was* Jesus who was nailed to the cross, he did not die as a consequence of it.

However, the possibility that Jesus did not die on the cross, strangely enough, does not make the average Christian happy. On the contrary, the very suggestion provokes a predictable welter of indignation and abuse. But the possibility that not only did Jesus *not die* on the cross but may not even have been crucified at all, is of course the heresy of heresies. Christians appear to have so much invested in this conception, that they desperately *want him to have died on the cross*. Yet when I first began to uncover evidence that Jesus may not have died in this way, I was awed and overjoyed. My heart rejoiced for him and sang a *Hallelujah!* But I found that most Christians preferred not to know about it.

It seems that the mythological aspect of Christianity, as learned in childhood, is more important to believers than the actual reality of the Master's teachings. The words of Jesus which are self-evidently authentic, strike home in the heart and soul. We have no need of blind faith in order to believe in them: we are touched. All other so-called 'historical facts' outside the teachings themselves might be better considered as tentative, until confirmed or otherwise. It would appear, however, that even modern man is in dire need of his myths in order to survive.

But the truth will out in any case. For Edgar Cayce, who foresaw the finding of the Dead Sea Scrolls – which were discovered shortly after his death – also stated there are still contemporary records to be found in the pyramids and in a hidden chamber near the Sphinx. These documents are said to contain the writings of close associates of Jesus and also: *"those records that are yet to be found, regarding the preparation of the Man, of the Christ."*[7] These scrolls will relate to the trials of his training in the temples of Egypt. The vociferous 'Doubting Thomases' would therefore do well to remain silent or they will look extremely foolish when these further documents are revealed.

As it is, the Dead Sea Scrolls have already shown that many of the teachings, and the very phrases Jesus used – which Christians believe to have originated with him – *already existed* in the Essene scriptures, dating from well over a hundred years before his birth. A close study of the Essene literature shows that Jesus was thoroughly familiar with their scriptures and that the Eucharistic breaking of the bread was a regular ritual of their communal meals. The documentary evidence once again corroborates the Edgar Cayce assertion that Jesus studied in the Essene communities.

AFTER THE RISING

Whatever the truth of the crucifixion, following the Bible story, Jesus evidently rose again in the same physical body of flesh as before. There was nothing supernatural about it, although highly coloured tales were later embroidered to make it seem so. Even if Jesus had been revitalised with spiritual power after his ordeal, his human body still needed 'fish and honeycomb' to nourish it, and his wounds were touchable by Thomas. Although Jesus was said to have made 'appearances' to Mary Magdalene and to two disciples on the road, these specious sightings are of doubtful validity, as the conflicting gospel writers seem unsure of their facts.

In any case, it is unlikely that Jesus would have been hanging about the tomb, to be caught again by the authorities, or be mobile enough the day after, to walk for several miles in the country with nail-wounds in his feet. And if the 'visitations' had been of a psychic nature – why then the need for disguise? Neither Mary nor the disciples were actually able to recognise the Master in these 'encounters' – but in the highly strung emotional state they were in, any one speaking in a scriptural manner – after the fashion of an Essene – might have been construed with hindsight to have been 'the Master' speaking. And this seems to have been the case; for the disciples said to each other afterwards: *"Did not our hearts burn within us, while he talked with us by the way, and while he opened to us the scriptures?"* (Luke 24:32) Here we have myth in the making.

DIVERGENT DETAILS IN THE GOSPELS

In one of the contradictory gospel accounts, it is held that a young messenger was left at the tomb to say that Jesus had gone on ahead to Galilee. This in itself is highly suspect, considering the condition Jesus must have been in after the crucifixion. He would have needed rest and healing. Unless he had not been crucified after all, in which case it is feasible. Except for the fact that in the other three gospels, Jesus and the disciples remain in Jerusalem, and come together in the 'Upper Room', where their meetings were clandestinely held.

Doubtless Jesus could not have been moved too far from the tomb in the state he was in, and it is not inconceivable that he was speedily brought to this house in the city to recover. There may well have been a secret chamber adjacent to the Upper Room, in which Jesus could have been treated by Essene physicians, since it is here that John's gospel has Jesus appear in their midst when the street-doors to the house were shut. Luke and Mark speak of the same event as being in Jerusalem. But Matthew has him meeting the disciples on a mountain in Galilee instead; which should have been a momentous occasion. But the gospel tails off lamely, having little else to say of this unlikely meeting.

Yet in Luke's version, Jesus has expressly told the disciples to *remain in Jerusalem* until they are endowed with spiritual power from above. But then, after the meal, he proceeds to lead them (presumably *walking*) along the road to *Bethany* (which is several miles south-east of Jerusalem, while Galilee is seventy odd miles north). On arriving in Bethany – where Jesus was accustomed to stay with Mary, Martha and Lazarus – Luke has him suddenly and unreasonably, *'carried up into heaven'*, rather than simply disappearing into the house of his friends. Jesus might have saved himself an unnecessary and painful walk if he had 'ascended' from Jerusalem, as Mark affirms.

However, John gives us a further contradictory tale. He says that Jesus first appears to the disciples on the Sunday evening at supper, but for some reason Thomas is not among them. This is the only gospel which mentions this 'fact'. (Mark says he ascended right there and then after supper). But John maintains that Jesus obligingly reappeared again, *eight days* later, in the same house, in order to prove to Thomas that he was actually made of flesh and blood. John further goes on to say that Jesus appears yet a *third* time in Galilee, where he does another fish-catching miracle and cooks supper, being evidently unmindful of the fact that the disciples did not return to being fishermen after the crucifixion, but dispersed as evangelists.

In this uncalled-for and rather spurious appendage to the text, we have another obvious interpolation of events out of sequence. It is evident that the author – or far more likely, a later copying scribe – has suddenly discovered a bit of manuscript that he has forgotten to incorporate into the main body of the text, and rather than rewrite the whole expensive scroll all over again, he has tacked this piece on to the end of the narrative, by using the device of inserting the vague linking words: *"Some time later, Jesus showed himself to his disciples once again . . ."* (*John* 21:1) And this artifice has been adopted as reality ever since.

This alleged event occurs quite 'some time' after Jesus has finally 'ascended into heaven' (variously from Jerusalem, from Bethany *and* from Galilee). To imagine that he returns from heaven some weeks later, just to do a bit of fishing and cook supper, is patently absurd. But I merely point out a few of these anomalies, with which the gospels are saturated from beginning to end, to awaken a little awareness that the gospels are not more reliable testimonies than the explanations of the journeyings of Jesus during the 'Lost Years', which Christian detractors choose to regard as 'fanciful'. It would seem that the more fanciful and garbled accounts of the 'ascension' were more in the nature of a hastily constructed ploy to put the Roman authorities off the track, than either a real occurrence or a well thought out finalé for the propagation of the faith; otherwise one would expect a lot more to have been made of this remarkable visual event.

But the account of Luke furnishes us with a valuable clue. If Jesus *did* leave Jerusalem for Bethany, it is more reasonable to assume that he would have spent some time with his best-

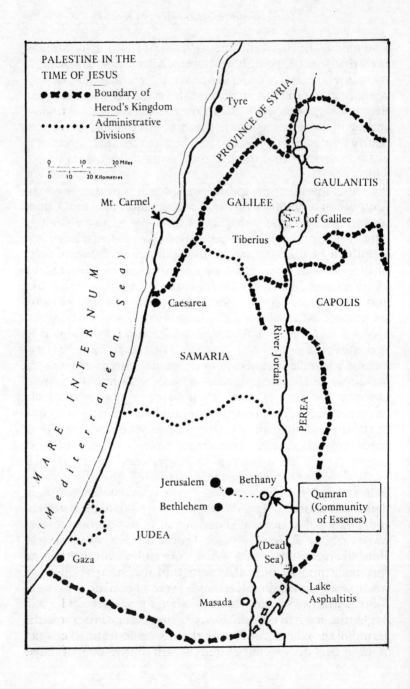

PALESTINE IN THE
TIME OF JESUS

●━✕━●━✕━● Boundary of
Herod's Kingdom

●●●●●●● Administrative
Divisions

0 ——— 10 ——— 20 Miles
0 ——— 10 ——— 20 Kilometres

Tyre

PROVINCE OF SYRIA

GAULANITIS

Mt. Carmel

GALILEE

Sea of Galilee

Tiberius

Caesarea

CAPOLIS

SAMARIA

River Jordan

PEREA

MARE INTERNUM
(Mediterranean Sea)

Jerusalem

Bethany

Qumran
(Community
of Essenes)

Bethlehem

JUDEA

(Dead
Sea)

Gaza

Masada

Lake
Asphaltitis

beloved disciples there, in the home of Mary as usual, and saying his last farewells before his final departure. As Bethany was also on the way to Qumran – the Community of Essenes – it is more than likely he removed himself there, and laid up for a time in one of the rock cells of the hermitage, before finally, and unobtrusively, crossing the nearby Jordan and leaving the country forever.

The miraculous 'Jesus Ointment' of which Swami Rama Thirta speaks, may well have been the main medicament for the healing of his wounds, prepared by the physicians of Qumran. This preparation existed throughout the East before the time of Christ and is still in use today. It is listed in literally hundreds of Eastern medical books as *Marham-i-Isa* (the Ointment of Jesus). Some of these books were compiled by early Christian medics, some by Magians, Jews, and some by Muslims; and the prescription, based on *myrrh* as the active ingredient, has been repeated in books on skin diseases until the present day.

Many of these works state that this ointment was used to heal the wounds of Jesus after the crucifixion, and the statement is repeated in a Latin pharmaceutical compendium of the first or second century. From this it can be understood that the observation that Jesus did not die on the cross was extremely widespread. A Sufi work exploring the life of Jesus, lists thirty-three Arabic and Persian medical books 'out of thousands' which reiterate the same sentiment.[20]

THE LOST TRIBES OF ISRAEL

After his life's mission in Israel was completed, the Hindu sages maintain that Jesus made his way back to Afghanistan and Kashmir, where he ended his days ministering to survivors of the 'Lost Tribes of Israel'. This is an extremely plausible notion, as Jesus stated early in his ministry that he was not sent to anyone other than 'the Lost Sheep of Israel', of whom the Afghans and Kashmiris were a remnant.

Such was my own impression when I first entered Herat in Afghanistan. I had the sensation of being plunged back into the period of the Christ, for among these Semitic-featured people, in their isolated world, I felt myself inside one of those wonderful illustrations found in old-fashioned Bibles. Nothing seemed to have changed among these people for two thousand years, for they still wore the same clothes and lived in the same way. Many other travellers and historians have noted the marked resemblance of the Afghanis to the Jews. And the Afghans themselves proudly trace their ancestry back to Abraham.

One tribe, which inhabits the Khyber mountain region on the border of Kashmir, is known as the *Youssoufszye* (the Tribe of Joseph) and call themselves the *'Ben-i-Israel'* (the 'Children of Israel') and were so recorded at the time of Genghis Khan.

History bears them out. Seven hundred years or so before the birth of Christ, countless numbers of Israelites were taken into captivity in successive raids by foreign potentates, finally culminating in King Nebuchadnezzar laying waste the whole country of Judah and deporting the entire population to his conquered colonies throughout the Babylonian Empire between 586 and 581 BC. When the Empire collapsed, many returned to their homeland and settled in Galilee. Large numbers of others of divers tribes escaped further on eastwards, to find freedom in the Ghaur (Ghor or Ghoree) hills, just north-west of Kabul, in Afghanistan.[21]

These people are said to have remained faithful to Jewish ways until AD 682[22], when many were converted to Islam, and gradually interbred with Moslems. Other tribes retained many vestiges of the Mosaic teachings, and even today, their codes of civil observance, their marriage laws, the keeping of a remarkably similar *Feast of the Passover* and other customs, all attest to their Semitic origins. Also the present *Pushtu* language which they speak, has been found to contain more root-words from Hebrew than from any other source. Similarly, the names of the towns and villages of these regions are based on Palestinian names. It is also curious to note that in Afghanistan and the northern provinces of India, it is the custom of truck drivers to paint fish (the symbol of Christ and the Piscean Age) on the sides of their wagons, as a protective talisman and sign of good fortune.

Thus, it is to these 'Lost Sheep of Israel' that Christ is said to have returned at the culmination of his life's mission: seemingly following in the footsteps of his predecessor Moses. For only thirty-five miles from Srinagar, the Kashmir capital, is what is considered to be the Tomb of *'The Prophet of the Book'* (namely, Moses), which is set on the summit of Mount Niltopp, and is still tended by an isolated Jewish community, believed to have been there since biblical times.

THE SUFI TOMB OF JESUS

In Srinagar itself, is a highly venerated shrine-tomb nearly 2,000 years old, which is said to contain the body of the Christ, and also that of a Christ-intoxicated Sufi saint of the fifteenth century, Nazir-ud-Din.[11][23] It is known as the *Tomb of Esah* – the name of Jesus *(Isa)* in Hindi. The tomb also bears a green plaque inscribed with the name of *Yus Asaf* (a derivative form of *Yasu* or *Yesu* – Jesus – coupled with *Asaf* derived from the Hebrew *Asaph* – 'the Gatherer'. Jesus was considered as the 'Gatherer of the Lost Tribes of Israel' from all the lands around. And it may be remembered, that *Asaph* was also one of the names given in the list of Jesus's incarnations in the Readings of Edgar Cayce.

It is another interesting 'cosmic coincidence' that Jesus spent his developing years in Egypt at Heliopolis – which means 'The City of the Sun', and is held to have died in Srinagar, which is the modern contraction of its ancient name *Surya-Nagar* – 'The City (or Place) of the Sun-God'.

THE HINDU MINISTRY OF THOMAS

It is also worthy of note that after Jesus left his disciples to spread the word far and wide, at least one of the disciples also went to India. An early Syrian document from the second century, known as *The Doctrine of the Apostles,* reads:

After the death of the Apostles, there were Guides and Rulers in the Churches; and whatever the Apostles communicated to them, and they had received from them, they taught to the multitudes. They, again, at their deaths also committed and delivered to their disciples after them, everything which they had received from the Apostles; also that James had written from Jerusalem and Simon from the city of Rome, and John from Ephesus and Mark from great Alexandria, and Andrew from Phrygia and Luke from Macedonia and *Thomas from India,* that the epistles of an Apostle might be received and read in the churches in every place.[24]

The document goes on to say that St Thomas evangelised the whole of India and all the countries bordering it (i.e., Afghanistan, Tibet, Nepal, Bhutan and Assam), *"even to the farthest sea".* This assertion is supported by another scriptural work entitled *The Acts of St Thomas,* dating from the late second, or early third century, which states: "When the Apostles had been for a time in Jerusalem, they divided the countries among them in order that each might preach in the region which fell to him; and India fell to the lot of Thomas."[24]

Evidently Thomas was not pleased with his lot and another passage has him complaining that he is a Hebrew, and unable to teach to the Hindus. And later in the same narrative he states obstinately: *"Withersoever thou wilt, O Lord, only to India I will not go . . ."* It might have been that he had a sinking premonition of his fate there. But it seems that he was persuaded to overcome his initial reactions and finally accepted what had come to him.

According to Church tradition, St Thomas arrived in India's southern state of Kerala in AD 52, where he is credited with founding the first Christian church. Even in the present day, Kerala is still the most strongly Christianised state of India and churches rise from the jungle everywhere. The Church followers still call themselves 'Thomas Christians'. Although Thomas also evangelised northern India, he could well have travelled there by sea, as there was a regular shipping route from the port of Alexandria in Egypt, to Quilon in Kerala, trading in silks and spices and sandalwood, and a Jewish community descended from the old traders still survives in Quilon today.

The *Acts of Thomas* describes his Indian travels, his conversion of one King 'Gundaphar' in north-west India and the founding of the seven major churches of Kerala, which are all still functioning. King Gundaphar was thought to be a legendary personage until the nineteenth century, when many coins were found in Afghanistan near Kabul, and in the southern Punjab, which bore the name of 'Gondophares' and some which are said to bear the name of Jesus. The coins are dated from AD 20 to 45, the period in which Thomas would have been travelling around India.

Thomas also came to be favoured by the king of the Madras region of Tamil Nadu, to which he moved, after living for a couple of years in Kerala. But there he aroused the jealousy of the king's priests and ministers who had Thomas run through with a lance, while at prayer at his sanctuary on a hill near Madras, when the king was away on state affairs. The hill on which Thomas was martyred is still known as 'St Thomas's Mount', and his body now lies beneath the flags of the Sant Thome (St Thomas) Cathedral in Mylapore, on the outskirts of Madras. The Cathedral is venerated as a Basilica by the Roman Catholic Church, because it has been accepted as standing over the Tomb of the Apostle.

ASSURANCE OF THE SECOND COMING

Such are the Christian links with the East, as I have come to understand them over the years. You may accept what you will. But are we honest enough with ourselves to accept that no religion is perfect? And that none has all the answers which will suit everyone? Can we accept that because of misconceptions and intellectual contrivance, there are twisted teachings in every tradition? And that it is precisely for this reason, that in every age of the world, there seems to be the 'resurrection' of a new prophet who comes to revitalise the old teachings gone astray? Just as Jesus came to fulfil and clarify the teachings of the Jewish prophets which had been perverted by the priesthood.

In our time – at the beginning of the Aquarian Age – there are many who feel Christianity to be in the same fallen condition now as the Mosaic religion was then. But should the Christ reappear as a new broom once again – as many now anticipate – who will there be to welcome him? Who is purified enough in heart to follow him? I fear that Christianity with its lack of openness to any other form of teaching but its own dogma, would be the last to recognise and accept him. Just as Jesus would doubtless find it difficult to recognise his own teaching in much of the present creed.

Given the present unfavourable climate, it would be sur-
prising if Jesus was masochistic enough to return and suffer the
same persecution all over again. And I say this in all sincere
tongue-in-cheekiness. But in actuality, in my heart of hearts, I
do not believe that he has ever been away. As Jesus himself
said: *"Where two or three are gathered together in my name, there am
I among you."* And when this is done with deep sincerity and
loving feeling, I feel this to be so. For he also said: *"Lo, I am
with you always, always."*

Most religions are centred on what the Masters *taught,* rather
than on the unreliable 'histories' surrounding their lives,
embroidered by successive generations of disciples. Therefore
to the sincere spiritual aspirant it actually matters very little (to
his life and growth) whether Jesus studied in Egypt or India, or
was born of a virgin, or was crucified or not, or ascended to
heaven from three places simultaneously, or died in Kashmir
at the age of one hundred and twenty as the prophet *Esah.* But
to Christians it seems to matter very much. Why else would
countless Christian historians have spent lifetimes in research
to try and prove the assertions of the Bible – and then hide
away some of their findings in the Vatican?

Much of the ethos of the Christian faith appears to be based
more on an embracing acceptance of these peripheral supposi-
tions than on the actual *content* of its spiritual message. If the
average religious follower actually *applied* the teachings of the
Christ in his own life, there would be no insular rigidity or
self-righteous separatism to overcome. But as things are, it is
of paramount importance to determine whether 'Jesus the
Traveller' studied the scriptures of other lands in order to
complete his wholistic visionary capacities – if such knowledge will assist in mellowing the rigidity of certain kinds of
prejudiced followers, and open them up to the spirit of spiritual cross-fertilisation and inter-religious support and study.
Such an awakening attitude might well herald a New Age for
mankind. We cannot – for example – claim to love God and
hate the Hindu (or 'the Russians', or the long-haired 'hippy'
who has often deliberately assumed an identification with the
Christ in his appearance and spiritually oriented lifestyle).

The fact remains, that the Christ image remains a powerful

force for good in the world. Therefore, although many things may have been altered in the 'historical' story of Jesus, the interpolations and concealments of the Church do not detract one iota from the power, the love, and the teachings of the Master himself. His achievement of having overcome all human frailties and the tempting voice of the ego, will still inspire mankind through all eternity. Our work is surely to follow in *his* footsteps? Are we here on earth to follow the statutes of a priestly doctrine, or to actually *put into practice the teachings of the Master?*

If we can understand this, there is no reason why we should want to defend, or hang on to, our chosen religion, like a drowning man to a straw, simply to feel ourselves in the right. Or to try and safeguard ourselves from falling apart, with a stick-on 'religious plaster' over the surface of our fears. Let each take up his cross and crucify this fear-producing sense-of-ego which separates us from all other men and faiths. For only opening ourselves to all, lets loose the love within our hearts.

In esoteric circles, the term 'Christ-Consciousness' has come to mean a *Universal Loving Power,* or *force-of-love,* which must remain resounding in our hearts, if we – as humankind – wish to draw once more the *physical* presence of this Master to our sphere. The Cayce Readings give the promise that the Christ *will* return again when the world is *ready* for his Coming. And: *"When China becomes the centre of Christianity . . . For he shall come as ye have seen him go, in the body he occupied in Galilee . . . The time no one knows, not even the Son Himself, only the Father. Not until his enemies – and the earth – are wholly in subjection to His will, his powers."*[7]

And what was the will of Jesus? As the Master said: *"A new commandment give I unto you: Love one another . . . Love the Lord thy God with all thine heart, with all thy strength, and love thy neighbour as thyself."*

This is the essence of the whole teaching of the Christ.

And this applies to all men and to *all* our earthly neighbours, of every land and every faith. 'East' and 'West' did not exist until we invented this arbitrary division. Man divides, God unites. Once there were just 'people' on the earth, and 'God-ness' everywhere. Each God-conscious being thus shared with another whatever he had learned by Grace, no matter from where he had come upon his globe. Therefore the sooner we forget all our partisan notions of 'East' and 'West', and 'my' religion and 'your' (obviously wrong) religion, and awaken to an evolving planetary consciousness, the better.

Surely the whole point of our existence is to achieve – or realise – our Union (Yoga) with the All – to become illumined – or to 'Walk at-One with God', no matter how, or by what teaching? All spiritual teachings are God-given, according to what we can receive of them into our hearts. Let us open ourselves to all spiritual truth then, wherever we find it. Ask not, was this man born blind, for such and such a reason? Ask rather, are we ourselves born blind? Can we not see that the whole of God's creation – the whole Guruverse (the teaching system of the universe) – is at our disposal; and not just one or other of its fragmented doctrines?

What I do not understand in the Bible, is revealed to me in the *Vedas,* and what I miss in the *Vedas* is clarified for me in the Bible: or the *Dhammapada,* the *Zend Avesta,* the *Koran,* the *Tao-te-Ching,* the *Torah* or the writings of the black or red man. No matter how, one way or another: *"Ye shall know the Truth, and the Truth shall make you free."*

Those whose hearts have ears to hear, let them hear.

THE WAY OF
SUNCONSCIOUSNESS

Healing the Sickness of the Soul

The other day I was taking a stroll through the market-place when I ran into one of my students. No sooner had I greeted him with a big hug than he fell to weeping on my shoulder. After he had cried himself out, I asked his trouble. He said he had been searching for me in case I could help him to understand what was happening to him. He explained: "For the past week my life seems totally void and useless. I don't know if I am dead or alive. Nothing has any meaning at all. It feels like I have an unfillable hole inside of me, an ache that never really goes away. Nothing is ever enough to fill the gap. I have had it before. Sometimes the emptiness of my existence fills me with a terror so strong I am not fit for anything. I wander about searching for I don't know what – some kind of answer to it all.

"It's not at all like the therapy I went through. I've felt all those pains and tears for the mummy and daddy who never came up with the goods when I needed them. But this is different. This feeling, this empty ache, I can't connect with anything. My wife was able to help me through the therapy period, but with this she is at a loss. She is a very sensitive person, but she just can't understand what this is and I can't explain to her how I feel. It's something much more than a need for long-lost parents. It's a longing – a reaching out for God knows what? I don't know *why* I exist or what existence is all about. Sometimes I feel sick with emptiness when it comes on me. I don't know what it is. Do you know anything that can help me?"

Alas, I knew only too well what was happening. My heart and I had passed through it many times. I explained as best I could in the blustery market-place and promised to write a few words to clarify things a little more and to help his wife to understand. It turned out to be an almost impossible undertaking and the task grew and grew in the doing. The following is the result.

This problem is one of the most prevalent maladies on this earth today, to which we are all prone on one level or another. It is one which, perhaps for lack of a medical name and a general inability to express its nature, is either ignored or greatly underestimated by both doctor and layman alike. This extremely lonely and distressing condition of being is what is known as 'soul-sickness'. Its advent has steered countless numbers of sufferers on to the spiritual path. In its deepest manifestations it is well known to the Christian mystics as 'the Dark Night of the Soul'.

Those who have known it, will instantly recognise what is meant by this expression. But how can one convey a sense of such 'sickness of the soul' to someone who has never been touched by the experience? How to define this seemingly indefinable sense of inner disquiet and deep anxiety? The roots of it lie deep and appear different for each of us on levels nearer the surface. But for many the onset may manifest in an underlying and ever-present forlornness in the face of existence. At times life appears totally meaningless and too incomprehensible to bear. This can often bring on bouts of overwhelming abjectness of spirit, in which one is rendered incapable of the simplest tasks, or stricken with the sense of trudging through purgatorial treacle when forcing oneself to see them through to the end.

I recall a girl so afflicted, who worked in a huge, impersonal business in a big-city high-rise office block. The lack of contact with her seemingly insensitive and superficial associates, caused her an agony of spirit through every working day. They lived in a matter-of-fact surface world, without depth, apparently untouched by the pains and poetry she felt in her own soul. Life was surely more than the empty-headed attitudes of those around her? One day, being too oppressed by her unreal lifestyle (and lacking the soul-food she needed) she stayed at home, distraught and numbed, unable to face the emptiness at work. Next morning when she went in and honestly tried to explain: 'I was ill with trying to decide what to do with my life', she inevitably got the sack.

Had she said she had toothache or food-poisoning, it would have been a different story. Physical ailments are something you can acceptably take time off work for, with all the attendant sympathy. But a sickness of the soul is sometimes worse to suffer, for the bodily symptoms can be more easily explained. But how can the soul-sick satisfactorily express the sense of dereliction – that empty, forsaken-child feeling — even to their nearest and dearest?

For the average medical practitioner 'soul-sickness' would be too vague and fuzzy an idea to be treatable. Thus many people without realising it, tend to create or bring on physical symptoms to gain the attention they need. Even for the majority of conventional psychiatrists and psychotherapists, the idea lies in an area where they are unable to tread, for lack of acquaintance with things of the spirit. And the only sympathy generally available from friends and family is of the "pull yourself together" variety; or from your doctor: "don't worry, it's just your *nerves*" (a tacit acknowledgement that he hasn't a clue), and you go away clutching an unconvincing little bottle of pills for bludgeoning your system into insensitivity.

Unrecognised and untreatable by the medical fraternity in general, soul-sickness seems to be on the increase all around the globe. Not only are the so-called 'civilised' nations suffering in this way, but also the more 'primitive' races when contaminated by our kind of world. In South America, where mechanised industry is eating into the rain forests and jungles at an alarming rate, the stone-age tribesmen of the Amazon, when confronted with a bewildering and relentless 'superior' culture and technology, are simply giving up the ghost and lying down to die in the forests, soul-sick unto death.

And perhaps here is one of the clues to this universal affliction. Not only is the physical habitat of these people being destroyed, but also their mental and spiritual 'climate' is being engulfed at a pace too great for their sensibilities to grasp. Can we not feel the echoes of this reverberating in the modern psyche too? As the inexorable Juggernaut (or *Jagganath*) of our technological society comes rolling over us, are we not sometimes seized by a breathless terror as it all becomes too much? *Stop the world I want to get off!* became a current phrase in recent years.

There seems to be an instinctual realisation that our mental, spiritual and physical environment is also being destroyed in the wake of scientific progress. Its benefits seem to be out-weighed by its negative aspects, like hazardous power plants (and their pollution) and horrendous military weaponry and stockpiling for bacterial plague warfare, which now gives us the capacity to destroy all life on earth a million times over. Such things place the majority of mankind in a helpless child-like dependence on the fragile sanity of the temporal powers that be. And these are only a few of the contributory factors towards a sickness of the soul.

We also live with 'wars and rumours of wars' and world disasters as our constant daily diet. As if that was not enough, we entertain ourselves with films of murder and mayhem. But does it really penetrate that all the garbage we allow into our minds creates the quality of our lives? For example, to cease-lessly feed ourselves on the scaremongering daily news (whether it be real or journalistically created hysteria simply for the sake of selling newspapers) is to inevitably cultivate a subtle sick-ness in the soul. Who can remain unaffected?

But we are told: "It is vitally important to know what is going on in the world." Perhaps, but I am not convinced. I spent ten years on the road, in remote areas of the world, not knowing anything but what was going on where I was, and do not feel any the worse for it. How does it improve the *quality* of my life to feed my fears on the daily news? With increased communications on a world-wide scale, we are now subject to instantaneous vicarious involvement in wars and disasters and political inanities all over the planet. We live in the karmic dreams of others. This only increases our own anxieties and paranoia, especially when we can do nothing about it. Or, on the other hand, an event in some far-flung corner of the globe suddenly sets people aflame all over the world, fermenting riots and reactionary violence in every country (which changes nothing at the *source* of the trouble), where otherwise it might have been only a passing local event and no one else need have been troubled by it.

Yet it seems we love to believe the slanted news and to rage and boil impotently. Every day we continue to agitate and enervate ourselves with the papers and the 'telly' for the whole of our lives, only to die at the end of it, having done nothing whatsoever about it, and never having lost our insecurity and tension through our belief in the 'importance' of keeping-up-with-the-news. And knowing-what's-going-on has not made one iota of difference to our lives, except perhaps to have shortened them by several years of anxiety.

It really depends on what we want from life. And at what level we choose to live in the world. Many by their inner power inhabit a world untouched by strife. *We each inhabit the world we create.* Let me cite the example of the typical mountain peasant I have encountered all over the earth. Without newspapers or television, he lives out his life in peace and purity amid the mountains, sheep and flowers, without any idea of what's going on elsewhere in the world. Who is to say his way of life is wrong? Whether he worries about what's going on or not, as far as the world is concerned the result is just the same. Except, perhaps, for the fact that the peasant has not increased the world's problems by throwing his own particular spanner into the works. Otherwise the only difference is that the news-eating impotent city-dweller has suffered all his life from things he can do nothing about, and the peasant has simply lived his life. No blame. The choice is ours.

Over-information-input-surfeit-sickness is another modern malady now disturbing the mental and spiritual equilibrium of growing numbers of people. The pace at which information is coming in is creating an underlying sense of hysteria in those who feel they cannot keep up. If more people left the news alone and minded their own business, there would be far less trouble in the world today. But we are expected to be responsible adults in the world and keep ourselves up to date. Unfortunately the majority of so-called 'adults' who are so busily doing just that and organising our world seem to be the major influences in its chaos.

How can it be otherwise, when they are basically driven by the pains of their past and infantile inner programming? Until they have put themselves to rights, their ego-prompted efforts can only act as spokes plunged into the wheels of the world. Although we may be well aware that many of our 'adult' attitudes and reactions to external affairs are based on our unresolved pains and problems from childhood, we rarely come to terms with them. In spite of ourselves, we still persist in those same reactions no matter how irrational. Thus the slavish impulsion to absorb the daily 'news' only serves to perpetuate the same pressurised mental-emotional climate our souls engendered in infancy, and which we then spew out through volcanic tension in our explosive relations with our work-associates or society.

For many, the maintenance of a self-justificatory sense of righteous indignation against others is the perfect and convenient smoke-screen which prevents them from needing to look at their own childish imperfections and uninvestigated neurotic tendencies. This kind of person safeguards himself from feeling the fact that he is soul-sick by the constant generation of self-righteous nervous tension. He opts for a coronary or a stroke instead. But the more introspective soul-sick sufferer – who does not use others as scapegoats – most often tends to have an inner climate of a melancholic 'poor me' kind of nature, which he may carry with him for the rest of his life, thus laying the foundation for much of the 'soul-sick' way in which he perceives whatever happens to him in the world today.

Happily a great many of these inner attitudes of childhood (and childish-adulthood) can now be uncovered and relieved by some of the more progressive forms of psychotherapy (i.e. *Primal, Gestalt, Psychosynthesis, Transactional Analysis, Bio-energetics*, etc.). But this is only half the story. These psychotherapeutically treatable aspects of inner distress mainly relate to a combination of any or all of the aforementioned psychological and emotional stress factors prevalent in the modern world.

However, soul-sickness is not solely a modern phenomenon. It appears to have existed throughout recorded history. Admittedly there have always been psychological stress factors burdening socially-structured man in every age of the world. But this is obviously not the whole picture since, even in non-stressful situations, people who have had no problems about money, work, food or accommodation, have also found themselves suffering from an acute existential emptiness. Even the rich and famous find no security in their wealth, power or position.

But this affliction seems mainly to affect only the more sensitive and (whether they are aware of it or not) the spiritually awakening members of the human race. And such beings have never been comprehended by their fellow man. From ancient times to the present day, those most harrowingly stricken to the core with existential agonies of the soul, have been those who (after surviving these 'growing pains') later became the world's mightiest spiritual teachers. It seems that for some unfortunate souls, from time to time, as they evolve higher and higher, the deeper and more profoundly they are plunged into the existential 'abyss of fire and water', as the spirit is tried and tempered on the 'Cosmic Anvil'.

It is hard to imagine that the hermits, ascetics and gurus who have undergone such spiritual sufferings, even after many years of inner work and isolation, are any longer pressurised by worldly problems or the left-over psychological traumas from childhood. There have evidently always been stronger forces at work. But of what nature? From whence comes this despair which racked the souls of mystics in the past and still continues to echo even in the urban hearts of our modern world? What is this feeling of emptiness, this unfillable hole in our existence?

Essentially, it is a sense of *separation*. This is the ultimate spiritual malady. Soul-sickness in essence, is a deeply disturbing sense of isolation from the Source of our being – from the very foundation for our existence. There seems to be in everyone an innate and tragic sense of cosmic estrangement from that unfathomable, Omnipresent *whatever-it-is* – from which arises all life and existence. And our seeming inability to feel at One with this Omnipresence is the heart of the existential dilemma. Even though we may be totally unaware of this situation on the conscious level, it is always there, subliminally resounding in the soul with subtle anguish.

It is therefore understandable why people in every level of society tend to band together in élitist cliques to be accepted as one of the 'in-crowd'. All of humanity feels the need to 'belong' in one way or another. In order to try and fill the aching void we form ourselves into circles, gangs and groups, join clubs, cults or religions, or even armies; perhaps becoming fervent nationalists, or fanatics of some other cause. But all these diversions can be seen as perverted forms of the usually un-realised drive for spiritual 'unification' (otherwise known as *yoga*). We seek instead some kind of 'roots' in the world, which only give us partial satisfaction in our palliative sense of togetherness. But for many, the palliatives are never enough. Nothing we do seems to fulfil the deepest needs of the soul.

But what exactly do we mean when we speak of 'soul'? Everyone blithely uses the term, although I have never seen or heard it anywhere satisfactorily defined. Nor have I encountered a preacher of any tradition who was able to precisely indicate its nature. Yet we all seem to have some intuitive sense of 'soul', no matter how hazy a notion it is. We know it to be the animating principle of all individual beings, without which the body is inert and falls apart, but what are its characteristics and relation to the Divinity?

For my own ease of comprehension I was given the following analogy when 'mentemplatively' gazing out of the window for an answer. In a similar way that clouds could be seen as a 'condensation' of the 'sky' – so 'soul' could be seen as a 'condensation' of the Omnipresence. If the pure universal Spirit – or Omnipresence – is visualised as the clear blue sky, then 'souls' could be likened to the relationship of the clouds which appear in it. And according to the 'atmospheric con-ditions' prevailing for their appearance, they go on expanding or contracting (in and out of various lifetimes) until eventually (on Realisation of their true nature), they evaporate back into the original clarity of pure Spirit, which they were all along.

My inner sense experiences 'soul' as something in the nature of a subtle spiritual 'force-field' which envelops, suffuses and holds together (temporarily) this complex package of body-mind, memory, intellect, will, ego-sense, subtle bodies, feelings and faculties and all that goes to make up the individual entity. The quality of this 'force-field' might be described as an 'atmos-pheric inner condition of reverential sensibility' which exerts a subtle influence on one's impression and expression of life. Soul seems ultimately not to be a 'thing' but a growth-inducing 'interior climate', the cultivation of which eventually brings about a blending of the sense-of-individual-being with the sense-of-Cosmic-Being.

One may sense it as the linking medium, which allows us to realise that our apparent individuality is in essence an indivisibility which cannot be divided from the Omnipresence, on account of it being of the same substantial nature. If we are at all aware, we cannot avoid feeling the condition of this inner atmosphere or 'Cloud of Knowing', through which we may know the All. Its operation may be experienced as a 'sensory mode of spiritual awareness', which acts in the manner of a rarified 'two-way transformer', 'stepping up' or 'stepping down' the free-flowing current of communication between oneself and the Omni-Self. Or at least, this is what would appear to be its function if we were not constantly keeping our receptive equipment virtually closed down to the two-way flow.

But being preoccupied with the ways of the world, our habitual tendency is to constrict the communication. The preoccupied mind acts like a vice on the soul, squeezing the channels shut. We have to realise that mind is a vice – not a virtue. A blockage in any circuit will build up pressure. The kind of pressure produced by impeding the flow between man and the Omnipresence results in a 'spiritual nausea' which epitomises the sensation of soul-sickness. And without understanding the processes at work the suffocating effect of this otherwise seemingly causeless conditions creates profound anxiety.

It sometimes happens that this feeling arises after having had a sudden and fear-inspiring glimpse of the 'actuality' – through a perhaps momentary shift of consciousness which has given one an inexpressibly acute awareness and awe of one's own existence. It is as if veils have been stripped away from this 'dream of life' as it appears to be – as manufactured by the mass thoughts or 'day dream' of humanity – and we suddenly 'see' the stark impossible wonder of our 'beingness' – or the terrifying absurdity of existing at all. There is no way to convey this unearthly experience. And such a glance into the void estranges us from all other dwellers on life's surface, for we are unable to express our awesome secret and no one we know could comprehend it anyway. But the shock of 'seeing' and the weird terror of its impact can precipitate anyone into existential anguish.

Although this experience does not consciously occur to the majority of sufferers from soul-sickness, I content that it is always uncomfortably near the subliminal surface. The veil is thin and its semi-perception exists as a fuzzily 'scrambled' undercurrent of consciousness in those susceptible to finer levels. Another influence to which we are susceptible is a malign conjunction of planets, which also has its effects on our inner climate, causing psycho-emotional disturbances, as does the full moon on unbalanced minds. When the planets are in such an alignment we find many people going thrugh troubles of the soul in the same period. But it is only a matter of time before the planets move out of phase and allow us to come to 'normal'.

Whatever its origins, soul-sicknes seems to 'stun' the sensibilities and smothers all sense of life and vitality in both body and soul. In this state, all the things towards which the average human aspires, appear utterly worthless. Even though suffering, one has the feeling of being an emotionless and unreachable zombie-like lone spaceman lost in the infinite void. A void in which the need to be reached is paramount. But at such times nothing and no one (of average consciousness) in the outer world has any hope of reaching through.

Of such souls, the mystically aware scientist Albert Einstein said: *"The individual feels the nothingness of human desires and aims ... He looks upon individual existence as a sort of prison and waits to experience the universe as a whole"*. Many experience this prison effect, but few realise *they are the universe* and need to expand into it.

This 'imprisoning' sensation of soul-sickness could perhaps be compared to the seemingly dry deadness of a caterpillar chrysalis. A sufferer's whole being is dried and deathly, yet at the same time an upheaval of anguished yearning is happening in his deepest sensitivities. Similarly, inside the dusty chrysalis, throughout the long dark night of winter, the churning cellular structure of the caterpillar is inexorably – unbelievably – metamorphosing into a butterfly. What can the poor caterpillar do but surrender itself to the process and wait on the workings of the Omnipresence? Sufferers from soul-sickness are in a similar position.

Yet without such workings on our spiritual sensibilities, we too would remain unevolved and unaware cabbage-like creatures. But even the cabbage-fed caterpillar after a lifetime of bondage to the cabbage world, eventually enters into a dark night of inner turmoil and emerges at last as a wondrous winged creature of the spring. And similarly so with us. One day our spring too, will come – in this lifetime or another. And it is this empty, soul-sick churning which serves to drive us on from worldly complacency towards the Light and flight of the soul.

Harrowing though the process may be, it is helpful if we can realise it as the pressure of the 'Presence' within, guiding us on in the way of spiritual evolution. The Omnipresence is at all times suffusing and sustaining our existence, whether we are aware of it or not. The realisation of every sage attests the fact that assuredly there will come a time when we too will come to experience it. Therefore everything is under perfect control. Why then are we always fighting the universe? Better we succumb to its processes gracefully. Why not allow it to do its work unimpeded by our constricting thoughts? For there is no doubt that both mental cringing-away-from-the-world and mental indulgence in the wearisome ways of the world, equally create a commingling of our cosmic and common anxieties and sow the seeds of soul-sickness to come.

When soul-sickness takes us over, all our spiritual practices seem to fail us. It seems then there is little we can do but surrender our souls to its dominion and see it through in as best a state of contemplative consciousness as we can muster. However, we must always be vigilant to see that the pressures of the present moment do not also bring up the spectres of sadness from the past. When we allow the mixing-stick of mind to stir up all our sorrow-associated melancholic memories from the reservoir of childhood feelings, we bring to bear an insupportable overload on the suffering of the present. It then becomes so easy to fall back into a self-pitying and melancholic inner climate if we have been accustomed to 'comforting' ourselves with such an atmosphere all our lives. But these 'historical' pains have no place in the problems of the present. And a self-pitying attitude is death to inner development and freedom from sadness. We have to gather all our strength to avoid wallowing in this way.

Unfortunately it is precisely this atmosphere engendered in childhood which is one of the commonest factors in the provocation of soul-sickness and its prolongation. A great many sufferers seem to have been dispossessed of love when they were children. Either their parents had been too brutish, coarse, dense and ignorant to understand the extra-special loving needs of a sensitive child or they were unwittingly too busily distant, inhibitedly shy of showing feelings, or too preoccupied with their own problems to give the child a sense of being accepted in the world. Thus the feeling of unfulfilled emptiness in the souls of such children remains as the sensory substratum of their existential experience. And it echoes throughout their lives like a bottomless well with no way to fill it up.

Even though, as adults, they may receive all the love and appreciation they most desperately need in compensation, they are often 'constitutionally' unable to absorb whatever love is given them. No matter how much love others may pour into them in the present, it somehow never seems to satisfy. Nor does it overcome their existential sense of separation. Even as lovers, they feel themselves as 'under glass'. They are unable to reach through. They feel themselves unable to give their partners more than a morsel of the 'love locked up' they have inside. Not having received it unconditionally – to a sufficiently satisfying degree – in their early years, they can neither give nor receive love easily. Much to their own dismay, they find they have an ingrown psychological barrier against the very thing they need the most.

At a deep and often unexplored level, love itself is sensed as something to be feared. It is felt to be some kind of threat, or bondage, or a manipulative power over one's life. Having once been trapped in the painfully vulnerable position of the child – of wanting love so desperately, and not getting it – the shut-off sufferer in his lingering child-mind sees love as a source of pain – and is not willing to expose himself totally to such a hurt again. Even though his adult mind now longs to do so, all his psychic forces are tensed up against abandonment to intimate relationship. In spite of himself, he can never fully 'connect'. He is always holding something back 'in reserve' and therefore remains forever 'encapsulated' in his isolated anguish on the inside of his 'psychic screen'.

Yet paradoxically people of this nature are capable of the most wonderful love for humanity in general. In fact, they feel it easier to love universally than to love intimately. Their tendency is to give themselves to great causes, or to all of humankind instead of to a single relationship. Many take to the spiritual path, steadily dissolving away their psychic screen by penetrating the mystery of Universal Love. The most ardent seekers of the Self thus bless the world by becoming Sages in the end. Others become the creative people in society: our artists, writers, poets, musicians, dancers, actors and the like, seeking from the depths of their souls to express their inner ache with works of beauty in the world. Many make the most wonderful practitioners in the caring professions, by endlessly giving out the tenderness their hearts most long to receive. In this attitude many are unconsciously expressing an intuitive understanding of the key to self-healing:

IF YOU WANT TO LIVE – GIVE! And give to others *what you need most.*

For the love we seek from others must first be found within ourselves. The only love we will ever be able to experience will come from within. And only love from deep within can fuse with love from without. It is therefore this inner love we have to foster if we want to *live*. At the unfelt, unsounded deeps of our inner well there lies an Eternal Spring – the Self – the Source of Love itself. If we cannot easily fill our well by the bucketful from the periodic love of others, we *can* with practice, find the way to overflow it from within. At some point we have to become aware of this and stop *seeking* love, by simply *being* love – by drawing on our own untapped reserves.

The Omnipresence is an unfailing spring – an energy flow

which manifests itself as Love through all forms of biological life throughout the cosmos. In the wild unspoiled spaces of this world you can feel the whole earth upsurging with the joy of it. Just as one can sense the landscape all but singing after rain. We are all animated by this energising flow. Therefore whether we are able to feel it or not, we *are* loved, because we are channelled through by love. It is *Conscious Love* which is growing us.

With all our silliness, irascibility and negativity, we are supported by the Omnipresence. Then why not try to align ourselves with it? If we seek fulfilment, its warmth will dissolve all barriers in the end. But to begin, we must find the way to remove our barriers from within, and let the Omnipresence in. Of course, it is already there, like electricity in the air. But first we have to let the current flow without restriction in ourselves, if it is to illumine the filament of our beings.

> The Hindu, Tibetan, Chinese and Japanese yoga texts consider there is a lunar force in the head and a solar force at the navel area or solar plexus. The Self-realised Sages say that the energies which move up and down between them, are balanced at the Heart-Centre – the seat of Consciousness.

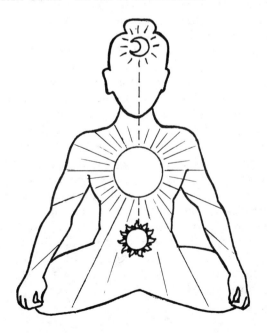

THE PRACTICE

First Phase: Loving your Heart

The way to awaken a sense of the Omnipresence in ourselves as a first step, is a wonderfully redeeming practice I call *Loving Your Heart*. This is to put all your attention in the subtle feeling you experience in your Heart-Centre. I do not speak of the physical heart, of course, but the very deepest centre of your being where you feel the essence of yourself to be. The Sages place this point two digits from the meridian into the right side of the chest, a finger-width lower than the nipple. But you can feel the place inwardly. Just concentrate on being *inside* the sentiment of your Heart of Hearts. Not with knitted brows and effort, but simply dissolve your mind down into that place and relax there. Let go all other feelings, except for feeling yourself *as* that central sensation of the Heart.

Just feel what the Heart feels. Experience it, bathe in it, identify with it. Then – magnify that feeling by *loving* it. No matter how tentative it may feel to begin with. Love it warmly. Care for it like a child. Like the child within which was never cared for enough. Care for it like you never cared for anything else. Loving your heart in this way may seem for some like a silly thing to do at first, but you may rest assured its practice is the doorway to the Self.

This is the practical method for achieving what for many has been the otherwise obscure instruction of the Sages – to 'abide in the Self'. We cannot visualise something as formless and abstract as the 'Self' in order to abide in it. Nor can we easily and naturally know it as the essential central nature of ourselves, when we have been conditioned to living in the sense-of-ego for so long. This problem has been a stumbling-block to many seekers desiring to do as the Masters prescribed. But as you persevere in this experience of self-centring, the Love-Light of the real Self rises softly like the sun within you, until your heart feels it might well near burst with joy.

As a beginning, it is helpful to remember to practise this each evening in bed before you go to sleep. And also each morning as you awaken. Let the sun rise within yourself to greet the day. And then evoke the feeling whenever you have a moment during the day.

ON THE INBREATH

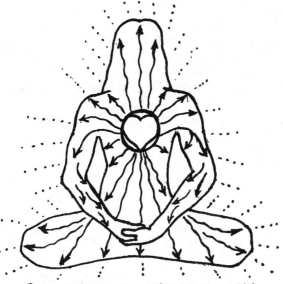

ON THE OUTBREATH

Second Phase: Samyama on the Inner Sun

After a short while, this practice of 'mentemplation' or *samyama* (fixation, concentration and identification) in the Heart-Centre becomes easy and instantaneous. Once you are established in it, then the effect can be intensified by visualising your breast as filled with a vibrant golden ball of loving light like the sun. Feel this *Inner Sun* as being fed with pulsing energy from within, and seeding the whole of your inner space with tiny vibrant particles of golden light. Visualise these charged particles, or 'lightrons', being diffused to lighten every corner of your body. Then feel them being drawn in again towards the Inner Sun with every long, slow in-drawing of the breath. Feel them as subtle waves of energy flowing away from inside the skin surface over all the body and feeding back into the Inner Sun. Imagine the sun increasng in size and becoming charged with energy and light on every inbreath.

Then with every long and steady outbreath you make, feel the 'lightrons' streaming forth with the loving forces of the Heart flowing outwards once again to every part of your body. And on the next inbreath, draw them in again from the extremities to the Heart, and then from the Heart to the extremities on the next outbreath. Continue in this way in a constant ebb and flow until you *feel* the coming and going.

Third Phase: The Sunconscious Way

As your positive spiritual energies build up by this practice, you can then begin to visualise this vibrant golden ball as radiating its rays outwards through the body wall in all directions. With every outward breath you breathe, be conscious of a mighty force of energy from the Sun-Self centre, pulsing waves of well-being out into the world. Feel that you are letting loose your 'lightrons' out into the hearts of all. And on the inbreath you are drawing them back in again, laden with the grateful goodwill of those whose day you may have lightened by your way of being. Feel that you are illuminating all the world around you. And very soon you *will* be.

Each time you step out of doors – and especially on grey or wet and windy days – prepare your way by invoking the Inner Sun. As you leave the house sing inside yourself: *"Here comes the Sun! Here comes the Noble Sun! Let it shine!"* And as you walk along the street, let your inner radiance shine out on everyone from your eyes – you will be surprised how many strangers feel impelled to bid you "Good-day!" as you pass. And you may know your light has touched them and returns to you again tenfold. Keeping your consciousness in the Inner Sun is the way to act *Sun*consciously in the world rather than *un*consciously, and creates a positive climate in the soul.

By keeping this image in mind – or rather, in Heart – at all times you consciously become what you are – an open channel for the Omnipresent loving energy to flow through. The practice automatically develops a constant inner climate of compassion and reverence for the wonder of life and all its manifest forms. As this is already the natural climate of the soul in any case, we only have to bring ourselves into attunement with it. Reverence is a sovereign remedy for all spiritual ills. Where there is reverence for all in the heart, fear cannot exist. When reverence is constant, the sense-of-ego (and thus mind and all its miseries) cannot survive.

It is therefore wise to cultivate association with those who express a sense of reverence in their way of being. If you know of anyone more spiritually evolved than yourself, or a saintly preceptor, go and bask in his or her presence at every opportunity. If they are not available, always hold them in that feeling of the Heart-centre. *Whatever you identify with, that you become.* The constant content of your mind colours the quality of your life. If you always identify with 'misery-me' you remain miserable. If you revere the loving quality of a Sage, you become sage-like. With Sunconscious inner attunement we can transform our soul-constricting sadness into reverential joy.

If you are surrounded by negativity, remain in the Inner Sun and out of the ego. Whenever possible leave the presence of others and go and sit on a mountain, or in a meadow by a stream. Lie on the earth and let it heal you. Sit in a wood or park and absorb the healing of the trees. The frequencies of sounds hidden in birdsong are also a healing balm for the heart. When you are suffering, plunge deep into the Heart-Sun-Centre and see if there is actually anyone there who is suffering. For without the participation of the mind (and the misery-magnifying memory) we may find there *is* no one there to experience it. Only the mind suffers. And it is mind in its maya* which makes obscuring 'clouds of unknowing' across the Inner Sun.

If the movement of mind is too insistent, we can verbally or mentally repeat a mantra until its turbulence subsides. A mantric word or phrase should be repeated not only at meditation times, but continuously, whenever the mental faculties are not required for practical purposes. If you have no personal mantra, then I offer this phrase in its place: *"I make my own joy"*. This may be repeated verbally or mentally as you go about and see where it takes you. Constantly repeat it in the centre of your Inner Sun visualisation. As you feel its positive effect in operation, its companion mantra: *"I am my own joy!"* might be substituted.

These are some of the ways in which rising soul-sickness may be transformed or kept at bay, although ultimately there is no permanent cure – except enlightenment, otherwise known as Self-realisation. And for that, to rest consciously and consistently in the Heart is all that need be done.

This is the direct route to the Self.

We recognise a Brother of the Spirit by the Sunlight in his eyes.

It matters not whatsoever a man may be . . . for I care not if he is a Christian, Buddhist, Hindu, Moslem or a Jew . . . that he walks upon the inner way with an open Heart is good enough for me. – And you?

---

* Maya is that power causing the process of mental illusion in which the so-called 'objective' phenomena of the universe are taken to be real, as distinct from the Omnipresence, whose consciousness is the 'mind-stuff' of which they are made and the light in which they are seen.

The Cosmic Communion
A Mentemplation for Soul Gatherings

In the deeps of our beings,
I AM.
Within the innermost reaches of our thoughts
　　　　　and thought-lessness,
I AM.
May we come to understand
　　　　　that there is no place where
I AM not.
For I AM the centre, and soul,
　　　and furthermost reaches of each and everyone of us
At the same time and in every dimension.
Those of us here gathered now,
I AM.
And those of whom we choose to disapprove,
　　　　　or call our enemies,
I AM, also.
For I AM the binding cord wherein the knowing of which,
　　　　allows no separation between Us and Them
For I AM you, and you are ME,
　　　　and WE are all together
In the knowing.
And those who wish to know
　　　　　but do not know as yet,
Be still,
And understand alone,
That – I AM.

This is the purpose of life

MUZ MURRAY

Chapter References

PROBLEMS ON THE PATH

1 *Talks with Sri Ramana Maharshi,* Swami Ramananda Saraswati (Sri Ramanashramam Press, Tamil Nadu, S. India.)
2 *Teachings of Ramana Maharshi,* Arthur Osborne (Rider, London, 1969).

ON CHANGING THE WORLD
THE WAY OF THE WISE MAN: REVELATION

1 *Talks with Sri Ramana Maharshi,* Swami Ramananda Saraswati (Sri Ramanashramam Press, Tamil Nadu, S. India.)
2 Greenpeace, 5 Caledonian Road, King's Cross, London, N1 (01 837 7557).
3 Green Deserts, Geoff's House, Rougham, Nr. Bury St. Edmunds, Suffolk. Also Green Deserts Global, P.O. Box 9844, Santa Fe, New Mexico 87504, USA. Phone: (505) 982 3104.
Other Worthy Institutions – The Woodland Trust, Westgate, Grantham, Lincolnshire NG31 6LL. (Phone: 0476-74297).
National Tree Campaign, 35 Belgrave Square, London SW1X 8QN.
Orb Foundation, Orb Housae, 13 Chapel Street, London SW1. (Funding and investigation of projects for planetary survival and harmonious existence.)
Earth Life Foundation, 10 Belgrave Square, London SW1X 8PH (Ecological charity for Preservation of the Planet, Rain-forests, etc.).
CND, 22-24 Underwood Street, London N1 7JG (Sane approaches to peace and disarmament) (01 250 4010).
War Registers International, 55 Dawes Street, London SE17 1EL (01 703 7189).
Friends of The Earth, 26-28 Underwood Street, London N1 7JQ. (01 490 1555).
4 Amnesty International, 5 Robert's Place, London EC1R 0EJ (01 251 8371).
5 Planetary Citizens, 777 United Nations Plaza, New York, NY 10017, USA.
6 *I Am That,* Sri Nisargadatta (Chetana Press, Bombay, 1978).

THE SCIENCE OF SOUND

1 *The Textbook of Yoga Psychology,* Ramamurti S. Mishra M.D. (Doubleday, New York)
2 *The Sufi Message,* Hazrat Inayat Khan (Barrie & Rockcliffe Ltd.)
3 *The Sound of Silence – An Introduction to Mantra –* a cassette by Muz

Murray, contains the pronunciation of the *Gayatri mantra* and method of chanting. A slightly different version can be heard on "*Agni-Hotra – The Healing Fire*" as used in the fire ceremony for mental and spiritual healing. Both cassettes available from Inner Garden Distributors, 30 Burton Avenue, North Walsham, Norfolk, NR28 0EP. (Send long stamped addressed envelope for brochure.)

SENSING THE INNER SOUND

1 Institutions and other teachers known to have knowledge in this area are Maharaj Charan Singh Ji (Radha Soami Satsanga, Beas, India); Darshan Singh (Surat Shabd Yoga); Guru Maharaj (Divine Light Mission); Sri Ramamurti (ICSA, Monroe, USA); Sri Darwin Gross (Eckankar, USA); Radha Soami Satsanga (Dayalbagh, Agra, India); Thakar Singh (India); Lifewave (UK) and many others.
2 *The Textbook of Yoga Psychology*, Sri Ramamurti S. Mishra (Doubleday, New York.)

HEALING THE HURTS OF MANY LIFETIMES

1 *Realms of the Human Unconscious*, Stanislav Grof (E. P. Dutton & Co. Inc. New York 1976)
2 Research Papers of Dr Graham Liggins, University of Auckland.
3 *Primal Man: The New Consciousness*, Dr Arthur Janov (Abacus UK)
4 *Twenty Cases Suggestive of Reincarnation*, Dr Ian Stevenson, MD (University of Virginia Press, USA)
For further reading on Birth, see *New Life* by Janet and Arthur Balaskas (Sidgwick & Jackson Ltd.) and *Birth Reborn* by Michel Odent (Souvenir Press, UK) or the books of Frédérick Leboyer. Further reading on Reincarnation: *More Cases Suggestive of Reincarnation* by Ian Stevenson (University of Virginia); *Edgar Cayce on Reincarnation* by Hugh Lynn Cayce (A.R.E. Press, Virginia) and *Reincarnation: An East-West Anthology* (Quest Books, 1975)

IS THE SPIRITUAL QUEST NEUROTIC?

1 *Pitfalls of Primal*, David Freundlich (*Primal Community* Vol. 1, No. 1)
2 *Primal Scream and Genital Character*, Charles R. Kelly (The Radix Institute, Santa Monica, California, USA.)
3 *Gestalt Is*, Fritz Perls, Ed. John O. Stephens (Bantam Books, USA.)
4 *Gestalt Therapy Verbatim*, Fritz Perls (Bantam Books, USA.)
5 *Primal Man: The New Consciousness*, Dr Arthur Janov & E. Michael Holden (Abacus, UK.)
6 *Hatha Yoga Pradipika*, Svatmarama Swami (c.1450 AD).
7 *Ramana Maharshi and The Path of Self-Knowledge*, Arthur Osborne (Rider, UK.)

EVOLVING OUT OF EGO

1 *The Textbook of Yoga Psychology*, Sri Ramamurti S. Mishra M.D. (Doubleday, New York.)

2 *Civilisation and Its Discontents*, Sigmund Freud (Hogarth Press).
3 *Collected Works of Carl Jung* (Vol. 9, Part 1)

OPENING THE INNER EYE

Reference tools for further development:

1 *Yoga Nidra* practice cassette by Muz Murray. Recommended for the deepest of relaxations. Send stamped addressed envelope (long) for brochure to Cosmicassettes, Inner Garden Distributors, 30 Burton Avenue, North Walsham, Norfolk, NR28 0EP, England.
2 *Fundamentals of Yoga* and *The Textbook of Yoga Psychology* (Doubleday, New York) both by Ramamurti S. Mishra, M.D., which give a thorough grounding in the theory and practical application of the subjects covered in this chapter.
3 *Agni-Hotra – The Healing Fire* cassette by Muz Murray, giving all details for the preparation of the sacred fire and method of chanting the mantras. (Also from Cosmicassettes, as above.)

ON THE SOULS OF ANIMALS

1 *The Philokalia* Vol. 1 (Faber & Faber, London 1979) from the *Ascetic Discourse* of St. Neilos the Ascetic of Sinai, p. 246.

THE UNKNOWN JOURNEYINGS OF JESUS

1 *The Man in The Sycamore Tree*, Edward Rice (Doubleday, New York, 1973).
2 *Honest to God*, John Robinson (S.C.M. Press, London, 1963).
3 *The Nag Hammadi Library*, Ed. James M. Robinson (Harper & Row, New York, 1978).
4 *The Divine Pymander of Hermes Trismegistus* (Shrine of Wisdom, Fintry, Brook, Nr. Godalming, Surrey, UK, 1955).
5 *Meister Eckhart* Vol. 1, Tr. Evans. (Element Books, Dorset).
6 *Thomas Merton on Mysticism*, Raymond Bailey (Doubleday, New York, 1976).
7 *Edgar Cayce's Story of Jesus*, Jeffrey Furst (Neville Spearman, London, 1968).
8 *The Aquarian Gospel of Jesus the Christ*, 'Levi' (L. N. Fowler, London, 1969).
9 *The Encyclopaedia of World Religions* (Octopus, London, 1975).
10 *Alexander the Great*, Robin Lane Fox (Futura, London, 1973).
11 *The Tomb of Jesus*, Sufi Mutiur Rahman Bengalee, MA (The Nazir Dawato Tabligh, Punjab, 1970).
12 *The Jesus Mystery*, Janet Bock (Aura Books, Los Angeles, 1980).
13 *The Unknown Life of Jesus Christ*, Nicholas Notovich (New York, Paris, London, 1890-4).
14 *Tibet, Tartary and Mongolia*, H. T. Princep (pp. 12-14).
15 *A Record of the Buddhist Religion practised in India and the Malaya Archipelago* AD 671, A. Ting, Tr. J. Takakusu (Clarendon Press, Oxford, 1896).

16 *The Children of Mu*, James Churchward (Neville Spearman, London, 1959).
17 *In the Woods of God-Realization*, Swami Rama Thirtha (Bhargava Bushan Press, Varanasi, India).
18 *The Passover Plot*, Dr Hugh Schonfield (Element Books, Dorset, 1985).
19 *The Armageddon Script*, Peter Lemesurier (Element Books, Dorset, 1981).
20 *Jesus in India*, Hazrat Mirza Ghulam Ahmad (Mirza Wasim Ahmad, Quadian, Punjab, India).
21 *The Races of Afghanistan*, H. W. Bellews (Thacker & Spink, Calcutta).
22 *Cyclopaedia of Geography*, James Bryce (Collins, London, 1880).
23 *Seeking the Master*, Muz Murray (Neville Spearman, Sudbury, 1980).
24 *In The Steps of St. Thomas*, Rev. H. D'Souza (Madras, India, 1972).